WOODY ALLEN

HIS FILMS AND CAREER

WOODY ALLEN
HIS FILMS AND CAREER

By Douglas Brode

CITADEL PRESS   SECAUCUS, NEW JERSEY

ACKNOWLEDGMENTS: With appreciation, to Debra Terwilliger, Nat Segaloff, Charles Joffe, Nat Tobin and *Crescent Advertising*, Ellen Goosenberg and *Showtime/Movie Channel*, Nevart Apikian and *The Syracuse Post-Standard*; and to American International Pictures, Paramount Pictures, Columbia Pictures, United Artists, and Orion. Also, the Academy of Motion Picture Arts and Sciences, and Larry Edmonds Bookstore.

Library of Congress Cataloging in Publication Data

Brode, Douglas, 1943-
    Woody Allen : his films and career.

    1. Allen, Woody.   2. Comedian—United States—
Biography.   3. Moving-picture producers and directors—
United States—Biography.   I. Title.
PN2287.A53B76   1985   791.43'028'0924 [B]   85-12769
    ISBN 0-8065-1067-6

Designed by Paul Chevannes

Published by Citadel Press
A division of Lyle Stuart Inc.
120 Enterprise Ave., Secaucus, N.J. 07094
In Canada: Musson Book Company
A division of General Publishing Co. Limited
Don Mills, Ontario

Queries regarding rights and permissions should be
addressed to: Lyle Stuart, 120 Enterprise Avenue,
Secaucus, N.J. 07094

Manufactured in the United States of America

10 9 8 7 6 5 4 3 2

For My Son
SHAUN LICHENSTEIN BRODE
who asked his Dad
to write him a book
about Woody

Woody as the "serious" host/narrator for the spy spoof, What's Up, Tiger Lily?

CONTENTS

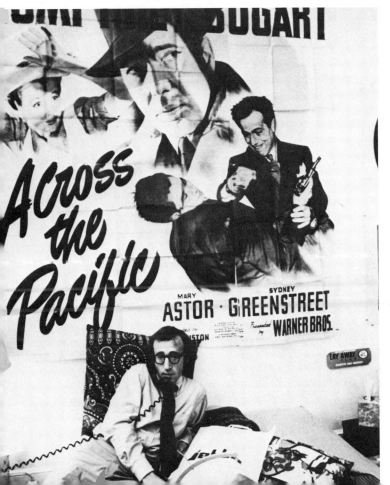

The young Woody Allen in his night club comic days.

THE PARADOX PRINCIPLE:

An Interpretation of Woody Allen

SISYPHUS AND HIS STONE

Woody Allen is an enigma. He hides from the public after fighting to achieve and maintain his celebrity status. He scoffed at the intellectual tributes critics heaped on his early films, then complained when they did not catch the serious underside of *Love and Death*. He has been accepted as the key comic consciousness of our times though his films make less money, and play to a considerably smaller audience, than those of any other comic filmmaker now working. He insists he is totally apolitical and in 1972 was the first star to sign up in support of George McGovern. We think we know him from watching his films, only to hear him insist that the apparently autobiographical characters in *Annie Hall*, *Manhattan*, and *Stardust Memories* are not meant to project himself at all. Even his name is an enigma: most sources say it is Allen Stewart Konigsberg, though others steadfastly maintain it's actually Haywood Allen. The purpose of this book is to break through some of the enigma surrounding Woody Allen and make this writer-director-actor a bit

more accessible. So, to start at the beginning:

Though the *Playbill* for the Broadway show *Play It Again, Sam* included in its capsule bio the information that Woody Allen is the son of a Latvian prince who emigrated to the United States following a pogrom at which he was the only one to show up, it seems pretty certain he was born December 1, 1935, and subsequently grew up in Flatbush, a lower-middle-class section of Brooklyn. His parents, Martin and Nettie, did not by all accounts ever once wear Groucho Marx masks in front of their child during his formative years, though even if they had worn them to the dinner table, Woody wouldn't have noticed. He didn't eat with the family, or associate with them much. After school, he later claimed, "I'd go right into my bedroom and shut the door. Consequently, I was able to get some things done." Those "things" included practicing magic—various card and coin tricks, and other sleight of hand shows—plus teaching himself to play the clarinet by listening to jazz records and jamming along with them.

Woody's father worked at many jobs, including a stint as a jewelry engraver and as a bartender at Sammy's Bowery Follies in Manhattan. Nettie (her maiden name was Cherry) also worked, as a bookkeeper in a Brooklyn floral shop. They were religious Jews, and young Allen attended Hebrew school for eight years. Woody's only sibling was a sister, who, like his first wife, would become a teacher, though he himself has expressed only disdain for formal education. He remembers Midwood High as "a school for emotionally disturbed teachers," and once told *Rolling Stone* magazine: "I loathed every day and regret every day I spent in school. I like to be taught to read and write and then be left alone." Understandably, then, he was never involved in extracurricular activities, but rather ran home to listen to *Fibber McGee and Molly* on the radio, or to play stickball and other sports on the street.

With his thick glasses and slight build, Woody might strike the uninitiated as someone who spent his childhood reading serious books. In fact, he read little but comics, and they weren't even *Classics Illustrated*; *Batman* and *Donald Duck* were his favorites. Woody would not begin reading the serious stuff until he realized, years later, that the women he enjoyed dating were the intelligent, educated girls; he didn't have a chance with them unless he could converse on their level. Yet he did demonstrate a talent for writing even at an early stage. When he handed in a composition for his high school English class, it was invariably chosen as a model for the other students and read by the teacher to the entire class. That was the extent of his scholastic achievement. When he left comic books behind, it was only to tackle the canon of Mickey Spillane. Eventually, he graduated with an overall C − average.

Before graduation, though, Woody had discovered the theatre—The Flatbush Theatre, to be precise, where he saw everything from movies to vaudeville acts. The comics who performed there gave him his first taste of "stand-up" comedy. Friends from that time recall seeing Woody rip open a candy box to jot down a joke he liked on the inside. After he'd leave the show, Woody would try to come up with comparable jokes of his own. One day, on an impulse, he mailed one of them to a newspaper and it ended up in print. The gag, published by Earl Wilson, went like this: "Woody Allen says he ate at a restaurant that had O.P.S. prices—other people's salaries." He had created the pen name to conceal his secret life from his classmates, but when Wilson kept mentioning the *nom de plume* in his column, and his gags were also picked up by Walter Winchell and Ed Sullivan, a press agent offered Woody a regular job writing one-liners.

David Alber, having noticed Woody's gags in the columns, tracked him down and was stunned to learn the bright new writer was a 15-year-old high school student. Every day after school, Woody would hop a subway into Manhattan, write some gags during the ride, knock off some more in Alber's office, then go home. Alber would then busily plant those gags in various newspaper columns, attributing the clever lines to his clients Arthur Murray, Sammy Kaye, and Guy Lombardo. This went on for two years, during which time Woody acquired a reputation as a speedy and supercompetent source of humorous material. He impressed enough people so that, at age seventeen, he was hired by NBC as a staff writer, first turning out material for Peter Lind Hayes, then for Herb Shriner.

Shortly, most of the big TV performers of the late fifties and early sixties were buying material from Woody: Sid Caesar, Kaye Ballard, Buddy Hackett, Art Carney, Carol Channing, Pat Boone, and Jack Paar among them. Before long, he was one of the regular writers for *The Tonight Show*. In the period between 1960 and 1962, Woody went from writing for *The Tonight Show* to appearing on it; between 1962 and 1964, he progressed from appearing as a guest to serving as a substitute host for Johnny Carson.

But at nineteen, Woody was still simultaneously flunking himself out of New York University and City College, getting married to Harlene Rosen, and entering a Writer Development Program at NBC where he soon worked his way up to a $350-a-week job. He made a name for himself working on scripts for Sid Caesar's *Your Show of Shows* (as did Neil Simon and Mel Brooks), and his reputation was soon lofty enough that he could, at age 22, command $1,500 a week as a gag writer for Garry Moore's then-popular show. Recalling Woody's work for him, Moore would later write to Steve Allen that "we rarely saw anything of him. Both his contributions and personal appearances were—well, random ... I recall that one late afternoon when Woody was discovered ambling through, on his way to God wot, the other writers tried literally to tie him into his office chair for the night to assure his presence at the next day's meeting. I was pretty close to the rest of the writing staff, but not with Woody. He is a will-o'-the-wisp in my memory...."

Then in 1962 came the decision that might have seemed to any outside observer an act of madness, but which would in time prove canny and correct: Woody quit his TV gag-writing job and left behind the stability of $2,000 a week in order to work as a stand-up comic at $150 a week—*if he was lucky*! Only two years later he would be earning a hefty $5,000 a week as one of the most sought after stand-up comics in the country, but there was no way of knowing that then. What inspired his decision? One element may have been watching Mort Sahl work, and being highly impressed. Sahl "changed the face of comedy the way Stravinsky changed music," Woody once said. "He

Woody with Johnny Carson, during one of Allen's frequent guest appearances on The Tonight Show *in the mid-1960's.*

Woody during the pre-Broadway tryouts for Play It Again, Sam, *with co-stars Barbara Brownell and Diana Walker.*

changed the rhythm of jokes.'' What impressed him most was Sahl's refusal to fit into the existing mold of a stand-up comic, Las Vegas style: the tuxedo, the glib attitude, the wise-guy delivery of gags written by other people. Mort broke the mold by creating his own material, drawn from the current political scene and his own neuroses, and casually wore his street clothes on stage instead of slipping into the cliché costume.

In addition, Woody had a strong personal feeling about how his own lines ought to be delivered, and sensed that in the TV comedies he collaborated on, his bits would invariably get lost in an overly cute, inoffensive routine. By becoming a performer, he could protect his work as a writer. And deep down, he must have sensed that, as silly as the notion sounded, he had the makings of a major star. His agents, Charles H. Joffe and Jack Rollins, also came to believe that Woody might make an excellent stand-up performer while listening to him elaborate on some of the wildly absurd experiences he managed to find himself in on a daily basis. Woody's

stories always left them rolling with laughter, convincing the two that if Allen could only overcome his innate shyness, he might become as popular a comic performer as he had already become a comic writer. But when Woody arrived for his first (unpaid) performance at Greenwich Village's small Duplex night club, he was so nervous that he had to be pushed onstage. The show was a disaster.

So were most of the shows that followed. For two years, Woody Allen the club comedian bombed out in front of audiences. Jack Rollins would later recall: ''He would stoically go through with his lines and do twenty-five minutes. He would get up there and wrap the cord around his neck as though he was going to choke himself.'' But in time, the Woody Allen act took hold, in part owing to what critic Mark Rowland would later describe as the fascinating juxtaposition of Woody's ''timid manner and the savage brilliance of his wit.'' His awkwardness onstage, at first considered detrimental to a comic, in time came to seem an asset; like Sahl, Woody changed people's notions about what a stand-up comic should be. When Bob Abel first interviewed the fledgling comic in the early sixties, he had been delighted when Woody likened his performing before an inert audience "to an intimate relationship between Sisyphus and his Stone."

From small clubs like The Duplex and The Bitter End, Woody graduated to Las Vegas showcases including Caesars Palace, then returned to TV, where he did variety shows (Ed Sullivan, Dean Martin) and talk shows (Dick Cavett, Johnny Carson), eventually writing and starring in a special for Kraft Music Hall. In the meantime, he had begun writing his parodic pieces for *Playboy* and *The New Yorker*, guided a pair of Broadway plays to success and saw his first movie ventures find a national audience. *Variety* proclaimed him in 1964 as being in the "first rank of cerebral comedians,"though he would reject the epithet "cerebral." In addition to his success with critics, Allen was enjoying remarkable financial success. From that first unpaid performance at The Duplex in 1962, he sky rocketed to $1,000 a week in the fall of 1963, $5,000 a week in the spring of 1964, and then $10,000 a performance later that same year. His hit night club act led to booking on both *That Was the Week That Was* and *The Jack Paar Show*; then, in the summer of 1964, he was signed as the first in a series of summer replacements to host *The Tonight Show* while Johnny Carson was on vacation, giving middle America its first major dose of Allenesque humor.

"Allen's act," Maurice Yacowar wrote of the early night club performances in his book *Loser Take All*, "seemed less a public performance than a private confession." The key word here, though, is "seemed," for Allen's talent was in performing a carefully calculated show that gave the audience an *illusion* of a spontaneous, improvised, intimate confessional. The act, though, *was* an act, and even Woody's later film persona must be viewed in the same way: the famous fatigues he wears are not some clothes he crawls into without noticing, but a carefully chosen costume that identifies him as perfectly as the tramp costume identified Chaplin. Intriguingly, they are almost the reverse of one another, costume-wise; Chaplin's running-character was a bum who dressed "up" on the social scale; Woody's running character is a member of the gotham high life who dresses "down" from what would be expected.

Woody as the host of "The Year 1967 in Review," telecast on The Kraft Music Hall, *NBC-TV, Wednesday, December 27, 1967.*

CHICKEN SOUP FOR THE SOUL

The Little Guy, a staple of American screen comedy ever since Chaplin first winked and waddled his way across the screen and into the hearts of viewers, has become as basic an icon to movie comedy as the tragic hero has always been to drama. Audiences may be charmed by the con-man cynicism of a W.C. Fields or delighted by the outrageous antics of the madcap Marx Brothers, but time and again they return to the small, vulnerable characters who suffer at the hands of a huge and oftentimes hostile world. Chaplin offered the world its first great incarnation of such an idea; Woody Allen stands as the greatest variation on that theme since Chaplin hung up his baggy pants. Understandably, then, the tendency to compare the two has been strong. Surprisingly, it's a comparison Allen has been less than comfortable with. "I can't tell you what I am," Woody once admitted to an interviewer who was trying to break through to the essence of the man, "but I can tell you what I'm not: I'm not Chaplinesque."

This, despite the fact that dozens of critics have, over the years, used just that epithet to describe his onscreen appeal. It's easy to see why people would like Woody to be another Chaplin—another admirable symbol of man's innate goodness, expressed through mime-like action—but as an actor, Woody works in a totally different manner, and his impact is far different. As Woody told *Cinema* magazine as early as 1973: "Because of the nature of Chaplin's background [he] came to the screen with a tremendous training in acrobatics. There's nothing in my background that's like that. My strength, if any, is lines. I could probably deliver lines better than Chaplin." Chaplin's medium was his body, Woody's is words. And he does with words, and with his own seemingly unappealing whine of a voice, what Chaplin achieved with his body.

So while there is a solid helping of physical comedy in the Allen films, especially the earlier ones, this element always remains subservient to his use of language, which of course marks not only his film projects but all of Woody's creative endeavors: the plays, the short stories, the essays, the stand-up routines. Woody is essentially a writer who, in films, has also chosen to appear, almost as an afterthought.

If Allen the artist resembles Chaplin, it is less in the superficial similarity of their Little Guy appeal than in the way the two men made movies. Despite his insistence that he is not Chaplinesque, Woody himself drew a comparison when, lunching with Sheila Graham at the Regency Hotel in August,

1969, he described his first directorial effort, *Take the Money and Run*, to her thusly: "I want a movie with belly laughs. I don't want to spend time forcing plot. If you look at Chaplin's movies, the early ones, you'll see there's only a thin plot line to hang the outrageously funny...scenes on." That same year, he told interviewer Arnold Reisman, "I'm a great fan of the Marx Brothers, but my direction is closer to Chaplin's." And he is correct. Like Chaplin, Woody began by directing knockabout comedies; like Chaplin, Woody added elements of melodrama to the mix; like Chaplin, Woody eventually tried a full-blown tragedy in which he did not himself appear (for Chaplin, *A Woman of Paris*, and for Woody, *Interiors*); like Chaplin, he was not afraid to risk alienating his audience by doing something other than what was expected of him.

"He was willing to fail," Woody has said admiringly of Chaplin. He might have been describing himself. Like Chaplin, Woody is ambitious and, in the eyes of the more critical, arrogant. Thematically, though, the two filmmakers differ. Charlie Chaplin has been tagged "the eternal optimist," while Janet Maslin noted the "singular pessimism" of Woody Allen's vision; he is, after all, the man who once claimed, "Life is, in the end, a concentration camp." Chaplin's character usually fails to get the girl, but still manages to walk down the road of life into a new sunrise and, despite his losses, kick up his heels happily. Woody very often gets the girl in the end, but that only adds to all his problems. One man loses in the worldly sense, but succeeds in his own heart; the other may win so far as the world is concerned, but remains the loser inside his psyche. Both, though, play on the audience's infatuation with losers, men who onscreen embody the fear of losing that haunts everyone, and which comedy can, at its best, exorcise from the audience's collective unconscious, objectifying it onscreen, making losing look laughable, thereby performing a healthy, positive function.

No wonder, then, that filmmaker Frank Pierson once called Woody's work "chicken soup for the soul," though more correctly it's for the psyche. Marc S. Reisch seems even closer to it when he refers to Woody the writer as "Camus, but with a sense of humor," for Woody's character is modern existential man placed in a comic context. And Albert Bermel wrote, in his huge volume *Farce*, that what Allen has done "in his embodiments of the Woody character is wring farce out of that American literary device gleaned from Dostoevsky, Strindberg, and Chekhov: the confession." Certainly, a sense of the confessional has been basic to Woody's appeal as far back as the night club days, and has run through such apparently autobiographical films as *Annie Hall* and *Manhattan*.

A recurring pose: Woody as a master chess player, in his debut film What's New, Pussycat?

"He takes us immediately into his confidence," Frank Pierson wrote, "slings his arm over our shoulder... and pours out those wonderful tales with their innate feel of man's fate unfolding, hilarious and heartbreaking." It is, of course, an act, polished and disciplined. "Seemingly spontaneous mannerisms are generally a part of Woody's act," Eric Lax wrote. "He will take off his glasses and rub his eyes at the same lines practically every time, and he will appear to have gotten confused over what comes next in the same story at the same point in each performance, all to good effect and the enhancement of his material." Woody gives his live audiences the illusion of improvisation, though he in fact has perfected every gesture, every inflection. The charm of his movies would grow from the same basic concept: though they would, at their best, appear freewheeling and unstructured, there is always the brain, wise as well as witty, controlling them.

Woody knows just what he is doing, and the critics who have tried to assess his appeal have distilled the impact for us in words. "A man whose comic vision of life is based on his absolute incapacity," *Newsweek* wrote of his work way back in 1964. And in that same magazine, Paul D. Zimmerman would write of Woody's confessional quality, now transferred to film, almost ten years later: "Allen's great comic strength lies in his willingness to dramatize his most intimate psychological tensions, to exaggerate them for comic effect, of course, but nonetheless to share the personal terrain of his own neuroses with his audience... [and] summon the laughter of recognition in each of us." The laughter of recognition: an important phrase, suggesting as it does that in baring his own

An acclaimed writer himself, who spends an extraordinary amount of time in front of his typewriter, Woody has not coincidentally appeared regularly as writers in his films.

soul, Woody touches everyone; that Woody's comedy clicks because his neuroses capture something of the larger issues of his age. Woody's comedy provides a catharsis by openly admitting all those fears of failure; by laughing out loud, his audience can come to terms with what they otherwise repress.

AN URBAN EVERYMAN

Richard Schickel (of *Life* and later *Time*), one of Woody's earliest and most tireless supporters, insisted: "Woody c'est moi," later calling Woody "a walking compendium of a generation's concerns, comically stated." Ever since, that has been the line of reasoning from which most claims of Allen's genius—the quality that sets him apart from the merely talented contemporaries he has surpassed—derive. People like or do not like Steve Martin, and go or refuse to go to his films accordingly. But there are people who do not like Woody Allen films who would nonetheless begrudgingly call him a genius. In this sense, Woody Allen goes beyond laughter.

In 1966, *Current Biography* saw in him a universal appeal: "He demonstrated a singular ability to distill humor from the small frustrations of daily life." At the same time, though, Woody seemed particularly concerned with the daily life of the particular era he, and we, were passing through. *Vanity Fair* noted the tendency to treat "Allen and his work as a sort of cultural barometer," while psychiatrist Dee Burton insisted, "Woody Allen is anxious about things that a lot of other people are thinking about."

Woody has been tagged a "comic polymorph," and certainly his humor seemed perfectly timed to the cultural explosion taking place around him. The mid-1960's was the era of Peter Max posters, of Lovin' Spoonful music, of Peter Fonda movies, and of Woody Allen humor, which seemed part and parcel of the hippie explosion that began as a subculture and then, by decade's end, spread to mainstream America. "I love their dances," Woody was quoted in a 1966 Los Angeles *Times* article as saying. "I love their music. There's nothing bad to say about them. Basically, their interests are creative ones. …I'd say teens are becoming more nonconformist. That's one of the good things about them today." Of course, within a few years those hippie styles would reach their peak and then, almost overnight, disappear: bell-bottom jeans and psychedelic-colored shirts would, along with the Nehru jacket, be tucked away in the back of closets. Significantly, Woody Allen would survive the cultural pendulum-swing. Peter Fonda can still stir up strong visual memories of that age, but Woody is as much a part of our culture today as he was then. He could delineate his times without being limited by them.

Perhaps that was because he did not so much symbolize the stereotypical images of the period, but rather gave us an image of an ordinary man trying to adjust to what was happening around him. In a *Life* cover story from 1969, Woody wrote about visiting a freak-out in Greenwich Village but was quick to assert: "I was freaking *in* at the time due to a bad sense of direction." Cute, certainly, but more than cute: the man who was perceived as a representation of his times in fact saw himself as being at odds with his times, of moving in another direction from those around him. Everyone wanted to appear at ease with what was ostensibly hip, though secretly many knew they were uncomfortable in their attempts to adjust. It is this tension between people as they really are and the images they know they are supposed to live up to that became the source of Woody's humor.

Woody spoke to a particular audience. As Steve Allen would argue: Woody "is digging into a vein that is almost his exclusive domain among American humorists and comedians; middle-class New York Jewish cultural experience, with its million-and-one emotional and psychological nuances." It was this cultural aspect of Allen's work that Jerry Stahl picked up on: "From a certain angle, it is our own psychic components that Woody's particular genius calls up from the shadows. This is what makes every new work an Event. Each Allen film, each short story, unveils nothing less than the latest wrinkle in our contemporary souls. When Alvy Singer [in *Annie Hall*] sneezes in the coke, we can all say 'Gesundheit!' to ourselves." Alvy Singer, the Woody Allen hero of the mid-1970's, is as out of touch with the hip, glib, complacent culture around him as an earlier Woody was when he freaked in instead of out.

Remarkably enough, though, Peter Biskind would eventually argue that "in the 70's, with such autobiographical sex comedies as *Play It Again, Sam*, *Annie Hall*, and *Manhattan*, [Woody] became a celebrant of the singles scene, an apostle of men's liberation, the poet laureate of what Christopher Lasch called 'the culture of narcissism.'" Joan Didion kicked off this anti-Allen backlash with a *New York Review of Books* article in which she argued: "Wisdom is hard to find. Happiness takes research. The message that large numbers of people are getting from *Manhattan* and *Interiors* and *Annie Hall* is that this kind of emotional shopping around is the proper business of life's better students, that adolescence can now extend to middle age." It is, of course, possible that large numbers of people are indeed getting just that message from the movies.

But Didion and Biskind are completely wrong in confusing a possible audience misinterpretation of a

WOODY ALLEN
DIANE KEATON
MICHAEL MURPHY
MARIEL HEMINGWAY
MERYL STREEP
ANNE BYRNE

"MANHATTAN" Music by GEORGE GERSHWIN

A JACK ROLLINS-CHARLES H. JOFFE Production

Written by WOODY ALLEN and MARSHALL BRICKMAN Directed by WOODY ALLEN

Produced by CHARLES H. JOFFE Executive Producer ROBERT GREENHUT Director of Photography GORDON WILLIS

The famous advertisement for Manhattan, *which Woody helped design and was approved by him prior to its release. Woody insists on total control of the commercials and other promotional material for his films, so they will not be misrepresented to the public by studio-style hype.*

work with the meaning of the work itself. Woody's films are attacks on the culture of narcissism, whether it is Alvy Singer sneezing in the coke (the substance, not the drink) in *Annie Hall* (the man offering him a snort, unmercifully satirized as pseudo-hip by Allen the writer-director, symbolizes the culture of narcissism) or Isaac Davis fighting to free himself from the superficial lifestyle of his attractive friends in *Manhattan.* As Woody told Frank Rich of *Time* in 1979: "At the personal level, I try to pay attention to the moral side of issues as they arise and try not to make a wrong choice. For instance, I don't think it's right to try to buy your way out of life's painful side by using drugs. I'm also against the concept of short marriages, and regard my own marriages as a sign of failure of some sort. Of course, I sell out as much as anyone—inside." What he rejects, then, is the notion of short-term couplings and the indulgence in drugs that are the hallmarks of the culture of narcissism.

If anything, he resembles both Dustin Hoffman and the late Rod Serling in confessing to a Jewish guilt complex coupled with a Protestant work ethic. During the shooting of *Bananas* in 1970, producer Jack Grossberg described Woody as "a compulsive worker," while agent Charles Joffe added: "He's not concerned with fame, stardom, money—only work." Interviewing Woody for a 1968 *TV Guide* article, Robert Higgins noted "a feeling of urgency—as if what he's doing at any moment is a gross interruption, something that's holding him back. Allen has no trouble naming the urgency. 'It's a need to work,' he says, 'to write. I'm *driven* to it. If I don't write every free minute, I have this terrible guilt. It's like—I don't know—if I don't write, I'll be sorry someday.'"

While on the road with *Play It Again, Sam* in 1969, he would finish a rehearsal or a performance and then, instead of going out drinking with the rest of the cast, would forego the chance to "unwind" and instead retreat to his room to knock off a short story. "I have absolutely Prussian self-discipline when it comes to my writing," he told interviewer Peter Hellman at that time.

Unable to go to a play or film to relax, he instead attentively analyzes what he sees, carrying notebooks into museums with him. Those endeavors that other people attend for pleasure provide him with, ironically, yet another source of grueling work. His idea of relaxing is reading Nietzsche. "I'm a middle-class filmmaker," he says without apology. "I'm not a druggie or a drinker." And, obviously, not a narcissist, either; the inner-contemplation that is evident in his heavier films is not indulgent self-interest but critical wrestling with his own psyche. To call him, as Biskind did, "a celebrant of the singles scene" misses the whole point. If anything,

Woody was to the seventies what Scott Fitzgerald was to the 1920's—a man who lived it and loved it, who (along with his beautiful Zelda) would become a key icon of his time (just as Woody and Diane Keaton would emerge, both in real life and in *Annie Hall,* as the perfect couple of the 1970's), and who wrote about it better than anyone else. But *The Great Gatsby* and *Tender Is the Night* are hardly superficial "celebrations" of the jazz age. They show the emptiness and hollowness underneath all the glamour and glitter of America's first decade of life in the fast lane.

Likewise, *Annie Hall* and *Manhattan* take similar approaches to the seventies. They appear "celebrations" of the lifestyle only to the superficial viewer, the same kind of audience that once actually dismissed Fitzgerald's greatest work, from the grittier and downbeat perspective of the thirties, as decadent celebrations of a shimmering era that had passed. Such critics noted Fitzgerald's accurate and exciting exposition of the surface of 1920's life without grasping his undercurrent of irony, his edge of anger, his patina of social (and self!) criticism. What impresses one about Woody is his ability to be, like Fitzgerald in the jazz age, at once an insider and an outsider, a member of that special community and its harshest critic, not its celebrant.

This makes Woody as much at odds with his times as he is a representation of them, a fascinating paradox if ever there was one.

MY TOASTER HATES ME

Why then does a relatively small but distinctively loyal audience feel such a strong sense of identification with Woody Allen? The answers are varied. "He makes the world laugh, even though he is a sufferer who makes fun of his pain," Peter Noble wrote in *Screen International.* Certainly, the Pagliacci quality is part of the appeal, as is the paradoxical element: "What Woody has succeeded in doing," Elliott Joseph wrote in *Genesis* magazine, "is combining a razor-sharp, instantaneous wit with a fabricated schlemiel-like personality, and having us all rolling in the aisles in sheer delight." Indeed, the word "schlemiel" pops up in many descriptions of Woody's screen persona, as does the fact that Woody's characters are very often losers in the game of life. Yacowar sees him as "a short, paranoid loser...a man who exists on the fringe of an unsympathetic and absurd world, and who is both teased and satisfied by improbable dreams."

To a degree, Woody's impact derives from his assumed identity as a victim of everyday objects other people can supposedly control. "My toaster hates me," he announced in one of his earliest stand-up routines. The line led directly to the depiction of mechanical objects in films like *Sleeper,* in

In his most famous film, Play It Again, Sam.

which he is at the mercy of every appliance that exists to make our lives easier and, more often than not, makes us quite thoroughly miserable. In the film version of *Play It Again, Sam* he added a scene which would have been quite impossible in the live-theatre version: Allen, as Allan Felix, prepares himself for a blind date by trying to blow-dry his hair, but is attacked by the machine. Once again, Woody provides a cathartic laugh for his audience: each of us has known such frustration, though assuredly not in so exaggerated a form. Nonetheless, comedy at its best works along the same lines as tragedy, moving the viewer to emotions of pity and fear. If we pity Woody for what he goes through with mechanical objects, we fear that we're almost as vulnerable, almost as incompetent at dealing with *things*. Woody realizes all our worst fears about incompetence with assorted technical apparatus, and the laughter an audience experiences is a kind of release.

This is what makes such moments mindful rather than mindless humor. Thus, Woody ironically turned failure into success by literally making failure the substance of his successful comic vision, as his initial awkwardness in front of an audience gave way to a carefully conceived image of awkwardness from a most self-assured talent. "The nervous tics, hunching posture and white-knuckled delivery emerged as part of a *persona*," according to Jerry Stahl. "A schnook was born." And the schlemiel-schnook was Allen's own distinct character. "As funny as his jokes and stories were," Leonard Maltin said of Woody's early night club appearances, "they could not be told by anyone else; they sprang from his individual character, and this character propelled him to success." While the character he created on stage and then honed in the films was certainly something of a schlemiel-schnook, Woody expressed discomfort when the press began describing that character as

24

though it were Woody Allen himself.

"I've never been that," he later insisted. "It's an appellation for the unimaginative to hang on me." Woody viewed the bits he did in night clubs and then in films as exaggerations of fantasies derived from his own life, presented within a humorous context. Believing that the character is Woody was as incorrect as thinking Groucho really ran around like Captain Spaulding or that Chaplin never spoke but spent his days shuffling about like a balletic tramp. And yet, since many of the characters Woody has written and portrayed have names like Alvy and Allan, it's hard not to think that what we're seeing is a slice-of-life, reconstructed for celluloid immortalization. At times, Woody himself has been responsible for the confusion. As early as 1964, Woody told the New York *Sunday News*: "My material is really true, except that it's exaggerated...." Three years later, while working on the as-yet-untitled script that would in time become *Play It Again, Sam*, Woody told A. H. Weiler of *The New York Times*: "It's a neurotic love story in which I play me." And in 1972, talking to Gene Shalit of *Ladies Home Journal*, Woody said of that play: "It's based on my own life experiences."

As "Little Jimmy Bond" in Casino Royale.

From the very beginning of his artistic career, Woody employed the premise of sharing his psychological and personal concerns as his approach, his technique, his style; his stand-up routines often began with his facing the audience and whispering confidingly, "A lot of significant things have occurred in my private life that I thought we could go over tonight...." Similarly, *Annie Hall* begins with his direct address to the audience, leading Bob Abel to state in *Cue*: "No filmmaker has been so autobiographical. Francois Truffaut has been reviewing—and rerunning—his own life script, but he doesn't play himself on screen."

If moviegoers wondered whether the character in *Bananas, Sleeper*, and *Love and Death* might be the real Woody, *Annie Hall* took the confusion to the breaking point. Robert Hatch insisted: "The first two or three times a fellow named Alvy Singer was mentioned....I blinked, wondering who the devil he was. It took me a while to catch on that he was the character Allen was playing, since it seemed so obvious that Allen was playing himself." Another critic argued that *Annie Hall* could only be understood as an autobiographical film, and that in order to appreciate it, a viewer had to come to the movie with considerable knowledge of Woody and Diane Keaton's relationship. "Of course, this is

completely untrue," Woody told Garson Kanin, "because I would say 80 percent of the film is totally fabricated." But when Kanin asked Jack Hall, Diane's father, about it, he answered: "It's 85 percent true—even to Dorothy and my mother" (Granny Hall). "The hero is called Alvy Singer," Penelope Gilliatt wrote in *The New Yorker*, "but biographically and neurotically he could pass for Woody Allen any day."

However, there are obvious differences between the events in the movie and what happened in real life. Woody and Diane did not meet after a tennis game, but when he was casting *Sam* and interviewing actresses for the lead. In real life, Diane was already something of a star when she met Woody, not the unknown of the film. She did not move to California, but continued to live in New York, after they broke up. Compression of events, as well as the rewriting of one's personal history to make it more accessible as drama (or comedy), is not only acceptable but absolutely necessary: The raw material of art is not art, but only raw material. As an artist, Woody had to add motivations that would make actions understandable to his audience, to structure his material by selecting what was worth including and eliminating what would be irrelevant to anyone but himself. When a *Newsweek* reporter raised the question of autobiographical elements at the film's premiere, Woody shrugged and said, "The movie is fictional" but "if people go out and say, 'Yes, it was based on his life' or 'Gee, isn't that amazing, a man makes up such a wild story,' that's fine with me, either way."

What can't be denied is that Allen's work, autobiographical or not, is clearly intended as self-expression. Take Woody's fear of physical abuse. "When I was a kid," he told *TV Guide* in 1968, "I had a *terrific* fear of being attacked, of suffering bodily harm. I couldn't pass an alley without thinking… something would jump out and snatch me away." In the movies, he is constantly being attacked by abusive characters: In *Take the Money and Run*, there are gangs of toughs; in *Bananas*, troublemakers on the subway; in *Play It Again, Sam*, a group of Hell's Angels. Even in a less cartoonish film like *Annie Hall*, there are people who verbally (if not physically) assault him on the streets, wanting Alvy's autograph ("Weren't you on the Johnny Carson show?") and the cool, menacing policeman who is as terrifying as the one Janet Leigh encounters in *Psycho*. All are variations on the single theme of the threat of physical abuse, just as all are grotesque nightmare visions drawn from Woody's imagination of characters who might assault him.

And they lead directly to the ultimate assault: The "fan" who, at the end of *Stardust Memories*, sighs sweetly, "You know, I'm you're greatest fan," just before blowing Woody's (ooops! Sandy's) brains out.

True, Woody has never experienced this. On one level, the presence of these infinitely variable symbols of a single given obsession are totally invented, and on another, they are highly personal, revealing what's on Woody's mind, then transforming his thoughts into art. What we see onscreen is more Woody's nightmare vision than his everyday reality. But as Freud would insist, those nightmares reveal more of the essence of a person than what happens to him while going about his daily business.

THE BLUEBIRD OF ANXIETY

The heart of Woody's appeal has always been his self-deprecation. "People forget me," Woody once claimed, "even while they're shaking hands with me." In fact, it's doubtful anyone who has ever met Woody has forgotten him, so obvious is his genius. Millions of people—especially Jewish men who come from similar backgrounds—wonder why they cannot, like Woody, turn the common cultural experiences they share with him into works of art, enjoy the adulation of audiences, experience the love of WASP movie-star goddesses that he can take for granted, enjoy the fame and fortune he has amassed. Such people—so near to Woody Allen in so many ways yet so far from what he has achieved—would give anything to be Woody Allen. But on the jacket flap of his book *Side Effects*, the bio blurb (obviously written by Woody himself) tells us: "His one regret in life is that he is not someone else." So who would he like to be? "I fantasize playing guard for the Knicks," Woody told *Rolling Stone* in 1976. "If I had my life to live over again, I'd rather be a black basketball player." But even if that impossible dream could come true, Woody Allen would inevitably find some way to make himself thoroughly miserable about it.

Because Woody Allen suffers from anhedonia, a psychological reaction to events which causes the sufferer to be unable to enjoy anything, even the most pleasurable of experiences. (*Anhedonia* was Woody's working title for the film that eventually became *Annie Hall*). "Early in life," Woody readily admits, "I was visited by the bluebird of anxiety." So it is anxiety, not happiness, that even the most positive of experiences generates. in fact, anhedonia is the basis for some of his best gags, as when in the short story "A Little Louder Please" Woody contrasts the joy of "engulfing a slab of the world's richest cheesecake" with "the guilty cholesterolish hallucination that I could hear my aorta congealing into a hocky puck."

Perhaps the key to Allen's anhedonia, artistically

expressed, can be seen in *Love and Death*, when Boris (Woody) and Sonia (Diane Keaton) drop their retarded friend off at the Village Idiots Convention, then drive on to try and change world politics by assassinating Napoleon. "It's easy to be happy," Woody sighs wistfully, "if your one concern in life is figuring out how much saliva to dribble." Ignorance, we know, is bliss, but the Woody Allen character (like Woody Allen himself) is not ignorant, and so can never be blissful.

Why, then, does Woody go on creating works of art? That is, why bother? One reason might be the pleasure some people derive from making movies, though that is not the case with Woody, who once

told me: "I hate everything about the moviemaking process but the writing. I hate the acting, the editing, the hours, the camera—everything. Sets are not fun. No one is amusing. It's a thoroughly unpleasant experience." How can he continue making movies, then? His answer is perfectly, perversely anhedonic: "I figure if I don't make movies now, I'll regret it later on. I mean, everybody in the world wants to be a filmmaker. How can I be egotistical enough to turn down the opportunity?"

Another reason for going through the painful work of directing is to protect the pleasurable work of writing. "I hated it," Woody would eventually say of what happened to his first screenplay, *What's New, Pussycat?* "and it was the reason I became a director"—

As Boris, the cowardly Russian in Love and Death.

that is, to protect his words.

On the set, then, Woody emerges as a natural leader rather than a dictator. Editor Ralph Rosenblum, comparing his work for the early Allen with the early Mel Brooks, recalls in *When The Shooting Stops* that Brooks was a petty tyrant who would not listen to the common sense of an experienced editor, so threatened was he by being in charge. Woody, he recalls, was all ears. And this is what marks the Allen approach to shooting a film: he is a perfect blend of the auteur (one man, one movie—it's my vision!) attitude and the collaborative approach to moviemaking. On the one hand, Woody is an auteur in that his singular sensibility suffuses everything; it is his world-view that ultimately gets up there on the screen.

On the other hand, he is a true collaborator, allowing actors to ad-lib, co-authors Mickey Rose or Marshall Brickman to add material, and editors to make suggestions that, if in line with his concept for the project, he will take. He is the first among equals. "The most revealing thing," cartoonist Joe Marthen of the *Inside Woody Allen* comic strip claims, "is that Woody chooses not to wield the incredible power he has when he works with other people."

Others, however, have spoken in less glowing terms. "On the set of his films," Natalie Gittelson wrote, "he politely but firmly distances himself from everyone but Diane Keaton, actor Michael Murphy, and other trusted friends. He delivers most of his orders to the technical crew through intermediaries. Otherwise, his anger might explode at mortal men and blow the production sky high." In addition to the aloofness Gittelson perceives, some observers complain about Woody's entire approach to moviemaking: "Woody Allen's repressive kind of control," Pauline Kael complained in her scathing review of *Interiors*, "is just what may keep him from making great movies." But for those who feel that Woody Allen *does* make great movies, his firm control over the filmmaking process is the key to his success.

Variety reported on October 21, 1973, that Allen has an almost mystical belief that his films shouldn't cost more than $1,100,000 per, and while that sum must, twelve years later, be adjusted for inflation, he continues to keep the budgets tight. In a 1982 *Family Weekly* article, he thought back to *Pussycat* and recalled: "When you're making a big picture for $4 million (a modest amount today, but a huge budget in 1964, when *Pussycat* was produced), there are a lot of people around and they tell you they are protecting their investment. They wanted a girl-girl sex-sex picture to make a fortune. I had something else in mind. They got a girl-girl picture which made a fortune."

Few of his films have made a fortune since, but all of them have turned out the way he wanted. "I have a nice gentleman's agreement with United Artists," he once claimed. "I've traded the idea of making millions in return for artistic control." Woody makes movies cheaply and each produces a small profit. As long as that goes on, UA (and later Orion) is happy. They leave him alone and he delivers a finished picture.

"When he's finished a script," manager and co-producer Jack Rollins explains, "he asks me to read it—but not until he's finished it!" Woody's other guardian angel, Charles Joffe, claims: "He's always saying to me, 'If I make a dollar profit, then I can go on to the next picture.'" In addition to overseeing everything from the first draft to the final print, Woody's concern for his films goes so far as to closely supervise the advertising and promotional ploys. "His gut feelings about what should be done with his films," Lloyd Leipzig, Vice-President of Advertising for United Artists and later Orion, says, "are always right; they work for him." For *Annie Hall*, Woody insisted on subdued print ads and absolutely no television spots until the film had already been running in theatres for several weeks, so that isolated scenes would not give a misleading conception of the film.

Fascinatingly, then, Woody has managed, at a time when money is tight and production companies prefer to keep a close eye on a project from script through editing, to make movies that do not even have a working title (WASP was the ironic reference for Woody Allen's 1984 Summer Picture) and refuses to let his backers know even the general plot line.

Early on, it all seemed pretty simple, "There's no great mystery to film directing," Woody told the Los Angeles *Herald-Examiner* in 1971. "In comedy all you have to do is subordinate everything to the joke.... Chaplin used to say, 'Tragedy is life in closeup and comedy is life in longshot.'...If you can just see it clearly, you're 90 percent home." And as long as he was filming relatively simple comedy, this directorial approach sufficed. There was a kitchen sink quality to those early films, as Allen would throw in wildly discordant gags—verbal jokes, silent comedy sequences, broad bits of physical slapstick, sudden bursts of social satire, parodies of old movies.

Those early films do suggest a searching for a style, one which eventually emerges in the more mature, more sophisticated works like *Manhattan* and *Zelig*. As Woody progressed, he would reject his earlier statements about there being no great mystery to film directing. "When I heard that Antonioni prepares a picture for six months," he confessed to *Cinema* in 1972, "I couldn't figure out what the hell he is doing for six months." With his first two or three movies,

Woody had been thrilled just to be able to make them, and only wanted the pictures to turn out funny. He didn't care about anything else except that the joke would work, the audience would laugh. Then, with *Everything You Always Wanted to Know About Sex*, he consciously tried to improve as a filmmaker—and, ironically, in the eyes of many critics produced a film that was less funny, and less satisfying, than many of his earlier, less visually sophisticated pictures.

The director at work: Woody on the set of Everything You Always Wanted to Know About Sex.

He had realized, for one thing, that he hadn't truly been a filmmaker at all, but he had been transferring (rather than translating) his words into movies, shooting what he had written (and what could just as easily have been stand-up material or a short story) rather than writing for the movie medium. ''It remains to be seen whether he can bring off the elaborate visuals he promises for *Sex*,'' Robert Mundy wrote in 1972, ''or whether his camera style will lapse from clumsiness into self-consciousness.'' But by this time, Woody was already embroiled in the chores, so much more complex than he had first

imagined, of a true filmmaker. "By the time I did *Love and Death*," he would tell *Take One* in 1978, "I was very concerned with the filmmaking aspect, and with wanting to do darker things, not deal with a lot of conventional stuff." But Mundy's warning was not to be ignored: in order to make truly successful films, Woody would have to tread a delicate path between the artless, enjoyable clumsiness of his early efforts and the self-conscious, overly arty effects that filmmakers often fall prey to when they take themselves too seriously, when they start thinking of themselves not as movie makers but as artists.

THE CONFRONTATION WITH SELF

Thus, what has clearly marked the work of Woody Allen is his insistence on continual growth, his constant reaching, for better or worse, beyond what he has already accomplished. Indeed, perceptive critics have long noted this. As early as 1969, in a review of Allen's first directorial effort, Joseph Morgenstern borrowed the key metaphor of *Take the Money and Run* and cleverly described Woody's future career in the language of the prison break-out pictures Allen was then parodying: "Occasionally Allen gives you the feeling that he's a prisoner of himself, that he'd like to break out into even more promising areas of movie fiction but finds himself hemmed in by his ideas of himself as a performer." The notion that Woody the clown prince of comedy and Woody the serious intellectual writer-director might be in conflict with one another indicate the tension which would exist throughout Woody's entire subsequent career.

Many of Woody's early gag ideas for films fail—if not to elicit a laugh, then to win a critic's admiration—because Allen was still essentially a prose writer who had enough prestige and power to turn his written words into pictures. Too often, though, these images took away from, rather than added to, the comic conceptions. As Leonard Maltin wrote in *The Great Movie Comedians* about the giant breast sequence from *Everything About Sex*: "this whole sequence draws few laughs, because it isn't really all that funny; in fact, like many of Allen's film gags, it is funnier when described than when seen firsthand. There is nothing inherently funny about the idea of a man having relations with rye bread, except in the absurdity of *saying* it. Actually, watching it onscreen is taking the joke one step too far, making what may be funny in abstract terms unfunny in three dimension...."

The point is well taken. Try to imagine one of the lines from a classic Allen monologue being filmed,

perhaps the one in which he argues that his wife is immature, and can prove it: Whenever he was taking a bath, she would walk in and sink his boats. That gag produced howls of laughter, because it was a perfect stand-up bit: a two-liner that can only produce laughter when spoken or read; a gag that depends, for its effect, on audience participation as the listener/reader mentally fills in the visual image. But if we were actually to see that image, the gag would no longer be funny. What Woody would have to do—and what, indeed, he *would* do—was learn to write for the camera, not merely use the camera to record the kind of writing he had already been doing.

Live theatre, be it a serious play or a stand-up routine, is "like literature," Woody would say in 1979. "It deals primarily with words. Film is about photography. It's a very different thing."

What's wrong with so many of the gags in early Allen films is that he merely films a written gag. When, in *Everything About Sex* mad doctor John Carradine announces that Woody's pretty companion (Heather McRea) is going to be mercilessly raped by boy scouts, the line produces a guffaw. But when the camera then cuts to an image of the scouts, it's merely a case of the visuals repeating the verbal gag without adding to it. In any good film—comedy or otherwise—the camera offers an entirely other dimension to what we hear on the soundtrack. Woody would in time learn this and, when he did, would cease to be a night club comedian given a camera and emerge as a true filmmaker.

As an actor, Woody has gradually but drastically changed his persona from Allan Felix in *Sam*, who could not get a date even on New Year's Eve (though he was married at the time), to Isaac Davis in *Manhattan*, who casually says, "I've never had any trouble getting girls." Even before that film's release, though, Janet Maslin noted in 1977 that "Woody Allen is outgrowing the droll, self-deprecating brand of comedy that has been his trademark." To understand the growth of the Woody Allen persona, it's important to note that when Professor Kugelmass, a character in one of Woody's award-winning short stories, complains, "I'm a man who needs romance," he could be speaking for all the Woody Allen heroes. Importantly, the "romance" the characters are searching for is not merely of the sexual-romantic variety, even though in the films it manifests itself in just this form. In 1972, *The New Yorker* pronounced that Woody "belongs to a contemporary offshoot of Romantic literature which could be called the literature of Neurotic Love. It has as strong a hold on American humor now as the language of the troubadours had on the poetry of Courtly Love, and Woody Allen is one of the funniest people

Woody Allen and friend in a starkly beautiful landscape that looks as if it could be right out of Wuthering Heights, *suggesting the philosophic and ''romantic'' quality that has too often been overlooked in his work.*

practicing it....The Woody Allen character is about a yearning for the unattainable (for prowess, for a sweet-natured love), which is the keystone of Romanticism.'' Kugelmass's mournful statement speaks for Woody in that both the character and the author are ''unlikely romantics,'' men in search not only of pretty girls but for the ideal as incarnate in the real, which is of course a search for the impossible dream.

Essentially, the romantic pursuit of a woman is only a philosophic-romantic inclination taking its most logical and obvious physical manifestation: Romanticism (in the philosophic sense of the word) is transformed, in the everyday world, into romanticism (in the physical sense of sexuality). In fact, though, the philosophic-romantic is a man who holds an ideal in his mind and tries to achieve that ideal. He is then emotionally or intellectually destroyed when he gets what he wants and finds that, in truth, it cannot measure up to what he imagined, because nothing in the real world can ever match the ideal of what it ought to be. In ''The Kugelmass Episode,'' a literature teacher wants to make love to that most fascinating of fictional characters, Emma Bovary, but when a magician makes this happen, the initially exciting affair quickly dissipates into disaster. This is very close to the notions of the British romantic poets, from Wordsworth to Coleridge; it's what Keats was talking about when he had his narrator look at a frozen portrait of men chasing (but never catching) women in the frozen image of a Grecian urn and conclude that ''heard memories are sweet, but those unheard sweeter still''; it's the terrible truth Jay Gatsby learns when, in Scott Fitzgerald's greatest novel, he finally gets the girl of his dreams and wishes he hadn't. Almost all Woody's work, literary or filmic, is written in this romantic spirit.

But it is only in the later films that the Woody Allen character emerges as a romantic hero rather than a sad victim of unfulfilled romantic yearnings. Noting this growth, Jack Kroll would claim that ''Woody has finally come to represent not the schlemiel he's so often been called, but an almost romantic figure.''

By admitting his homeliness (in conventional definitions of sex appeal), Woody served as a scapegoat for all of society at large, since most people fear they don't measure up; and in so doing, Woody not only helped other people accept themselves but also changed the definition of what constitutes beauty, emerging as a romantic figure in the process. in 1969, *Time* could type him as ''an incarnation of the schlemiel, a born super-stupe'' and get away with it. But ten years later Natalie Gittelson would note for *The New York Times* that Woody ''has shed his adolescent

insecurity. He has largely given up the slapstick and sight gags which, although often hilarious, were also a defense against the confrontation with self.'' That confrontation has been basic to Woody the writer-director as well as Woody the star. Woody once said about Chaplin (the filmmaker, not the actor) that ''he was preoccupied with developing. He was willing to take many chances and he often failed. Some of his movies were quite terrible. But he was always trying to grow. And whatever he did, you felt in contact with an interesting artist.'' It's hard not to believe Woody's interpretation of Chaplin can also serve as Woody's projection of the kind of artist he wanted to be.

A few years later, he would go even further when talking to *Newsweek*: ''It's important not to get into that terrible syndrome where you're a creator of hits—then I think you're dead. I think it's important for any filmmaker or playwright to do a lot of stuff and to fail miserably a portion of the time. It's a healthy sign you're trying to grow. So I'm willing to be publicly humiliated.'' And, on more than one occasion, he has been. The critics almost unanimously panned *Interiors* and *Stardust Memories*.

But Woody's natural comedic talents were, in his mind, getting in the way of his heavier ambitions as a filmmaker. As early as 1970, Woody noted that ''The fun in directing is to get 'fancy.' But you have to present the comedian in as clear and simple way as possible. In directing something serious, you can indulge yourself. It's not too much fun directing comedy.'' Part of the reason it's less fun—less likely that the director can set up some spectacular shot—is because, as he'd declare two years later, ''Comedy films are unlike other films: what's important in a comedy is the content of the shot, not the shot itself.''

Pauline Kael was one of the earliest critics to note that Woody's growth as a technical artist was, paradoxically, accompanied by a lessening of his impact as a humorist. Reviewing *Sleeper* (the first film in which Woody attempted to get a little ''fancy'') she simultaneously criticized and celebrated the film, balancing her complaints with compliments: ''If it sounds like a contradiction to say that *Sleeper* is a small classic and yet not exhilarating—well, I can't completely explain that. Comedy is impossibly mysterious; *Sleeper* is a beautiful little piece of work—it shows a development of skills in our finest comedy-maker—and yet it's mild, and doesn't quite take off.'' Woody, meanwhile, was going through a most frustrating period, trying to resolve his serious inclinations with his comedic gifts. ''Some things can be expressed in a funny way,'' he claimed, ''but I'd hate to think I could only make amusing films. I'm too much a fan of serious films.''

Those serious films include the works of

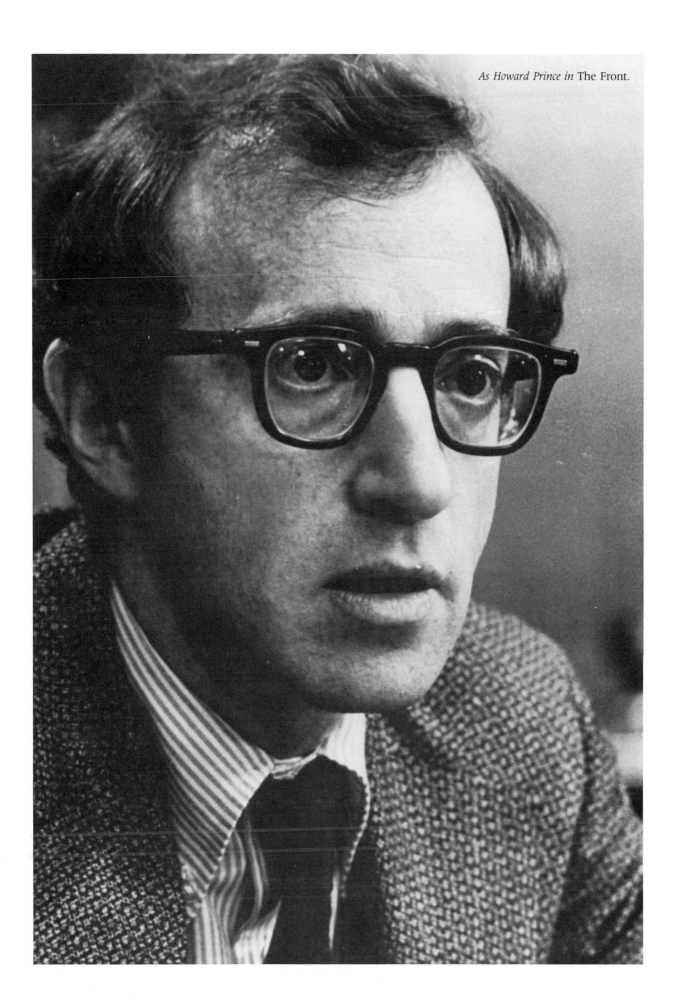

As Howard Prince in The Front.

Bergman, whom Woody would emulate with *Interiors*, the totally dramatic film which would divide critics and fans alike. "It's a personal view," Woody once told *Esquire*, "but I have a lesser opinion of comedy....I get more enjoyment out of a film like *Persona* (Bergman) than *The General* (Keaton) or *City Lights* (Chaplin). A comedy, for me, has the quality of being a little dessert, a diversion....The real meat and potatoes are serious films." Woody's comment is naïve at best, outrageous and angering at worst. Comedy can be (and at its best, which includes much of Woody Allen, always has been) as meaningful, as insightful, as complex, as multi-layered as drama.

Why does Woody Allen denigrate the form to which he seems most naturally inclined, and has been graced with such enormous gifts? Perhaps it is his anhedonia again. The Jewish intellectual who would rather have been a black ballplayer is not so far removed from the world-class comedian who thinks it would be better to have been born a world-class tragedian. Moreover, the fact that our greatest comic artist feels the need to downplay his form and wax rhapsodic about the alternative is a paradox,

one of those incomprehensible and absurd contradictions that mark Woody Allen's life and work. Indeed, to understand the impact of Woody Allen's humor—how it works its effect on us—it is necessary to first catalogue some of the more significant paradoxes and come to realize that what I shall call The Paradox Principle is the basis of his approach, whether one considers the philosophic base of his most successful work or the technique with which that work is expressed.

GOD AND CARPETING

On the eve of *Annie Hall*'s release, Woody described to me a scene he had cut for the sake of the film's "flow," but which, if included, might have revealed the most insightful image of himself Woody has yet offered. At that famous New York literary-set party to which Alvy and Robin go, Alvy slips away from the pretentious conversation and, alone in the bedroom, watches a ball game on TV. What's missing from the final print is that televised game, as a groggy Alvy/Allen mentally perceives it as a contest between the New York Knicks and members of the intellectual Establishment, who are of course trounced royally. "I wanted to show the grace

As the title character in Broadway Danny Rose.

and beauty of the Knicks, and how what they do makes any accomplishments of the intellectual community look ridiculous and insignificant by comparison," Woody told me. Fair enough, as social satire; but the *paradox* comes in the fact that in the sequence, Woody plays on the side of the intellectuals. And therein rests the rub: Woody anhedonically accepts that he is a part of everything he feels compelled to criticize.

For instance, some observers have experienced confusion in trying to understand how, in a single film, the Woody Allen hero may alternately describe himself as a superstud and a washout with women. But his near-paranoid (and totally paradoxical) pendulum swings are at the heart of his humor. The way in which the character (and most of us watching) wants to perceive himself, and on the other hand the way in which he feels he may appear to people, cause the real man in the middle to bounce back and forth from moments of elation, when he feels he may almost be living up to his media-created ideal (Bogart, James Bond, etc.), to fear of total failure. Likewise, Woody can crack an audience up with a line like "Sex is a beautiful thing between two people...between five, it's *fantastic*!" And then, when asked to list his all-time turn-offs, immediately assert that "group sex" is one of them. Paradoxical, to say the least; but it makes clear the distinction between Woody the popular entertainer, who makes us laugh nervously at our hopes and fears, and Allen the serious, philosophic moral artist, the man of conservative lifestyle who is a political liberal.

"We empathize with this five-foot-five-inch, skinny, bespectacled, confused-looking, wispy redhead," Elliott Joseph wrote in *Genesis* magazine, and "we laugh at him and with him as he tells us how people kick sand in his face at the beach. But at the same time we admire him, because he is a champion for us all, a wonderful, contradictory loser-winner." The loser-winner: what phrase could better capture Woody's paradoxical persona?

But how many of us made $350 a week in the early sixties, before inflation set in? The point is, that loser onstage or in the films is not a window into Woody's soul, but a mirror held up to the audience. Everyone occasionally feels, in his darkest hour, that he's a loser in the game of life, and Woody allows us to laugh at that self-pitying aspect of ourselves by encouraging the audience to laugh at him. Everybody's favorite "loser" was able, however, as early as 1966 to move into a spacious six-room duplex apartment in the East Seventies, decorate it in Louis XIV downstairs while upstairs include a den complete with billiard table and film projector, at a cost of over $100,000. Unlike so many writers and/or

performers who achieve success (if at all) only after a lengthy struggle, Woody succeeded at everything he attempted almost immediately, critically as well as commercially: He received the highly esteemed Sylvania Award in 1957 for his scripting of a *Sid Caesar Show* when he was only twenty-one, the youngest performer ever to receive this coveted recognition.

Paradox: Woody flunked out of his literature class at City College and then, several years later, won the O. Henry award for the best American short story of 1976–77 ("The Kugelmass Episode"). Paradox: a 1967 *Reader's Digest* story typed him as having been "a puny, sensitive youngster" who had not been "much for athletics," when in fact Woody had not only been fond of sports but was also very good at them, including the roughest sport of all, boxing, qualifying for the Golden Gloves tournament but dropping out only because his father would not sign the release form. Paradox: Woody is so removed from practical matters and financial affairs that, according to *Time*, he gave producer-manager-friend Charles Joffe the power of attorney to sign "all his contracts and even his divorce papers." But Woody inspired Michael Blowen of the *Boston Globe* to write "Allen's attention to business details is legendary" and a former United Artists executive to comment that Woody's "business sense is extraordinary. He knows that his fiscal conservatism and pre-planning are what allow him to make other movies." Paradox: Woody is famous for his seeming lack of interest in clothing, though *McCall's* once noted that his famed crumpled-corduroy jacket actually came from Brooks Brothers. Paradox: even as a youth, he was at cross-purposes with himself, rooting for the New York Giants from across town against the local team, the Brooklyn Dodgers, whenever the two played. Paradox: Woody escorting First Lady Betty Ford to a benefit, as compared to Woody telling *Rolling Stone* that "Ford was the guy who I remembered being on the wrong side of every issue—utterly unqualified to be president of the United States by any stretch of the imagination." Paradox: Woody attending that event in tuxedo and tennis shoes. Paradox: at the same time the young Woody contemplated joining the FBI, he also seriously considered life as a criminal.

Even Woody's movies are paradoxical. At a time when Hollywood movies were glossy, Woody's films were rough-edged. *Take the Money* stood out in an era of airport pictures, the last of the big expensive formula films; several years later, when the post-*Animal House* Hollywood had gone self-consciously crude, Woody reminded us of the élan and elegance of the past with his graceful, glamorous *Manhattan*. When I once asked Woody what kind of movies he hates the most, he answered without hesitation that he can't stand those slow-moving, overly artsy, ennui-ridden European

35

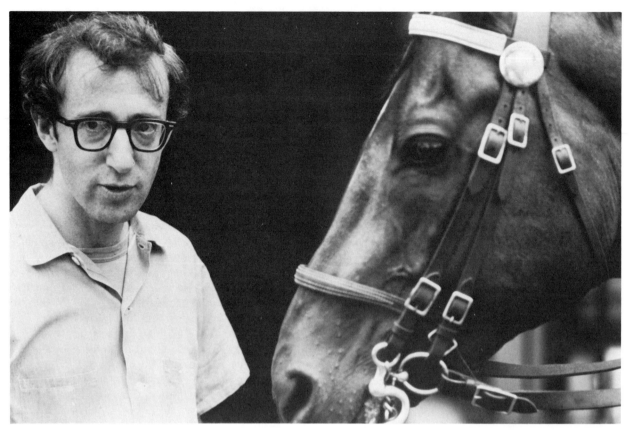

Woody Allen and friend. Who looks the more nervous?

films that exhaust an audience with portraits of sophisticated people's self-important but meaningless lives. From this, I assumed he meant Michelangelo Antonioni, but was too well-mannered to name him. When I then asked him who his favorite moviemakers were, he quickly asserted that Antonioni was one of them. Astounded, I asked Woody how he could reconcile loving Antonioni with hating the very kind of movies Antonioni is famous for making, to which he shrugged and said, "I know, it doesn't make any sense, does it?" He was himself aware of the paradoxical quality of his statements, and couldn't reconcile them.

Likewise, it's paradoxical that Woody's favorite comics are Bob Hope, the symbol of the old-time slick professionals, and Mort Sahl, the representative of the new breed of scruffy counter-culture comedians. Woody's own approach is a paradoxical union of the two styles. Understandable, then, that some of the most telling comments about Woody remark on the paradoxical nature of his appeal: Yacowar notes that "the club comedian and Kafka converge in Woody Allen," while Pauline Kael concluded that there is a "running war between the tame and the surreal—between Woody Allen the frightened nice guy trying to keep the peace and Woody Allen the

wiseacre whose subversive fantasies keep jumping out of his mouth."

One of the most significant paradoxes in Allen's work is the element of Jewishness that pervades his films. "He's vacillated in his attitudes toward Jews and gentiles," Peter Biskind wrote, "one moment sentimentalizing Jews as lifesaving agents of passion and vigor, capable of revitalizing desiccated WASPs, as he does in *Interiors*, the next denigrating them for their vulgarity, as he does in *Stardust Memories*, or romanticizing WASPs as vessels of truth and beauty, put on earth to redeem eternally ambivalent Jews, as he does in *Manhattan*." That "vacillation" may in fact be only one more aspect of the paradox principle.

"I don't have that Jewish obsession," he calmly stated in 1976. "I use my background when it's expedient for me in my work. But it's not really an obsession of mine and I never had that obsession with Gentile women." That may come as a shock to Diane Keaton and Mia Farrow, those WASP goddesses who have graced Allen's art and life. And in paradoxical contrast to this comment, there is Woody's gag-line in which he describes himself as "a Jewish intellectual with a penchant for fascist women." But that's merely one more paradox.

And paradoxical is certainly the word to describe Woody's relationships with women, at least as they

Woody faces the press at a conference promoting one of his films. (PHOTO BY PAUL SCHUMACH)

are reflected in his films. A sado-masochistic streak can be detected in his 1965 comment to the Los Angeles *Times* about the type of women he's attracted to: "Very pretty, very bright, witty girls who are spoiled and mean and will give me a hard time no matter how much affection I squander on them." But when asked to describe his appeal for the opposite sex, he told Don Alpert that same year: "A certain type of woman likes me. The type that has cut her wrist at least once. I appeal to women in proportion to the times they have attempted suicide." In the late sixties, when nobody questioned the validity of *Playboy* magazine and the lifestyle it preached (and, indeed, "liberated" women were the ones who claimed that magazine, which Woody often wrote for, was healthy and positive), the pursuit of beautiful girls in Woody's plays and films was unquestionably accepted. "How he loves his women!" Frank Pierson sighed. "He mocks them, pays them lavish compliments and slaps them down, watches them with the fascination of prey yearning to be devoured."

But in the seventies, when Women's Lib made itself felt, there came a backlash against both Hugh Hefner's publication and Woody Allen's work. "Women in Woody Allen's movies were little more than projections of male lust," *Ms.* huffed. By 1980, Vivian Gornick of *The Village Voice* scoffed, "I could no longer find his ridiculing pursuit of women *funny*." One of the few writers who looked beyond the obvious was theatre critic Ross Wetzsteon, who explained:

"The jokes seem to be saying that Woody Allen always wants to get laid, but that women keep rejecting him, so he feels like a schlemiel." *Feeling* like a schlemiel when rejected by an autonomous woman who will not always respond on cue makes sense of Woody's paradoxical image of himself as a schlemiel and a stud: "Woody Allen tells us that although we may have trouble with women (and we all feel we do), we don't have trouble with our sexuality.... Allen assures us, then, of what we most want to hear, that no matter how often we suffer sexual confusion, embarrassment, or downright rejection, these fiascos don't make us any less *masculine*."

Wetzsteon perfectly reconciles the paradoxical elements of Woody's approach to the opposite sex. But many of the paradoxes can't ever be completely resolved, and that's the basis of their appeal. "My parents," an Allen gag goes, "were simple people. They believed in God and carpeting." The audience laughs, because of the paradox: they believed in the most spiritual and the most practical—as do, in the end, we all.

The paradox principle extends from Woody's personality to the basic technique he uses for film-making: His best moments, comic or otherwise, are those in which the image and words contradict one another. In his most memorable movie gags—the ones that not only perfectly express his own unique vision of life but which also make the most of the sound-film's possibilities for contrapuntal effect—the humor is not in the images or in the words so much as it exists in the relationship of the one to the other.

The repressed lover as bookworm: Woody Allen as Victor Shakapopolis.

WHAT'S NEW, PUSSYCAT?

A UNITED ARTISTS RELEASE (1965)

CAST:

Peter Sellers *(Fritz Fassbender)*; Peter O'Toole *(Michael James)*; Romy Schneider *(Carol Werner)*; Capucine *(Renée Lefebvre)*; Paula Prentiss *(Liz Bien)*; Woody Allen *(Victor Shakapopolis)*; Ursula Andress *(Rita)*; Edra Gale *(Anna Fassbender)*; Catherine Schaake *(Jacqueline)*; Jess Hahn *(Perry Werner)*; Nicole Karen *(Tempest O'Brien)*; Jean Paredes *(Marcel)*; Jacqueline Fogt *(Charlotte)*; Jacques Balutin *(Etienne)*; Annette Poivre *(Emma)*; Sabine Sun *(Beautiful Nurse)*; Tanya Lopert *(Miss Lewis)*; Colin Drake *(Durell)*; Louise Lasser *(The Nutcracker)*; Richard Saint-Bris *(The Mayor)*; Francoise Hardy *(Mayor's Secretary)*; Richard Burton *(Man in Bar)*.

CREDITS:

Producer, Charles K. Feldman; director, Clive Donner; screenplay, Woody Allen; photography, Jean Badal; music, Burt Bacharach; editor, Fergus McDonnell; sound, William-Robert Sive; art director, Jacques Saulnier; special effects, Bob MacDonald; color by Technicolor, Scope; running time, 106 minutes; A Famous Artists Production.

After catching Woody's acclaimed stand-up act at The Blue Angel, Hollywood producer Charles K. Feldman agreed to put up the money for a movie Woody would write. Feldman's concept was a comedy vehicle designed specifically for Hollywood's latest heart-throb, Warren Beatty, who would star in the film and say the line he always used when called by young women on the phone: "What's new, Pussycat?" Because of scheduling conflicts and artistic differences, Beatty eventually dropped out of the project, though there is a certain irony in the fact that Woody's first screen-writing experience came in fabricating a project for the man who would eventually end up with Allen's inamorata, Diane Keaton, and whom Allen would savagely satirize with the Paul Simon character in *Annie Hall*. Woody himself would later describe his work as "a Marx Brothers type-script, kind of crazy," but he had no power in the industry at that time, and it would be drastically rewritten, so much so that he would in time speak only negatively of the entire experience.

He told *Boston After Dark* five years later: "I loathe everyone and everything concerned with it and they all loathe me....They butchered my script. They wrenched it into a commercial package....It ended up in the hands of establishment people who were hep, not hip. I couldn't go to see it for a year." Ironically also, Woody's first film, which established him in Hollywood, did so as an inversion of all the movies that would follow: they were critically acclaimed but not particularly well attended; *Pussycat* was the biggest

A romantic hero: Victor woos Jacqueline (Catherine Schaake) and paves the way for future amorous heroes from Allen.

A cerebral comic: In his first screen appearance, Allen (as Victor) plays chess with a beautiful Parisian, though his eyes reveal his amatory interest. His idol Michael (Peter O'Toole) offers guidance as Bogie will later do for Allan Felix.

grossing comedy ever at the time, though largely damned by critics.

Indeed, it was the highbrow critics—those who would in time become Woody's greatest supporters—who had the nastiest things to say about it. Stanley Kauffmann of *The New Republic* wrote that "the script is by the night club comic Woody Allen, who also appears in the picture as his usual self-conscious intellectual bumbler, and it is to him that the film owes its unconventional air as well as its occasional funny lines.... However, most of the script is made up of material that probably reads hilariously but does not play successfully. This often happens to good humorous writers: S. J. Perelman's sketches, knitted by him into a play called *The Beauty Part*, simply reminded us of how funny they were to read. Allen's material might be funny either read by us or spoken by him with *all* the lines colored by his oblique, self-deprecating humor. When the lines are assigned to different actors, who have to give them even farcical reality, who have to act out, with their bodies, ideas that only *sound* funny when spoken by an intelligent weakling, most of the script is reduced to good intention." In complaining that Woody failed to write specifically for the movie medium here, Kauffmann provided constructive criticism; Woody would in fact progress, learning to understand the cinematic form and practice it with most impressive results.

Most critics, however, took the route Hollis Alpert assumed in *Saturday Review*, attacking the overall aura of the film rather than pinpointing a specific aesthetic problem. "Everyone involved presumably felt they were having a lot of stylish fun with this non-plot, and maybe that's the trouble," he chided. "So admiring are they of their freedom that they all come out stilted and artificial, and almost entirely unfunny. The madder the pace set by the director, the more the would-be comedy creaks, and eventually it collapses into a yawning pit of boredom." Whereas Alpert's anger expressed that of the more intellectual critic, many members of the popular press—those who view their jobs less as the artistic consciousness of the serious set than as purveyors and predictors of popular taste—also took such a view, as when Judith Crist of the New York *Herald-Tribune* dismissed the movie as "a shrieking, reeking conglomeration of dirty jokes, dreary camp and blatant ambi-sexuality wrapped around a tediously plodding plot and stale comedy routines." Bosley Crowther of *The New York Times* specifically took Woody to task, claiming the famed night club comedian "is formally charged with the minor offense of having written what is alleged to be the screenplay.... But Mr. Allen can deny it, if he wants to, and he is bound to be believed. He can simply state that no one in his right mind could have written this excuse for

A bedraggled Michael (Peter O'Toole) encounters a shocked but fascinated Carol (Romy Schneider).

a script," echoing Crist's complaint about "stale comedy" with his own assertion that there were "too many imitative tricks."

Woody's tendency to include in his films all sorts of famous tricks of the trade that had been employed by great filmmakers of the past—both comic and non-comedic techniques—has been at the center of Allen criticism since *Pussycat*. Some critics insist that he is not the innovative and original voice he's been cracked up to be but only a cinematic copycat, while others view his absorption of film history as the basis of his point of view, as he learns from all previous moviemakers and then serves up films that are state-

The perfect masochist: Victor takes a job helping the strippers at the Crazy Horse Saloon get into their costumes, remaining so near and yet so far.

to the tail of an old tom." Similarly, Richard Schickel, who would in time become Woody's most ardent supporter, attacked his first film effort, labelling it "a star-filled, expensive, vulgar non-movie" (a description Woody would probably agree to), then arguing specifically: "Its makers have obviously appreciated the works of such masters as The Marx Brothers. Who hasn't? But what they missed therein was the relentless internal logic, the compulsive concern for sticking to the truth of the basic characterizations that was the real strength of the old-timers. When they engaged in a chase, they chased *for* something, they did not run aimlessly around, hoping to stumble on the reason for their activity while it proceeded. *Pussycat* has no internal rationale or logic. It only wants to be fashionable."

Perhaps. Then again, Schickel may miss the point of the movie. Though Woody and director Clive Donner do revive the conventions of classic screen comedy here (not only the Marx Brothers but Mack Sennett as well) they would merely be imitators and nostalgists if they served up such lovingly remembered clichés at face value. Instead, Woody resuscitates the old movie styles by focusing them on a subject of, about, and for the 1960's. The point about old movies is, as Schickel correctly points out, that everyone chased for something, mainly because they were produced in an era when people generally believed there was unquestionably something worth chasing around for. True also that Woody's characters run aimlessly around, though that is less the criticism Schickel intends than an apt description of both Woody's own comic vision and the life view that would surface in the revolutionary 1960's. Woody's comic presence would, in subsequent pictures, emerge as a man steeped in past traditions trying to adjust to the untraditional present.

Newsweek, on the other hand, would insist that "the whole nasty business is tricked up to look like an exotic flowering of the avant-garde cinema—frenetic, disjointed" but that it instead "batters the senses with the mindless insistence of a discothèque loudspeaker." It's also possible, though, to take the film as a freewheeling spoof of the mid-sixties as an era, and the cinematic style developing at that time when the commercial success of *Dr. Strangelove* and *A Hard Day's Night* caused the big studios to finally forsake their stodgy styles and instead try (however strained their attempts might be) to make their big pictures in techniques borrowed from little films. Certainly, the public didn't listen to the put-downs, lining up to see a picture they considered the perfect large-scale comedic entertainment for its particular time, in terms of the cast, the concerns, and the craftsmanship. A few critics writing in the popular press did react in the same vein as the

ments about film. *Time* took a negative view of this tendency with *Pussycat* (they would, over the years, change their tune), complaining that "in his disappointing double debut as a scenarist and second banana, Nightclub Comedian Woody Allen has written a small flat role for himself and fleshed it out with perhaps a dozen workable gags," describing the film's style as a desperate "rummaging eclectically through a whole range of comedy styles, like a man tying tin cans

audiences. James Powers of the *Hollywood Reporter* hailed it as "a wild and wonderful romantic farce," noting in particular that "Woody Allen, who did the merry script, is also a funny performer." George H. Jackson of the Los Angeles *Herald-Examiner* called it "the wildest, wackiest comedy to come along in memory...a madcap mixture of farce, fantasy, slapstick..." and praised the "highly imaginative screenplay by Woody Allen." Richard Gertner of the *Motion Picture Herald* had kind words, too: "Sex and psychoanalysis have been satirized in movies before, but neither has in a long time taken a drubbing delivered with quite the same ferocity and lack of let-up that they get without mercy" in *Pussycat*, calling the result "one of the most hilarious pictures to hit the screen in recent years."

And at least one highbrow critic—the always unpredictable, always outrageous, always fascinating Raymond Durgnat—came out in the film's defense: "In a word," he explained in *Films and Filming*, "this is a post-TW3 [TV's experimental *That Was The Week That Was*] picture, homing in, like *The Knack*, on a new lifestyle...It's about a world of shamelessness, and not simply about sex. Where most people, however free in their own thoughts, are, in fact, scared stiff of letting other people know about their immoral desires, their irresponsibilities, their spats, kinks and phobias, what's new about *What's New* is that it's about people who, instead of hiding them, display them as proudly as peacocks, and, instead of ridiculing or resenting them in others, tolerate and enjoy them, so becoming as good-natured and obliging as they are colorful. The cavaliers ride again. It's interesting not just because it's the Kinsey Report as it might have been filmed by Mack Sennett, but because it's a festive escape from the general anxiety to be, or at least to appear to be, 'normal' and 'well-adjusted.'"

Durgnat's perceptive analysis defines, with amazing foresight, precisely the theme most critics would in time come to see as the essence of Woody's comic vision, strongly suggesting that *Pussycat*—despite its grandiose production values and extravagant all-star approach—comes closer to being a Woody Allen film than anyone, Woody included, would care to admit. Peter O'Toole has claimed that he and Peter Sellers actually improvised much of the dialogue on-location, but there are plenty of lines that certainly sound like vintage Woody Allen, while the situations themselves express an Allenesque vision of life's absurdities. *Pussycat* is best viewed as a collage of concerns, an initial presentation of ideas still in fragment form which would be developed during the next two decades as Woody matured as a filmmaker and a screenwriter.

In fact, a plot synopsis of the comedy's basic "situation" at once expressed Allen's "anhedonia" theme. Michael James (Peter O'Toole) is a fashion reporter living in Paris, where he constantly finds himself surrounded by beautiful women. This should make him happy; instead, it makes him miserable, since he's in love with Carol (Romy Schneider), a bright and beautiful woman (and a sort of European Annie Hall) who is clearly the

The recurring Allen theme of psychoanalysis is introduced in the very first film, as Dr. Fritz Fassbender (Peter Sellers) listens to the problems of patient Michael James (Peter O'Toole).

perfect mate: intelligent and oversexed. But he cannot properly enjoy Carol any more than he can take pleasure in the various pussycats who pass in and out of his life: His love for her makes him feel guilty about flirting with them, while his desire for them makes it impossible to fully commit himself to Carol. The anhedonic inability to enjoy even the most pleasurable of situations also bothers his best friend, Victor (Woody), who gets a job helping the Crazy Horse Saloon stripteasers into their bizarre costumes, putting him nearer the women he lusts after than most other men can get, yet so far away since they perceive him only as a bumbling fool.

Romantic love, Woody here suggests, is one primary cause of anhedonia, since everyone in the film loves somebody he or she cannot have. Victor loves Carol who loves Michael who is in turn pursued by the elegant, sophisticated nymphomanic Renée (Capucine) who is the love object of Michael's psychiatrist, Fritz Fassbender (Peter Sellers), who desperately wants to be more like the patient he is, paradoxically, attempting to cure. We want, the film insists, what we cannot have, simply because we cannot have it, and that makes it valuable; so people who could, if they only would, be perfectly happy with someone who loves them, instead find ample opportunity to be miserable over an impossible dream.

Michael's situation suggests the tragic plight of the modern male as he will be depicted in future Woody Allen movies: wanting both the excitement of casual affairs with women like Liz Bien (Paula Prentiss), a frigid striptreaser with a penchant for writing radical poetry and attempting suicide at the drop of a hat, and also the safe, sane normalcy of life in the slow lane, enjoying a long-time lasting relationship with the right woman. Michael's anhedonic romantic problem is paradoxical in much the same way Alvy Singer's is in *Annie Hall*: he also tries to keep the relationship from getting too thick until Annie rebels at his inability to commit and leaves, at which point he does a quick about-face and desperately pursues her.

By the time of *Annie Hall*, of course, Woody would have grown enough to play the romantic hero, rather than cast himself as the hero's schlemiel-like sidekick. Alvy Singer, like Michael, has the kind of problem poor Victor can only wish he had to deal with, and the implied statement is that being successful at romancing women does not provide any more happiness or satisfaction than being unsuccessful with women: they are only two opposing forms of misery. Both Michael and Alvy serve as Woody's representations of the modern male, torn by the paradoxically polar attitudes the media has barraged him with since birth: the need,

In another prelude to Play It Again, Sam, *would-be ladies man Woody gets advice on how to handle women from a conventional cinema hero (Peter O'Toole).*

like all those unattached heroes of TV detective and western shows, to be free and unattached; and the need, like the heroes of all those TV family shows, to be committed.

Another problem facing Victor is that he's in love with his best friend's woman. As in *Play It Again, Sam*, which will eventually offer a more personal serving of the themes glossily commercialized in *Pussycat*, Victor wants his friend's woman and hates himself for wanting her. In *Pussycat*, he tries and fails to bed her; in *Sam*, Allan Felix succeeds, then goes through paroxysms of guilt afterwards; in *Manhattan*, Isaac Davis refuses to date the friend's woman until he's sure they have broken up. The progression of attitudes toward what is essentially a single comic-dramatic situation shows the growth not only of the Woody Allen character, but also of Allen the artist. In time, Allen's character will learn to reject the value system he accepted without reservation in the swinging sixties as he undergoes a moral education on his way to the enlightened eighties.

Also tying *Pussycat* to *Sam* is the notion of the

Woody Allen character's attempting to live up to an impossible ideal, a media-created image of what a male ought to be like and which, in fact, *nobody* is like in real life. In *Sam*, of course, it's Bogart; in *Casino Royale*, James Bond. That notion might not at first seem to fit in *Pussycat*, where Peter O'Toole is playing a specific character, however successful with women that character might be. But that O'Toole is really playing Peter O'Toole pretending to be Michael, rather than seriously creating a comedic characterization, is established early-on when O'Toole/Michael enters a bar and encounters an unbilled Richard Burton. In actuality, Burton and O'Toole were pals who co-starred in *Beckett* a year earlier. Here, O'Toole asks, "Don't I know you?" and then tells Burton to "Give my regards to what's-'er-name," a reference of course to Elizabeth Taylor. More than a gag, this is a wink to the audience that O'Toole will never totally submerge into the character of Michael, but on some level will remain O'Toole the movie star. He is the ideal Victor aspires to, the dream of what Victor would like to become (and, in *Annie Hall*, what he *will* become), while Fassbender is the nightmare vision of the exasperating lecher Victor fears people may perceive him as.

There is a thin red line, then, between the sex symbol of Michael and the dirty old man of Fritz, and it is Victor who unhappily straddles that line.

A fascination with food, and a tendency to use it as a symbol for sex, is apparent in this shot showing Victor grasping a banana (the foodstuff that will later provide a film title) as an alternative to the sex enjoyed by Michael and Carol.

Food is also associated with death: Victor's meal is interrupted by Fritz, who plans to commit suicide owing to sexual dissatisfaction.

The recurring fear of marriage in Allen's films is first symbolized by Anna (Edra Gale), Valkyrie-like wife of Fritz Fassbender.

Another nightmare vision of marriage: Monsieur Lefebvre tends toward madness owing to the infidelities of his beautiful wife (Capucine).

"A personal friend of James Bond" (Ursula Andress) turns the madness into a swinging sixties orgy.

As Carol, Romy Schneider presents the first screen incarnation of the Woody Allen image of women: flirtatious, intelligent, neurotic, and ready for marriage.

In the madcap finale, Michael and Carol lead the cast on a go-cart chase across the French countryside.

Anhedonia at work: Michael is miserable because he is so
successful with women, whereas Renée wants him because he
is the only man she can't have.

Michael wants only to be true to Carol...

...but nonetheless finds himself joining Fritz at a strip show.

Looking like the skinny guy at the beach who is afraid a musclebound giant will kick sand in his face, Victor cowers as a Nazi Neanderthal flirts with Carol.

That Michael and Fritz are manifestations of the Victor/Allen character is made clear by the fact that, at times, both wear Woody's famous glasses, a clear high-sign to the audience that they "are him." In flashback, we even see Michael as a boy in glasses impressing his English teacher with an essay, surely an autobiographical touch, exaggerated for comic effect. That scene is portrayed as one of his confessions to the doctor, but when the camera cuts back to the present, O'Toole is without glasses and Sellers is now wearing them.

At the same time, Michael is a combination of two elements that will be divided into separate figures in the forthcoming *Sam*: the best friend Dick, whose woman Allen/Allan wants, and the ideal "Bogie" he longs to be like. But if *Play It Again, Sam* shows Allen the artist hung up on old movies, so too does *Pussycat*: even the setting, Paris, is the city Bogart told Bergman they'd always have memories of. And the Paris of *Pussycat* is less an image of the real city than a backdrop of movie mythology, a silver screen incarnation of the land of romance. Likewise, the entire film attests to the remarkable impact of movies: the way in which ordinary lives often become aborted attempts to live up to those patterns schematized for us by the "lives" glimpsed in films. "Shall I get dressed," Carol asks Michael while stepping out of her shower, "or is it

foreign movie time?" The idea of the sexual act performed not as an original and spontaneous meeting of mates but as an attempt to capture in the flesh those idealized onscreen couplings is basic to the film's—and Allen's—viewpoint.

This theme is carried through the entire film. When Michael meets Victor at a café, Toulouse-Lautrec and Vincent Van Gogh (with bandaged ear) sit at the next table, giving the city the movie sensibility of *Moulin Rouge* and *Lust For Life*. When Fassbender courts the aloof Renée, her huffy attitude toward him plays off the audience's remembrance of the similar Sellers-Capucine relationship in *The Pink Panther* two years earlier. The audience is constantly acknowledged, as when O'Toole, trapped by two women, turns to the viewer and groans: "As a man's life goes down the drain…You Are There!" Acknowledged too are Woody's favorite films: Fellini's *8½*, the inspiration for *Stardust Memories* a full fifteen years later, is in evidence here, as O'Toole—in black garb and whip, looking remarkably like Marcello Mastroianni in the 1963 film—tries to control his varied women. When Ursula Andress finally pops down as a parachuting nymphomaniac, wearing a cobraskin catsuit, she's introduced as "a personal friend of James Bond": Andress played the female lead in the first Bond film, *Dr. No*.

The film, then, is very much a film of the sixties: a self-conscious work of High Camp for an era in

Fritz is obsessed with Renée, who is in love with Michael, who…

which Bond would soon be joined by the *Batman* TV series and the psychedelic sights and sounds of an emerging pop culture. *Pussycat* even begins with a Tiffany-style slide show, played out to the sound of Burt Bacharach music photographed against art nouveau decors, while the characters sport Beatle wigs and Carnaby Street fashions. Frenetic fluff, perhaps, but perfectly concocted with a clever if calculated eye on an emerging audience sensibility.

Even within this crowd-pleaser, Woody is able to convey, if in what he would consider a compromised form, his ideas on such subjects as marriage. This theme, which will run through his upcoming films, is introduced in the opening sequence, when Fassbender and his Brunhilde-type wife (Edra Gale) fight. "I've hated you from the moment I married you," he screams, suggesting they may have been quite happy before that. No wonder then that his patient, Michael, hesitates, even though Carol is in a hurry. "No reason why people can't discuss the subject of marriage without it turning into a Third World War," she sighs. But it always does for them, and the problem is not that he doesn't love her, only that he has trouble committing himself to the terrify-

The final orgy sequence.

ing notion of a lifelong state without other women. "When will you be old enough to assume the responsibility of marriage?" Carol demands; we can't be sure if she's a tender trap or if he's an arrested adolescent. Many future Woody Allen heroes will also face that question.

There's much evidence that Michael's fears are not imaginary. There is Renée's husband, who is the only man she doesn't want, and who at one point screams, "My wife—I kill her!" Or Carol's parents: so set, so square, so...sterile! Ultimately, of course, there's no way around it: Michael and Carol do marry at the end. Then, they immediately have their first fight. In Allen's twisted fairytales, there is no "happily-ever-after." But there are women—plenty of them—and the film reveals both Allen's love for and fear of them. Carol is so appealing, but will she in time turn into her mother, faithful and sexless? The opposite possibility is Renée, who castrates her husband but is promiscuous with almost everybody else.

Liz is Allen's perfectly paradoxical female; a frigid nymphomaniac, who likes to turn a man on, then when he's aroused put him down. Even non-sexually, her paradox is perfect: she simultaneously self-destructs and tries to insure her survival, consuming vast quantities of alcohol with wheat germ added. All the women are desirable, though each in a way creates a sense of dread for the male with a 1960's sensibility. That is something Woody will in time try to shed: Michael can play around and then, when Carol tries the same thing, complain, "It's different for a girl," but later Allen heroes will go beyond that double standard. Other elements introduced in this film will always be with him, for example, the ambiguous attitude toward the analyst, here seen rolling around hysterically on the floor before his patient arrives; he is a precursor of the analyst in *Manhattan* who calls patients at three in the morning and sobs over the phone.

There is also Woody's fear of machines; he is inept behind the wheel of his sport car and a go-cart, paving the way for future problems. And, there's the concept of a successful man who wants to quit his glamorous but superficial career so he can work on "serious" art. This notion will find its perfect incarnation in Ike Davis who, in *Manhattan*, does just this; the germination point is Michael, who wants to quit his journalist's job because "I know I've got a novel in me." Most important, Woody suggests the relationship between sex and death, with food serving as a bridge, that will shortly come to dominate his films: Victor, eating dinner alone because he is sexually unfulfilled, encounters Fritz, who is about to attempt suicide out of sexual frustration. Their midnight confrontation on the

banks of the Seine sets up the notion that death and eating are alternatives to the sexual experience, and thus handy metaphors for it.

It's impossible to discuss the paradox principle here in terms of Allen's visuals working against his verbals, since he is not credited with creating this film's images. Suffice it to say, then, that the very concept of *Pussycat* is a paradox: Woody Allen's personal little script blown up into a huge, commercial crowd-pleaser.

Food, Sex, and Death:
WHAT'S UP, TIGER LILY?

American International Pictures (1966)

CAST:

Tatsuya Mihashi *(Phil Moskowitz)*; Mie Hana/Hama *(Terry Yaki)*; Akiko Wakayabayashi *(Suki Yaki)*; Tadao Nakamaru *(Shepherd Wong)*; Susumu Kurobe *(Wing Fat)*.

CREDITS:

Executive producer (American version), Henry G. Saperstein; associate producer, Woody Allen; music, Jack Lewis with songs by The Lovin' Spoonful; sound, Glen Glenn Sound Co.; title sequence, Murakami-Wolf, Phil Norman; production conception, Ben Shapiro; production manager, Jerry Goldstein; director (Japanese version, *Kagi No Kagi*), Senkichi Taniguchi; screenplay, Hideo Ando; photography, Kazuo Yamada; producer, Tomoyuki Tanaka for Toho; re-release director, Woody Allen; American editor, Richard Krown; new screenplay and dubbing, Woody Allen, Frank Buxton, Len Maxwell, Louise Lasser, Mickey Rose, Julie Bennett, Bryna Wilson; Eastmancolor, Scope; 79 minutes.

American-International Pictures was, in the mid-sixties, the shlockmeister of Hollywood studios. While other companies were assembling the likes of *The Sound of Music, Beckett*, or even *What's New, Pussycat*, A.I.P. was busily purveying such lurid lowbrow low-budgeters as *The Wild Angels, The Trip*, and *Maryjane*, movies that exploited then-current social trends. Sometimes, their results bordered on the

Woody Allen grows tight-lipped while hosting the dubbed Japanese spy movie.

surrealistic, thanks to the lack of restrictions placed on directors like Roger Corman, allowing them to experiment with new techniques and innovative styles. After all, when the budgets were that slight and the break-even point extremely easy to reach, producers Samuel Z. Arkoff and James Nicholson could afford to allow filmmakers vast freedom. After the restrictions imposed on him by United Artists during the production of *Pussycat*, freedom was precisely what Woody Allen was looking for.

Meanwhile, a comic talent like Woody was precisely what A.I.P. needed. One of their executive producers, Henry G. Saperstein, traveled to Japan where he conferred with the people at Toho productions, a company best described as the Oriental equivalent of A.I.P., turning out cheaply made monster movies of the *Godzilla* variety and also quickie imitations of the immensely popular James Bond films. A.I.P. and Toho occasionally worked in tandem, the American company picking up distribution rights to the Japanese company's features and vice-versa. When Saperstein returned, he brought with him a very bad Bondish adventure film called *Kagi No Kagi* (in various sources alternately translated as *Key Is the Key* and *Key of Keys*), which Toho was about to market in their own territory and which they hoped A.I.P. could do some-

Sex and food are tied together as, in the film's epilogue, Allen studies an apple, ignoring China Lee's striptease...

...until his appetite shifts and he turns from the partially eaten apple to bite her luscious body.

thing with at the drive-in circuit and double bill theatres Stateside. On closer inspection, though, Saperstein felt the film was simply too awful to do any business, especially since the market had already been flooded with cheap Bond imitations.

Toho had already dubbed the film into English, calling it *A Keg of Powder*, but when Saperstein screened the print for A.I.P. executives, instead of getting seriously involved with the film's combination of sadism and suspense, they could not control their laughter, and even began shouting comical retorts to the dumb dialogue of the actors onscreen. Indeed, the experience of watching the film—which would have been very bad if they tried to take it "straight"— became an enjoyable one under the circumstances, and Saperstein was struck with the idea of altering the film so it could be released with just such an approach grafted onto the print. Thus, he called in Allen to view

the film, but ran it for him with the soundtrack turned off. Wouldn't it be fun, they decided, to try and turn a bad film into a good one by creating a totally new and completely comical soundtrack that would undercut the already ridiculous but relatively sober goings-on onscreen? In other words, turn an unconsciously bad film into a self-consciously bad (and therefore good) one in which the Japanese actors visually performed one story while Woody and a group of American actors verbally performed a totally different one.

Woody agreed it might be a fun experiment, and *What's Up, Tiger Lily?* was born. Unfortunately for Allen, the results were not as happy as hoped for. His original idea for the project was to do it in a fast, furious, frenetic sixty minutes, because he firmly believed that the concept could not sustain its comic premise beyond that limit. "I wanted to do it in one hour," he later insisted, "but the producer wanted a commercial venture so he padded it." Convinced such a film could not be effectively marketed, Saperstein added sequences from other Japanese adventure films and also inserted several scenes featuring a popular American pop group of that time, The Lovin' Spoonful,

Phil Moskowitz (Tatsuya Mihashi) is surrounded by Japanese beauties, including Terry Yaki (Mie Hana/Hama, far right) and Suki Yaki (Akiko Wakayabayashi, left).

performing songs (supposedly, at the night club the Japanese characters go to) accompanied by frug and twist dances. This was, ostensibly, to draw in the youthful audience that would be attracted to the Spoonful, just as Woody's name would lure the intellectuals who favored his work, while indiscriminate audiences might also show up for the action sequences. But the movie became inflated beyond Woody's razor-sharp concept of a perfectly controlled spoof, and eventually he went so far as to sue the producers for tampering with his work.

Certainly, the critics' reaction tended to bear out his disappointment, for while the film was met with generally favorable reviews, acknowledging his witty dialogue, they also tended to complain the film needed to be about twenty minutes shorter than its

80-minute length. "The idea for this satirical adventure is so bright," Howard Thompson complained in *The New York Times*, "it's a real pity that the picture doesn't hold up, even with some truly hilarious moments, specifically wisecracks, courtesy of Woody Allen and a battery of six comic writers." Likewise, in a generally rave review, Kevin Thomas of the Los Angeles *Times* finally admitted that even though the film only runs 80 minutes, "its one joke wears a bit by the end." But most critics responded favorably. William Weaver of the *Hollywood Reporter* acclaimed the film as "razor-sharp, exaggerated, ironic, raffish, bold, bawdy, crude, nude, raucous, ribald, sophisticated, slapstick, slick, smart, inside and outside comedy put together by Allen, working with no holds barred and none untried," acknowledging the incredibly eclectic way in which Allen worked, a point many critics had made (some quite negatively) in describing *Pussycat* as a film that clearly revealed Allen as a film writer in search of a style. Weaver also acknowledged that Woody was in the forefront of a hip new kind of comedy, to be "roared at or resented, according to individual taste." Ironic, of course, from today's perspective, since movie

("She was even better in The Sound of Music.*") In a scene recalling the Crazy Horse Saloon confrontation from* Pussycat, *adversaries Shepherd Wong (Tadao Nakamaru) and Wing Fat (Susumu Kurobe) cease their fighting to enjoy a stripper's show.*

comedy has become increasingly vulgar and Woody Allen, once thought of as being too outlandishly bawdy for some taste, seems downright conservative by comparison. Perhaps Arthur Knight of *Saturday Review* best summarized the overall reaction to the film when he wrote, "I found myself not only pleased but grateful to comedian Woody Allen for a marvelously unpretentious little movie that sets its sights modestly, then scores bull's-eye after bull's-eye all the way....Allen's sense of fun is at once low-keyed, far-out, and hip. He neatly turns his Japanese source, made in patent imitation of the James Bond films, back upon itself to be a travesty of *all* James Bond films....It is a *reductio ad absurdum* that delights as it deflates, and all the more so because what is being reduced is so obviously absurd in the first place. Allen's humor is without malice and without effort; and if some of his puns are terrible, there is an added fillip of fun in the realization that he is every bit as aware of it as we are." In this last assertion, Knight is undoubtedly referring to the scene in which the bound hero tells a man about to

Bondage: Phil and the girls are tied up by enemy agents, adding to the Japanese film's kinky sensibility.

torture him that in considering the two competing gangsters, Wing Fat is no better than Shepherd Wong, and "Two Wongs don't make a right." We would groan at the bad gag if the torturer did not *himself* groan at it, making for hysterical results.

Mostly, though, the humor in the film is related to two concepts that might at first appear to have little to do with one another, but which are paradoxically yoked together by Allen. "Food and sex," Woody once told Mel Gussow, "are always good for a laugh." Woody's script is based (consciously or unconsciously on his part) on the notion that if either sex or food is good for a laugh on its own, a purposeful confusion of the two concepts will be doubly funny. "I was always thinking about food or sex," Woody once guiltily admitted when asked about whether he had paid attention as a schoolboy; *Tiger Lily* works as a perversely clever presentation of adolescent fantasies about the two equally appealing vices.

Movies like *Tom Jones* have, through its famed eating sequence, slyly commented on how sexy food can be; psychiatrists often suggest that people not engaged in regular sexual activity tend to overeat as an unconscious alternative, food becoming a substitute for

sex. In a sense, then, satisfaction of the two very different kinds of "appetites"—which at first seem to have nothing to do with one another—is actually a single desire taking two possible routes. Woody acknowledges this again and again in *Tiger Lily*. Even the film's basic plot line makes it clear: The extremely sexy genre of the James Bond thriller is shifted and even subverted when the object of everyone's search is not a missing piece of microfilm or an atomic secret but a recipe for the world's best egg salad. Phil Moscowitz, "lovable rogue" (Tatsuya Mihashi), must retrieve the document in order to save a country that has yet to be officially acknowledged ("We're on the waiting list—when one opens up, we'll get it—the people are still locked in crates"). To get them a spot on the globe ("Preferably between Spain and Greece—somewhere warm!") Phil must go up against two gangsters: one, Shepherd Wong (Tadao Nakamaru), addicted to egg salad; the other, Wing Fat (Susumu Kurobe), addicted to beautiful women. In paralleling the gangsters' obsessions with food and sex, Woody sets up an immediate

relationship between the two. And when the two sexy female stars of the film are introduced, their names carry on this parallel: Terry Yaki (Mie Hana/Hama) and her equally delicious (pun intended!) sister Suki Yaki (Akiko Wakayabayashi) are named after popular oriental foods, and certainly each woman is (pun again intended) a dish.

Indeed, there is even a hint of an Allen theme that will emerge in *Love and Death*, where Woody will take the food/sex concept further by emphasizing the dark relationship of both these pleasant pastimes to the threat of death. "One last request," a dying gangster coughs in *Tiger Lily*. "Don't use embalming fluid on me—I wanna be stuffed with crabmeat." A wonderfully wild, absurd gag, to be sure, but more than that a hint of the emerging Allen vision. Indeed, the fear of death (that would progressively come to haunt the films) and the notion of marriage as a kind of death-in-life (already suggested in *Pussycat*) are inherent in one of the film's wackiest gag lines: "I was going to marry her," a gangster wails after learning that his new lover is actually an enemy spy. "I'd already put a deposit on twin cemetary plots." The line could belong to Boris in *Love and Death*. But even as early as its opening sequence, *Tiger Lily* introduces both a theme and a

A bevy of oriental beauties add to the ersatz James Bond quality.

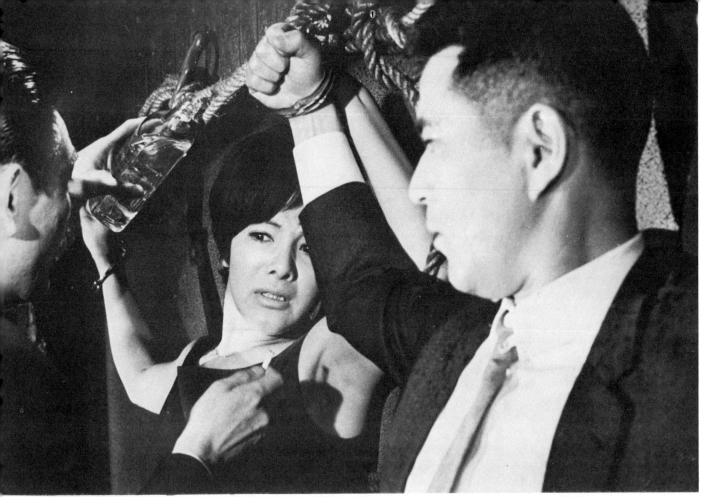

Another instance of mainstream-movie kinkiness, as the heroine is menaced by a match-wielding villain. Phil is unable to help.

Terry Yaki and Phil enjoy a sex interlude ("Thank you, for clearing up my sinuses.")

Phil enjoys sex (on left) and violence (the right) simultaneously.

American teenagers twist to the sounds of The Lovin' Spoonful, added to the American version to pad out the movie.

Phil and Terry attempt to capture their enemies through technological spying devices.

Kiss kiss. Bang bang.

concurrent technique which will be developed in his first true directorial effort, *Take the Money*, and which will reach its apex in the masterpiece *Zelig*: the mock documentary. After some nonsensically enjoyable goings on in which a beautiful Japanese girl is tied to a log and then passively driven towards a buzzsaw by the villain, Woody is interviewed in a straight-faced fashion about his work on the film we are about to see. Woody is here seen sitting in the kind of posh study usually employed to suggest the intellectuality of the filmed speaker, and rambles on about how his film (which of course turns out to be a cheapo-cheapo exploitation flick) was made, allowing for some sharp satire on the pretensions of filmmakers who inflate the value of their work in interview situations. This, and the later interruptions of Woody into the plot-line, make clear that we are not so much seeing a film as a documentary about the making of the film.

At the same time, though, we are not only introduced to an upcoming theme but also reminded of one already explored in *Pussycat*: Allen's insistence on making us conscious of the fact that we are indeed watching a movie. Just as, in *Pussycat*, the words "Author's Message" appeared onscreen when Peter O'Toole began talking about the need to forsake superficial affairs for true love, so in *Tiger Lily* we see a

stripteaser's breasts covered with the words "Foreign Version." The film's very first verbal gag goes for a similar approach: When one of the gangsters watching this girl notes that she's fantastic, the other smilingly replies: "Yeah, but she was even better in *The Sound of Music*." The film's indebtedness to old films (and not only those of the spy genre) is clear whenever the karate fights begin: "Saracan pig...Spartan dog..." Phil huffs, and his words are funny because they derive from sword-and-sandal costume films, and are marvelously turned into malapropisms by their placement here (when he adds "Turkish Taffy," it's wonderfully absurd).

Even Phil's line for introducing himself to people—"Phil Moscowitz, lovable rogue"—is a homage to old movies, in which characters are neatly tagged with simplistic labels for the audience to immediately identify characters as types rather than people. In addition to making the audience constantly aware they are watching a movie, Allen also borrows a bit from the *Road* films with Bing Crosby and Allen's favorite, Bob Hope, in which the characters constantly acknowledged being trapped in a film. "I

Woody's constant fear of machines is suggested early-on in the way his sound-track kids the complex technological equipment of the spies.

A villain offers a Peter Lorre imitation as a means of torturing our heroes.

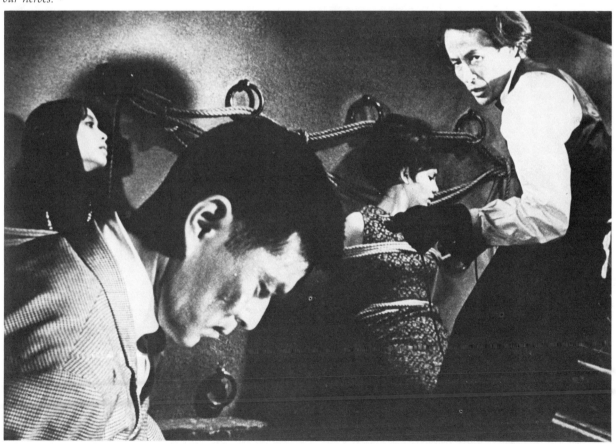

63

was almost shot and killed, just before the opening credits,'' Phil tells a friend. Later, Phil takes one of the Yaki girls to a tower, and just before two people walk by, Woody has him say: "This is the obligatory scene—the director always has to walk through with his wife.'' A couple wanders by and Phil mutters under his breath, ''Egomaniac.''

Essentially, movies operate thanks to the willing suspension of the viewer's disbelief; we know we're watching a film but are willing to forget it, at least on some level. Woody subverts our normal reaction, and in so doing makes us more aware of the way in which movies in particular, and media in general, manipulate us in order to work their effect.

To achieve this, Woody must make us aware that no movies exists in a vacuum: each one is part of our ongoing love affair, as a nation, with the very *idea* of movies. So a bad guy with a snake, clearly modelled

(even by the makers of the original Japanese film) on the various villains played over the years by Peter Lorre, is given by Woody a voice clearly in imitation of Peter Lorre's and at one point the character actually complains, "Oh, my throat—this Peter Lorre imitation is killing me.'' Likewise, another villain grabs a girl and holds a gun to her head, but in Woody's version he is not trying to harm the girl, only acting out a James Cagney imitation. "Wing, do you think I'll win an award for my acting in this film?'' Phil asks, but he's then beaten for being such a lousy actor as other movie tough guys (''Sonny Tufts…John Wayne…'') are recalled.

Finally, near the end, Woody solidifies all his various hints of self-consciousness about the cinematic context when he envokes that most famous of theatrical devices: James Barrie's classic bit from *Peter Pan*, in which the audience is begged to applaud if they believe in fairies to save Tinker Bell's life. Here, the audience is told that if they applaud, Phil's gun will magically be reloaded so he can win the day. Taken together, these seemingly random gags form a statement: Woody's serious theme, expressed through a

The shooting of the big shipboard finale. (''Where did you get that suit, from an ambulance driver.'')

succession of jokes built upon a single premise and therefore taking on a line, an arc, during the film's progression. Future films will take further the notion that the proper subject of movies is, for Allen, the very experience of watching a movie.

This is the reason why a key "trick" he plays is so significant. At one point, the film appears to rip, and the audience viewing the film in a theatre for the first time actually believes for a moment that they see the shadows of people up in the projection booth accidentally projected onto the screen. It takes a moment to realize that this is in fact part of the movie, as Woody and Louise Lasser portray adulterous lovers, trying to sneak some romantic moments up there in the booth, only to have their images unknowingly shared with a moviehouse full of people. The intermingling of the fictional and the factual, the way in which private moments become impossible in a world where anything can be turned, by the media, into public entertainment, will develop in each successive film. Likewise, Woody takes a snipe at those who would overanalyze films (his included) when, in mid-movie, we find ourselves back in the study, and that pompous interviewer asks him if he would care to explain the meaning of the movie so far. "No," Woody tells him matter-of-factly, and it's back to the action.

Much of that action concerns the sexual situations, and *What's Up, Tiger Lily?* can be viewed as a companion piece to the similarly titled *What's New, Pussycat?* in terms of revealing Allen's early attitude toward women. In *Loser Takes All*, Maurice Yacowar brilliantly explains the title sequence in terms of this very theme: "Here a cartoon Woody dons glasses and cavorts across a variety of pin-up pictures. Though he ogles these large ladies, lies on their breasts, and pulls credit lines out of their navels and cleavage, he nevertheless remains generically removed from them. He is an animated, moving figure while they are still-life images (in photographs). This is a visualization of Allen's common pretense to frustration with women, who seem to exist on another level and are unresponsive to him." Sometimes, though, the women are viewed as responsive in ways that send out conflicting messages to men, and in these sequences Woody comically visualizes and verbalizes the frustration not only he but most men experience when trying to understand the female psyche.

In *Pussycat*, Peter O'Toole attempted to make sense of Paula Prentiss's acting like a nymphomaniac in public and then revealing she is frigid in private, working very hard to arouse him, then growing angry when he responds. Her equivalent in *Tiger Lily* is Terry, who upon finding herself alone with Phil tells him, "I'd like to tear your clothes off and make violent love to you right now!" When he's foolish enough to take her at her word, she then acts disappointed with him: "Phil, all you *ever* think about is sex." When he begins, with difficulty, to pull back, she immediately notices a phallic symbol out the window: "Wow! Look at the smokestack on that ship!" Later, one of the girls, while exercising, joyously announces, "Boy, am I a great piece!" And even the final credit sequence carries on the theme: Woody, usually the lecher who lusts after beautiful women who refuse to respond, turns the tables by chewing on an apple while China Lee (an extremely popular *Playboy* model at that time) strips. But when he finally begins to respond, she is immediately less interested.

China Lee's appearance also solidifies another theme that has been the source for many gags throughout the film: cultural confusion. She is, in fact, a Chinese girl appearing as a footnote to a Japanese movie. Earlier, Woody featured this theme in a sequence featuring the two villains in confrontation: "Are you Chinese?" "Japanese." "You sure? You're not Chinese?" The characters are unsure of their cultural context, and they have a right to be. Any film in which the main character is an Oriental with a Jewish name is going to make much of such confusion, so the naming allows Woody to introduce what will become a key theme: assimilation of Jews into non-Jewish lifestyles. One character, who has been acting like a true Oriental throughout, reverts back to his origins when shot: "I'm dying—call my rabbi." He is only the first crude representation of a type of character Woody will develop fully in future pictures.

The very notion of *Tiger Lily* is a paradox—a Jewish soundtrack set against Oriental visuals—and naturally paradoxes run rampant through the film. This is clear from one of the earliest, and best, gags: A beautiful woman, clad only in a bath towel, walks up to Phil and opens the towel, Bardot-style. Instead of whatever seductive line existed in the original, she says something uproariously inappropriate: "Name three presidents."

If the experience of *Pussycat* made clear that Woody would never be happy working within the collaborative system of big-budget moviemaking, *Tiger Lily* convinced him that even working on a low-budget project would not necessarily insure that his vision would come across uncompromised unless he seized total control, which he would shortly do. But before that happened, he would be involved with two more projects in which his unique style would be misused. And compared to those upcoming fiascos, both the overextravagant *Pussycat* and the more modest *Tiger Lily* seem (their compromises duly noted) relatively successful expressions of Woody Allen's vision.

Woody Allen as Little Jimmy Bond.

In Bondage:
CASINO ROYALE
Columbia Pictures (1967)

CAST:

Peter Sellers *(Evelyn Tremble)*; Ursula Andress *(Vesper Lynd)*; David Niven *(Sir James Bond)*; Orson Welles *(Le Chiffre)*; Joanna Pettet *(Mata Bond)*; Deborah Kerr *(Widow McTarry)*; Daliah Lavi *(The Detainer)*; Woody Allen *(Jimmy Bond)*; William Holden *(Ransome)*; Charles Boyer *(Le Grand)*; John Huston *(''M'')*; Kurt Kaznar *(Smernov)*; George Raft *(Himself)*; Jean-Paul Belmondo *(French Foreign Legion Soldier)*; Terence Cooper *(Agent .007)*; Barbara Bouchet *(Miss Moneypenny)*; Angela Scoular *(Buttercup)*; Gabriella Licudi *(Eliza)*; Tracey Crisp *(Heather)*; Jacqueline Bisset *(Miss Goodthighs)*; Anna Quayle *(Frau Hoffner)*; Bernard Cribbens *(Taxi Driver)*; Tracy Reed *(Fang Leader)*; Percy Herbert *(First Piper)*; Man in Bar *(Peter O'Toole)*.

CREDITS:

Producers, Charles K. Feldman and Jerry Bresler; directors, John Huston, Kenneth Hughes, Val Guest, Robert Parrish, Joseph McGrath; screenplay, Wolf Mankowitz, John Law, Michael Sayers, suggested by the novel by Ian Fleming; photography, Jack Hildyard; editor, Bill Lenny; production designer, Michael Ayringer; special effects, Cliff Richardson, Roy Whybrow; music, Burt Bacharach; titles, montage, Richard Williams; Technicolor, Panavision; 131 minutes, A Famous Artists Production.

Published in 1953, *Casino Royale* was the novel that first brought Ian Fleming recognition as a writer. This was due in part to the unique hero he created, in part to his ability to weave a solid spy storyline, and, in part, to the one classic sequence he fashioned, in which James Bond faces SMERSH villain Le Chiffre across a baccarat table. The screen rights to the book were sold almost immediately but, for complex reasons, the movie never got made, even though a "dry run" was performed on television some two years later in a one-hour drama starring Barry Nelson as Agent 007. The projected movie version was to have been made in black and white, for at most two million dollars. In the meantime, though, Albert "Cubby" Broccoli and Harry Saltzman had bought the rights to the remainder of the Bond series (*Casino Royale*, having already been optioned apart from the series that was to

Naughty Little Jimmy combines his obsession with beautiful women with his incompetence with machines when he straps The Detainer (Daliah Lavi) into a torture bed.

An early incarnation of the unlikely romantic: Little Jimmy embraces The Detainer...

...and proves that even short and homely men can succeed sexually.

follow, was the only book they could not negotiate for), which, beginning with *Dr. No* in 1963, emerged as an extremely successful line of films, each one topping the previous entry in terms of audience appeal.

So when Charles K. Feldman finally brought *Casino Royale* to the screen in 1967, he ignored the story's potential for relatively "straight" spy drama, despite the fact that most fans of the Bond books feel that it features the strongest storyline of any in the series, and would probably have made for a very fine film if shot as a Sean Connery vehicle in much the same style as *From Russia, With Love*. Instead, Feldman attempted a spoof on the order of his hit of two years earlier, *What's New, Pussycat?* crossing the best qualities of the popular Bond series with the appeal of that highly successful comedy. It was necessary, then, to get

Sir James Bond (David Niven) and Miss Moneypenny (Barbara Bouchet) encounter the nefarious Little Jimmy.

Without his glasses, Little Jimmy is helpless and harmless.

not only people already associated with the Bond genre to appear, but also to reunite the *Pussycat* crew. Ursula Andress, of course, was absolutely necessary, being a veteran of both *Dr. No* and *Pussycat*. Peter Sellers was seduced into performing, while Burt Bacharach returned to do the music again, and was inspired to compose "The Look of Love"—the film's fabulous song—after gazing at Ursula Andress, while Richard Williams came up with similar pop-art titles. Peter O'Toole was even persuaded to make the kind of cameo in *Casino Royale* his friend Richard Burton had contributed to *Pussycat*. And finally Woody Allen, who had expressed only harsh words for what Feldman and company had done to his *Pussycat* script, joined the throng.

Master of disguises Evelyn Tremble (Peter Sellers) dresses up like Henry Toulouse-Lautrec, and is accompanied by the deadly beauty Vesper Lynd (Ursula Andress).

Little Jimmy gets his just desserts.

In fact, Woody spoke quite optimistically about the project, at least early on. On June 9, 1966, Earl Wilson carried the following entry in his syndicated column: he asked Woody (at Gallagher's) if Allen were one of the writers on the film. "I'm one of the only people *not* writing it," Wilson quoted Allen as telling him, adding that Ben Hecht had originally been hired to write the film, then was replaced by several sets of writers as diverse directors were hired, each to work separately, and with different performers, on specific sections of the film, creating the possibility that the final result might be a cinematic patchwork quilt. "I don't know who my writers are," Woody continued. "I hear they are $5,000,000 over budget now. There's not a tiny role that isn't played by a big star. Charlie Feldman has spared no expense to make it an opulent production." And Charlie Feldman has spared

Little Jimmy tries to prove himself a suitable cowboy . . .

70

...but has trouble dealing with the real thing...

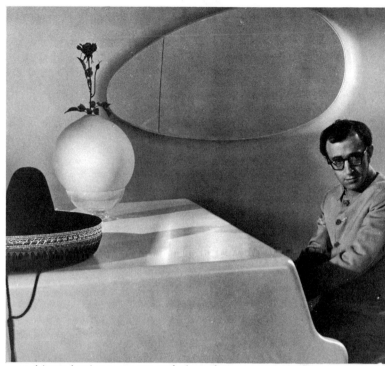

...and instead retires to a more aesthetic pastime.

no expense when it came to insuring Woody Allen would be on hand when he was needed. Woody was ceremoniously flown to Europe and set up in a hotel at the film company's expense, then left alone while Feldman and his people continued to try and throw some sort of a workable script together. Woody did not waste the time, though; he spent his time composing essays and stories and delineating the first drafts of future scripts. After it was all over, Woody would take a dimmer view of the film: "An unredeemingly moronic enterprise" is how he described it in *Woody Allen: An American Comedy*, a documentary about Woody by Harold Mantell.

Actually, the plot that was finally devised sounds ripe with possibilities for effective parodying of James Bond as a pop culture hero. Though there is in the film a character meant to parallel Sean Connery's menacing machismo interpretation of Bond (Terence Cooper), the central character is in fact Sir James Bond (David Niven), a retired secret service agent of the old order who finds scant humor in the fact that some "imposter" has been buzzing about, maligning the family name, degrading the patriotic enterprise of gentlemanly spying by employing it as a means to seduce women. Sir James decides to do away with the enemy agents at SMERSH in his own more traditional, low key, genteel, even celibate style. To do this, he enlists the

Ursula Andress captures the qualities of the Woody Allen woman: flirtatious...

...aloof...

aid of a series of people, each of whom temporarily "becomes" James Bond. They include Mata Bond (Joanna Pettit), his own daughter by Mata Hara, along with an unassuming Baccarat genius named Evelyn Tremble (Peter Sellers) who may just be able to best the loathsome enemy agent, Le Chiffre (Orson Welles), in a climactic game.

How horrible it is for Sir James to learn, then, that the real brains behind the enemy organization is none other than his own physically tiny and psychologically twisted nephew, Little Jimmy Bond (Woody).

The relationship of the Woody Allen persona to the James Bond icon serves as predecessor to the similar relationship between that persona and the Bogart icon in *Play It Again, Sam*. After all, Bond replaced Bogie as the pop culture image of proper masculine behavior. In the 1960's, the spy metamorphosed into an internationalized jet-set/*Playboy*-era version of what the private eye had been for the 1940's; the movie spies had as little to do with the murky business of actual spying as movies like *The Maltese Falcon* and *The Big Sleep* had to do with the day-to-day work of most gumshoes. In both cases, what's notable is that a popular ideal of masculinity perfectly expressed the values and sensibility of each era: Bogart's surface cynicism covering his deeper sentimental streak, Connery's cool seduction of women masking his character's contempt for the opposite sex; Bogart's apparent rugged individualism quickly dropped when society at large is in trouble and he willingly leaps into the fray out of a sense of community, Bond's apparent loyalty to the general social order existing only as an excuse that allows him to legally perform the sadistic acts of the criminal class he fights against.

The Woody Allen persona represents, in both films, the public that desperately tries to live up to the image and is constantly frustrated by his inability to do so. In the (by comparison) more realistic style of *Sam*, the Woody persona ineffectively emulates the Bogart image in everyday situations and strikes out with women as a result, finally growing enough to reject the ideal and operate as his own man; in the spoofy, High Camp cartoon context of *Casino Royale*, the Woody persona grows so frustrated by his incompetence at trying to live up to the hero that he gives in and becomes a villain instead, if only by reason of insanity. Indeed, it's possible that, in the midst of the

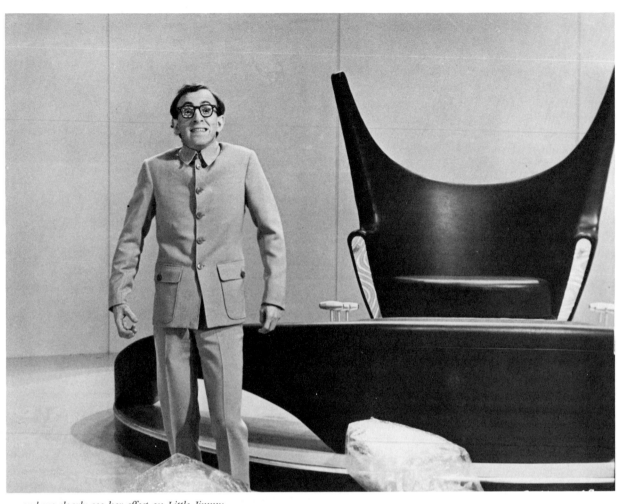

. . . and we clearly see her effect on Little Jimmy . . .

who goes ga-ga over the gorgeous girl.

mess of a movie then being manufactured, Woody noted in its conception a possibility that Feldman and the others overlooked, and out of the Allen/Bond relationship came the germination for an idea that would happily lead to *Sam*. If that's so, then *Casino Royale*, however horrible it may be, has a *raison d'etre*.

And the film certainly needs one, because it reaches beyond the merely bad; this is truly an abomination. As *Time* magazine put it: "With so many egos—including five directors—competing for attention, the picture soon degenerates into an incoherent and vulgar vaudeville. Each actor frantically does his

bit and then gets offstage to make room for the jugglers....This kind of keystone cop-out was done faster and funnier 34 years ago when the Marx Brothers made *Duck Soup*. But in those days comedies consisted of scenes and not herds." *Newsweek* managed even harsher words, labelling the film "The persecution and assassination of James Bond by the inmates of *Casino Royale*," as critic Howard Junker described the film as "burbling like a hyperthyroid idiot." Moira Walsh complained in *America* that "The story line is virtually undecipherable....*Casino Royale* is an aimless collection of disconnected skits and gags...labored and silly, especially against the backdrop of overpoweringly handsome and expensive-looking 'Pop-art' sets." In *Commonweal*, Philip T. Hartung insisted it was "a lot of

Little Jimmy's sinister plot to take over the world—or at least its women—by eliminating every man who is taller than he is.

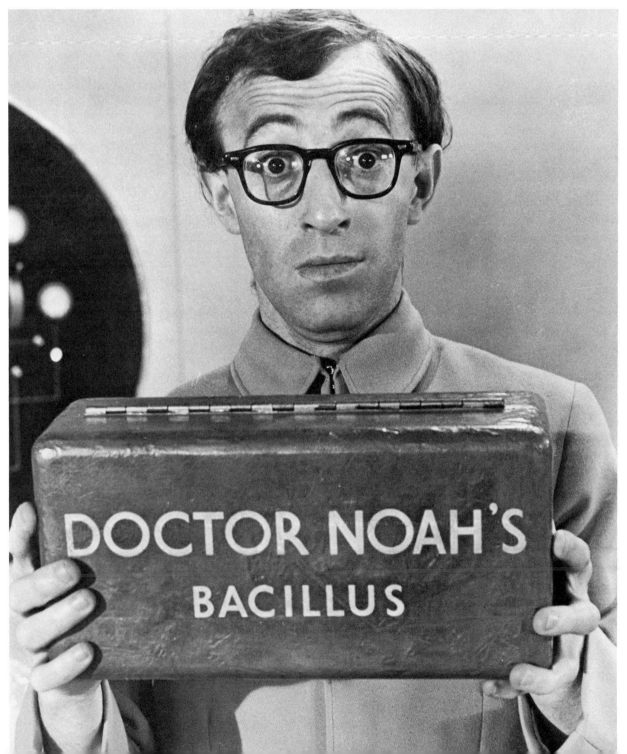

sound and fury signifying nothing," likening the film to the old-fashioned movie extravaganzas in which past Hollywood producers had thrown in everything except the kitchen sink; "instead of a sink, however, they have a toilet...."

There was, of course, the rare critic who leaped to the film's defense. Brendan Gill of *The New Yorker* insisted that "*Casino Royale* is a very funny picture, and no two ways about it...one would have to be a misanthrope with a toothache...not to find *some*thing to laugh at....I enjoyed being run over by it for two hours and ten minutes." Most critics would have been quick to identify themselves as misanthropes, though, and most viewers felt the same way. Like *What's New, Pussycat?*, *Casino Royale* received mostly negative reviews but, unlike *Pussycat*, *Casino* flopped at the box-office. Both films may reflect a similar Hollywood-commercialized notion of how movies ought to be made: overextravagant, impersonal, grandiose and gimmicky. But the box-office records tell something, too, for the public—not prejudiced by a built-in hostility toward anything that reeks of commercialization but, to the contrary, attracted to just such projects—enjoys a large serving of hokum if it works, if it plays to an audience, and, if, in the case of comedy, it's funny.

There's no question that, while Woody himself may resent the elaborate visualization his sparse script was given, *Pussycat* worked perfectly as an effective Hollywoodization of Woody Allen humor. *Casino*, on the other hand, is truly terrible, not because it's big and gaudy and over-ornate, but because it doesn't work, doesn't play—is not funny. Other than Woody's two brief sequences, the film consistently falls flat, like a bottle of expensive champagne that, when opened, turns out to have had some slow leak that's dissipated all the expected fizz. Everything except Allen's presence is forced, desperate, hysterical, hollow.

But in his improvised bits, Woody does at least get to deliver a few lines that are unmistakably his own. "We'll run amuck," he tells a companion at one point; then, considering, he adds, "and if you're too tired, we'll walk amuck." His ability to point out, in a Marx Brothers fashion, the absurdity of our language is equalled only by his constant concern with dying: ordered to step before a firing squad, he declines, insisting he has a "low threshold of death." Likewise, his physical comedy is effective. At one point, he burps out pastel mini-balloons while gorgeous Daliah Lavi force feeds him a time bomb pill: food, sex, and death all together. At another, he self-righteously makes a speech on the rights of everyone (regardless of race, creed, or religion) to free dental care, while the stage on which he stands lecturing moves skyward, revealing four harmoniz-ing singers beneath, thereby giving us a logical explanation for the illogical presence of music in the scene. This is another example of Allen's insistence on drawing attention to cinema conventions, making his audience self-conscious about them. At the end, when all the other Bonds move heavenward, Jimmy Bond is seen on the descent, Woody's victory being that here he did manage to have his comic character killed off, despite the fact that he had little control over this movie. Even in his own first writer-director effort, the upcoming *Take The Money*, he would be unable to share with the public his intended death scene of the Allen character.

Woody was allowed to ad-lib his early "execution" scene (about to be shot by the firing squad, he laughingly leaps over the wall, then finds himself facing *another* firing squad) and also wrote the grand finale for Feldman, though his work was at first scrapped as being too farcical for the film's concept, then was at least in part revived when Feldman realized the only way his travesty could be salvaged was to take a farcical approach. And a surprising number of Woody's deeply personal themes are presented, however, briefly, in his segments. In addition to the ineptness he (and we) feel in comparison to the larger-than-life movie myths like Bond, there is also Woody's regularly recurring ineptness with mechanical objects. Here, the theme takes the form of his being unable to handle either a player piano or a mechanical horse; this sets the pace for his confrontation with the hair-dryer in *Sam* and with every conceivable modern appliance in *Sleeper*. His early love/hate feelings for women are obvious when he entraps The Detainer (Daliah Lavi), then alternately tries to seduce her and sadistically torture her, while his obsession with beautiful women and corresponding frustration at not being the kind of physical specimen women are ordinarily attracted to is present in his fiendish plot to make all women gorgeous and eliminate all men taller than he is. Woody's obsessive interest in death, which will progressively come to dominate the films as they grow ever darker, is made clear in both the firing squad sequence with which he opens the film and his descent to hell which ends it, as Little Jimmy Bond becomes the first Woody Allen hero to stare the grim reaper in the face. Likewise, the paradox is present as Woody plays a hero at the beginning and a villain at the end.

Indeed, Woody's sequences are so good that, were they removed from the film proper and anthologized in a program on Woody Allen humor, they would leave any audience laughing wildly. But they appear here as the framing device for a fat, formless, flatulent film. By appearing in *Casino Royale*, Woody placed himself in bondage in more ways than one.

The Innocents Abroad:

DON'T DRINK THE WATER

An Avco Embassy Film (1969)

CAST:

Jackie Gleason *(Walter Hollander)*; Estelle Parsons *(Marian Hollander)*; Ted Bessel *(Axel Magee)*; Joan Delaney *(Susan Hollander)*; Michael Constantine *(Krojack)*; Howard St. John *(Ambassador Magee)*; Danny Meehan *(Kilroy)*; Richard Libertini *(Father Drobney)*; Pierre Olaf *(The Chef)*; Avery Schreiber *(The Sultan)*; Mark Gordon *(Merik)*; Phil Leeds *(Sam)*; Howard Morris *(pilot of escape plane)*.

CREDITS:

Producer, Charles H. Joffe; associate producer, Jack Grossberg; executive producer, Joseph E. Levine; director, Howard Morris; screenplay by R. S. Allen and Harvey Bullock, from Woody Allen's play; director of photography, Harvey Genkins; operating cameraman, Urs Furfer; casting director, Jay Wolf; editorial supervision, Ralph Rosenblum; music by Pat Williams; title song, lyrics by Kelly Gordon and music by Pat Williams, sung by Jake Holmes; set design, Robert Gundlach; costume design, Gene Coffin; title design, Richard Williams; color by Berkey Pathé; running time 98 minutes; Rating, G.

An Enormous Restaurant: Caterer Walter Hollander (Jackie Gleason) and his wife Marion (Estelle Parsons) find themselves about to be "devoured" by world politics they can't understand.

During the filming of *Casino Royale*, Woody sat around for six months, on salary in Europe, while Feldman's producers tried to figure out how they could use him in a brief sequence. But Woody didn't waste the time: the European locales set him to imagining how his own parents might react to being on the continent, and by the time he flew home, he had *Don't Drink the Water* ready for Broadway. Previously, Woody had contributed some sketches to a staged revue, but this was his first attempt at a full-scale play. That his conception was flawed became clear in *Variety's* review of the show's tryout in Philadelphia, when their October 5, 1966, notice praised Woody's talent while pointing out a problem: "The author reveals both an ear and imagination attuned to the times....But while the laugh lines are fresh and frequently inventive, story and staging format suggest pre-World War II farce." Most of the future reviews of the show would take the same approach.

The play opened on November 19, and Broadway audiences as well as critics were treated to the tribulations of a "typical" American family of tourists, forced to seek refuge in the American Embassy of a mythical Iron Curtain country called Vulgaria, after mistakenly being suspected of spying, then protected by a singularly inept son of the absent ambassador. Woody appeared to be combining two past classics, *Teahouse of the August Moon* and *You Can't Take It With You*, in terms of plot, while layering on his own unique blend of comic word play. "Looney merriment is the only aim," William Glover of the Associated Press wrote. "Since its author, Woody Allen, is a gagman of renown in night clubs, movies and television, the results are mostly dandy. If the machinery wheezes occasionally, another guffaw soon sets things right." And while he noted that the play lacked a clear comic-dramatic line, he brushed this off, insisting that the plot developments "just set up situations for a string of lively Allen quips, topical and inventive."

Taking the opposite approach, Richard Watts, Jr., of the New York *Post*, complimented the high quality of the comedy lines but scolded Woody for the play's failings: Woody Allen "is a master of bright and hilarious dialogue," he wrote, "and has provided so much material for laughter in his farcical comedy...that it is upsetting to find that the final result falls disturbingly short of satisfaction....The fun grows too mechanical for its own good." Norman Nadel of the New York *World Journal Tribune* loudly complained that "It's not a comedy, in the sense of an organized, humorous play, although there is a plot. Rather, it is a massive accumulation of club" and stand-up comedy bits passed off as a play. Woody, who is far better at accepting constructive criticism than most writers,

The Allenesque hero Axel Magee (Ted Bessell) tries to help the Hollanders return to the U.S.

The film's director, Howard Morris, does a cameo role as the pilot who will fly the disguised Hollanders to safety.

came to accept this attitude toward his first experiment at playwriting: "There's always got to be something beyond the laughs or people will get bored," he told the Los Angeles *Times* in 1969. "That was the trouble to some extent in *Don't Drink the Water*. It was one laugh on top of the next. Every line was a joke. The problem was, every time a laugh didn't work, the thing went down the toilet." His next play would rectify that: in

Marion catches a quick nap while Axel works on a plan of escape.

Sam, we care so much about the three focal characters that even if a gag fails to go over, we stick with the play on the level of emotional involvement.

But while the Hollander family could have been made real as well as funny, emotionally involving as well as comically cartoonish, either Woody did not think to do this or had not yet honed his writing skills to the point where he could pull it off. *The Wall Street Journal* noted that the show was "fine for gag lovers, but not quite so fine for those who expect comedies to have some structure," while Walter Kerr of the New York *Times* similarly complained that "Playwrite Allen has given [Lou Jacobi and the cast] lines, lines, lines, nothing but lines," and while many of them were very funny in the manner we'd expect from a top night club talent, "what's fundamentally

wrong" is that now these gags were being passed off as theatrical dialogue, placed in the mouths not of true characters but quickly-sketched-in living cartoons who served only to toss back and forth the kind of comic patter Allen did himself in his monologues.

Still, Kerr was at least able to praise all the "successful incidental jests" though he felt they never added up to a true play. But almost three years to the day later, when the film version opened, Roger Greenspun of the *Times* could not even venture that claim. For if the play's flaws were ones of construction and conception, the movie version managed to muff even the best of Woody's gags so that the "incidental jests" could no longer be called "successful."

Indeed, in retrospect from the vantage point of a very poor film, the play began to glow in the memory, as Greenspun claimed that "those lively offspring of Woody Allen's imagination came to dull

The Hollanders' daughter Susan (Joan Delaney, third from left) has fallen in love with Axel by the time the family makes good its escape.

Father Drobney (Richard Libertini) is crazy enough to be kept in a straight-jacket.

and clamorous ends in Howard Morris's inept movie version.'' Morris, an acting member of Sid Caesar's stellar stock company when Woody was employed as a writer for that group, had little experience transforming a popular Broadway play to the very different medium of the movies. As Greenspun concluded, Morris did not so much heighten what had been best in Woody's awkward but entertaining first effort as a playwright, but unaccountably went against the grain of what was good: ''Given a comedy built upon hapless wisecracks and more or less sophisticated one-liners, Morris has directed his attention to sloppy sight gags,'' making for a film that ''looks like nothing so much as a terribly ambitious high school production.''

Most critics tended to concur. Charles Champlin of the Los Angeles *Times* noted that ''the real problem is that a claustrophobic stage play has been opened up without any special inventiveness. The plot is still the stage plot, implying all the physical limitations of the stage. The chase sequences are not just unimaginative, they are banal. What was required was enrichment, not mere adaptation. The whole production has a chintzy look about it,'' and the final effect, he argued, was ''a flat, forced and tepid potion.'' Barry Glasser, writing in the *Motion Picture Herald*, noted that in the film version, ''the pacing lacks the antic, nimble agility so vital to the confusion of farce,'' while the ''vehicle's farcical spontaneity is unfortunately blunted by the expansion of the play and uneven direction.'' *Time* concurred, taking an interesting if debatable line of reasoning: ''Woody Allen may well be the funniest

man in America. But he is not the funniest writer in America, and between the two titles lies a profound gap.'' One critic who would undoubtedly disagree is Stanley Kauffmann, whose reviews of Woody's work consistently suggest that he hurts his projects by appearing in them. Kauffmann's assessments usually begin with the premise that Woody *is* the funniest writer in America, though not necessarily the funniest man. Woody fanatics, of course, will disagree both with *Time*'s unsigned critic and with Kauffmann. But *Time* does at least point to a fascinating situation: why didn't Woody portray Axel either in the play (where he was performed by Tony Roberts) or the film (Ted Bessel had the role)? In his book on *Farce*, Albert Bermel argues that Axel Magee, incompetent son of an acclaimed ambassador, ''is the first developed version of Allen's schnook hero to whom beautiful girls unaccountably surrender. This character, disguised as himself, always drops sharp quips at his own expense.... As a loser who wins, he has a lot in common'' with the varied Allen heroes who would emerge beginning in *Take The Money*, and of whom Victor in *Pussycat* serves as precursor. Even the name, Axel, reminds us of the names of so many Allen alter egos—Allan in *Sam*, Alvy in *Annie Hall*—who sport names reminiscent of Allen's own. Allen chose not to play Axel, even though he certainly seems to have written the character as a vehicle for himself.

Perhaps the problem with doing the role on Broadway was that, in guiding his first full-length play to the stage, Woody wanted to save his energy for the more significant task of writing; when it

Soviet officer Krojack (Michael Constantine) and Ambassador Magee (Howard St. John) must be dealt with before the escape can work.

came time to do the film version, he was convinced it would not be successful. His refusal to have anything to do with the film project—not only acting in it, but also adapting it or directing—suggests this may be so. "I get dozens of requests to write *Water* as a screenplay," he told *Boston After Dark* in 1969, "but I have no interest in doing it. I wrote it as a play and I have no desire to re-work it into something else." That, apparently, included acting as well, though *Water* would benefit from his presence. Ted Bessel is a good and underrated comic performer, but he's extremely handsome in a conventional way, and that fact makes all the father's gruff complaints that his daughter is getting interested in a nebbishy loser seem silly rather than funny. And while Jackie Gleason is a fine comic performer, his casting causes the film to take on a "Honeymooners visit Europe" quality, whereas in the original stage version, Lou Jacobi was free to create a totally new and unique character, not merely do a variation on Ralph Kramden.

Indeed, the only real interest of the film is as an early, if unsuccessful, variation on the key themes Woody had already scratched the surface of in three previous pictures, and which would continue through his career. Axel is himself a good dry run for Virgil in *Take The Money* who, despite his homeliness, will attract more than one beautiful woman, just as future Allen heroes will. Axel also has problems with a more successful and conventional father, the first image of such parent-child clashes that will parade their way through the pictures. Food is a key theme here: Walter Hollander is, after all, a caterer from Jersey, and his entire life is based on food. In *Love and Death*, Boris will describe life as "an enormous restaurant," in which every creature in the world is busily eating something smaller than itself while unknowingly about to be devoured by something larger. The food imagery, and the function of eating, in the films suggest this is not a fleeting comparison, but an essential image for understanding Woody's work. Making Hollander a caterer, of all the possible middleclass careers he could have had, is a source for more than just humor; he is a cog in the workings of that enormous restaurant. The "hunger" is emotional as well as physical: he "devours" his daughter by trying to control her life, and is "devoured" by the Reds who surround him.

81

In addition, Hollander is also an artist—"the potato salad Picasso," his colleagues non-sarcastically call him—and like Peter O'Toole in *Pussycat* ("I have a novel in me!") he is the typical Allen hero who must try to balance at-odds interests. In *Pussycat*, Michael James cannot reconcile his enjoyment of the hedonist/swinger's good life with his deeper, sometimes depressing desire to create serious art; Hollander hopes to happily blend the businessman side of himself with the artistic urge by being a Picasso who works in the highly lucrative potato salad field. Art you can eat will always sell; business and aesthetics are not necessarily at odds, as Woody himself—a most practical businessman-filmmaker as well as a most serious aesthetic one—can tell you. It may not be altogether wrong to see Hollander as a projection of Woody's fears, because *Water* is, at least by implication, about the perishability of art: not only Hollander's food-art, which despite his extreme and delicate care will be hastily and carelessly devoured in one room of that worldwide restaurant, but books and films as well. Once, when someone suggested to Alfred Hitchcock that he would achieve lasting immortality through his films, he shrugged, shook his head, and insisted: "In fifty years, it will all be disintegrating in the cans." In a similar vein but in his unique voice, Woody insisted he did not want to achieve "immortality through art, but through not dying." Art is only the false hope of leaving something for after you are gone, and Hollander's perishable potato salad masterpeices offer an image of that.

As an artist, Hollander even tries to innovate: "I was the first to make a bridegroom out of potato

Axel confronts Krojack…

salad," he says in the play, where the line received more laughs than when, in the film version, it was changed to "pot cheese." Either way, though, the notion of the need to innovate, rather than merely repeat, will haunt Woody's heroes and Woody himself, who would eventually insult some of his fans with his more esoteric experiments like *Interiors* and *Stardust Memories*. In addition to art, *Water* is also about magic: Father Drobney (played both onstage and in the film by Richard Libertini), who has been hiding from the Reds in the embassy for a full six years, tries to amuse everyone with magic tricks; the hero of Woody's later play, *The Floating Light Bulb*, is—like Woody himself—something of a magician. By having the magician in *Water* also be a man of the cloth, Woody introduces the religion theme that will surface in later films, and also suggests that magic and religion are two aspects, the one secular and the other sacred, of the same basic force. The paradox principle is included by having Father Drobney represent the two, and then furthered when Drobney, the good man of God, shouts "Damn!" when angered.

In addition to the initial misunderstanding that convinces the Reds that Hollander and his family are spies—they are photographing each other at the airport, and Red security chief Krojack (Michael Constantine) assumes they're actually snapping films of the Russian planes—most of the problems grow from Axel's honest statement to Krojack that "You spy on us, we spy on you," which Krojack assumes is an admission of Hollander's guilt. The theme of communication, and its near impossibility in our modern world, is augmented by another concern: It is the man who tries to be honest, and moral, who causes all the problems in an amoral

world which cannot comprehend such qualities. Understandably, then, the communication gap reaches the point of absurdity when the Reds analyze Hollander's notebooks, which outline future catering plans, and try to "crack the code."

"I had an incredible sense of failure," Woody has said of himself as a child; "She's kissing a failure," Hollander screams to his wife (Estelle Parsons) when he notices his pretty daughter Susan (Joan Delaney) kissing Axel. She's the first of many Allen heroines to fall in love with a nebbish, and Axel is the first loser who eventually wins. Indeed, Susan will spur Axel to his great final success, just as Nancy (Louise Lasser) in *Bananas* will turn the loser Fielding Mellish into a winner in the political scheme of things.

Role playing becomes significant, as the characters must pass themselves off as the Randall family in order to escape, and pretty Susan must even make herself look like a boy—a ploy from ancient comedy, to be sure, but one given a Woody Allen twist here. Marriage becomes a key theme: "When you get married," Hollander insists, "you give up happiness," anhedonically suggesting that the "happy ending" marriage of Axel and Susan may not be as sweet as it seems. Woody's oft-expressed cynicism of politics is inherent when we realize that Axel's father and Krojack are equally corrupt power brokers. Hollander, the complacent middleclass Silent American, grows loud and even radicalized by what he sees, telling the State Department officials, "I don't work for you—you work for me!" The tendency toward movie parody comes across when Gleason breaks into a James Cagney imitation, while self-consciousness about the film experience is clear

...but only manages to convince him the Hollanders are indeed guilty.

when the chef (Pierre Olaf), seeing Axel kiss Susan while she's disguised as a boy, shrugs and looks at the viewer, saying: "Well, that's the State Department for you." Even the assimilation theme is present, as the problems begin because the Hollanders, presumably Jewish suburbanites, are unable to fit into a totally different culture. Paradoxically, while they are stuck in a country called Vulgaria, they are themselves ironically viewed by Allen as vulgarians: the father wishing he were in Miami Beach, the mother dabbling in high culture she cannot comprehend, the daughter looking for an excuse to attract boys. Susan's boyfriend who sees them off at the airport sports Woody Allen style glasses, and the film even partakes of that autobiographical coloring which will become such an issue in later Allen films like *Annie Hall*. Woody later announced that the play was a projection of what would have happened had his mother, father, and sister visited Europe; when they indeed went a year later, he claimed that they perfectly lived up to his musings.

Still, no amount of thematic exploration can make this appear anything other than an unappealing footnote to Allen's film work. Even his failures like *Stardust Memories* are fascinating in a way *Water* is not. The movie is frantic and unfunny, a witless and worthless example of a slight Broadway play turned into a strained film. And because Gleason (much like the character he plays) did not want to leave his beloved Miami Beach, the film had to be shot there, on indoor locations, so *Water* does not even boast the lovely European locales that might have lent it some charm. Did all of this disturb Allen? Not if his comments are to be believed. "As long as they pay," he said after the film's release, "it doesn't bother me for a second."

The Road Not Taken:

TAKE THE MONEY AND RUN

A Palomar Picture (1969)

CAST:

Woody Allen *(Virgil Starkwell)*; Janet Margolin *(Louise)*; Marcel Hillaire *(Fritz)*; Jacqueline Hyde *(Miss Blair, the blackmailer)*; Lonny Chapman *(Jake)*; Jan Merlin *(Al)*; James Anderson *(Chain Gang Warden)*; Howard Storm *(Fred)*; Mark Gordon *(Vince)*; Micil Murphy *(Frank)*; Minnow Moskowitz *(Joe Agneta)*; Nate Jacobson *(The Judge)*; Grace Bauer *(Farm House Lady)*; Ethel Sokolow *(Mother Starkwell)*; Henry Leff *(Father Starkwell)*; Don Frazier *(The Psychiatrist)*; Mike O'Dowd *(Michael Sullivan)*; Louise Lasser *(Kay Lewis)*; Jackson Beck *(The Narrator)*.

A family portrait: Virgil with wife Louise (Janet Margolin) and son.

Woody Allen as Virgil Starkwell, criminal.

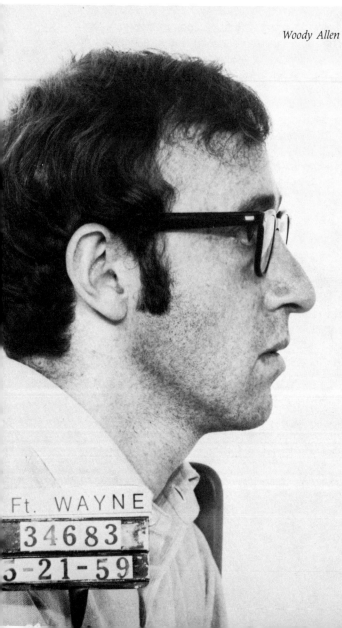

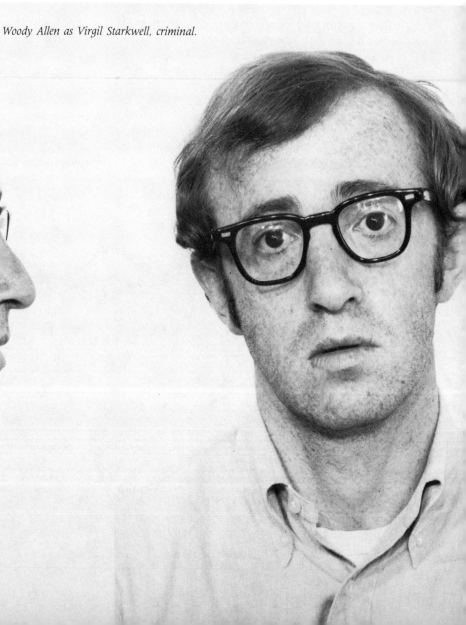

CREDITS:

Producer, Charles H. Joffe; associate producer, Jack Grossberg; executive producer, Sidney Glazier; director, Woody Allen; original screenplay, Woody Allen and Mickey Rose; director of photography, Lester Shorr, A.S.C.; editorial consultant, Ralph Rosenblum; supervising film editor, James T. Heckert; music, Marvin Hamlisch; art director, Fred Harpman; special effects, A. D. Flowers; set direction, Marvin March; sound, Bud Alper; color by Technicolor, Movielab; running time 85 minutes; MPAA Rating: M.

"The first unadulterated 'Woody' movie" is the way *Current Biography* describes *Take the Money and Run.* Certainly, with Woody co-authoring the script (with Mickey Rose) and directing, as well as playing the lead, his vision came through in a way it did not in the earlier pictures. Woody also established his technique of efficient and inexpensive shooting, bringing in a film budgeted at a modest $2,000,000 at a mere $1,600,000 and a week ahead of schedule. Woody saved time and

Virgil and film director Fritz (Marcel Hillaire) contrive a surrealistic technique for robbing a bank: pretending to shoot a film about a bank robbery.

finances by using a single-truck mobile studio, designed and built by cameraman Fouad Said in order to film weekly TV shows like *I Spy* more quickly. Woody's was the first feature film (other than a Hawaiian-lensed quickie, *Kona Coast*) to be shot in this style. At the time, Associate Producer Jack Grossberg told *Variety* that *Money* "would have taken 70 days instead of 50" without the one-unit studiomobile, and that "it also saved us hiring 15 to 20 more people a day. We had a total crew of 45 men" instead of the usual 100 or more.

Despite his oft-expressed contempt for the sloppiness of most TV work, Woody here used a piece of TV technology, and it worked not only financially but also aesthetically: the lightweight Arriflex cameras gave the film an extremely natural, documentary look, perfectly appropriate to a film that is a satire on TV documentaries. Said's studiomobile was rented at $1,500 a day, which included the technician-operator, and the single unit could then, as reporter Rick Setlowe noted at the time, "replace a caravan of cameras, sound, electric, grip, and generator trucks." It could also be ready to move from one location to another in 15 minutes, thereby allowing Allen to cover as many as six different locations on any day, two or three times the usual for a Hollywood film. "There were no technical hangups and I

Virgil's abortive attempt at an armored car robbery.

had all the lights, camera and dollies I needed," Woody claimed.

New York and Florida had been considered as possible shooting sights, but when Woody and Grossberg estimated the film would cost $500,000 more if sequences were shot there, they decided to do everything in the San Francisco area, working hard to make locations look like various areas of the country as widespread as Jersey, Ohio, Baltimore, and Georgia. In San Quentin, Woody grew depressed at the youthfulness of the inmates (the average age of the 4,000 prisoners was 24) but closely followed the warden's advice to keep cast and crew apart from the criminals, to avoid being taken as hostages. There were no serious incidents, though Woody and his people were constantly mistaken for actual guards or prisoners.

Throughout the shooting period, Woody and his team balanced their scripted work with improvisa-

tion. "We have a script," he told interviewer Kevin Thomas at the time, "but use it only as a guideline... in lots of cases we'll shoot alternatives—as many as three different jokes for the same spot. How can you take the chance on just one joke? But there's a lot of improvisation in the dialog scenes. 'Aw, let's wing it' became the company philosophy after a while." Woody, of course, had at this point never so much as looked through a viewfinder, and took a flippant attitude about it all: "I am operating on the principle that the less you know about directing, the better off you are," he said.

Initial critical reaction was mixed but mostly positive. Many reviewers noted that Woody worked in a scattergun style here, loading up his comic shotgun with gags instead of buckshot, then firing them at the audience, hoping enough would hit to do the job and that it wouldn't matter how many others flew off ineffectually. No wonder critic Mark Rowland referred to the film as Woody's "choppy but inspired debut as a director," noting it was "less

During a prison experiment, Virgil turns into a rabbi: one more case of the visuals "following" the verbal gag.

a movie than a collection of frequently hilarious vignettes." A few critics were tough: Pauline Kael, in *The New Yorker*, dismissed it as "a limply good-natured little nothing of a comedy, soft as sneakers," while *Variety* complained that "a few good laughs in an 85-minute film do not a comedy make." Others were kinder, as when Stanley Newman in *Cue* insisted, "Allen has created a frame for his talents that really works—enough discipline to provide point and focus and enough freedom for his comic genius to run amuck," while Kevin Thomas of the Los Angeles *Times* noted that "Starkwell is so appealingly hapless you don't think of him as a criminal at all but rather as a kind of everyman in which we can all recognize our sense of frustrated helplessness at being at the mercy of a toweringly indifferent universe….It is, in a very true sense, a film of the absurd."

In a review that praised *Money* as "a very funny movie," Vincent Canby of *The New York Times* also described it as "the cinematic equivalent to one of Allen's best night club monologues." Indeed, the film succeeds when Allen is able to find cinematic equivalents to his monologues, fails when he merely films the kind of humor he had already been practicing onstage. Woody often reveals an early (and therefore understandable) lack of comprehension of the difference between movie gags and stage or club humor. For instance, when the narrator solemnly explains that a vaccine Virgil experimented with in prison temporarily turned him into a rabbi, the line itself is funny as monologue-type verbal humor. But when the camera "follows" the gag line by showing us an identical verbal gag—Woody dressed as a rabbi—it only repeats, and therefore diminishes, the impact of the spoken gag. Likewise, when Virgil attempts to rob a bank and breaks into the vault only to find, as the narrator first tells us, "a family of gypsies living there," we then see the gypsies and it hurts rather than heightens the comic effect.

For a first film, though, what's impressive is the number of gags that are not only funny but also perfectly cinematic, making use of the paradox principle as it applies to sound film techniques: the humor derives from the discrepancy between what

Parents in masks: Virgil's embarrassed mother and father (Ethel Sokolow and Henry Leff) don Groucho disguises before they face the camera.

we see and what we hear. For example, there is the beautiful contrast between Virgil and Louise (Janet Margolin) on their first meeting, lovingly walking together in the park in an image that is overly lyrical to the point of being maudlin; this would be terribly mawkish moviemaking except that we hear, as a voice-over, Virgil/Woody telling us "within fifteen minutes I wanted to marry her...after half an hour, I gave up all thoughts of stealing her purse." The classic Allen cynicism comically contradicts the gooey, sickly-sweet visuals, and by undercutting them makes a sophisticated final effect out of what would otherwise have been trite and clichéd. Earlier, when the young Virgil tries to master the cello, we *hear* the horrible attempts at making music but only *see* the outside of his house, until the instrument finally comes flying through the glass windows when Virgil is too depressed to continue playing. To see him playing would only repeat (and thereby lessen) what we hear; the sequence is effective because we *don't* see how Virgil is making those incredibly bizarre sounds until a former music teacher verbally confides Virgil was blowing into the cello. Saving the humor for the verbal gag, rather than doubling verbals and visuals, demonstrates Woody's early implicit feel for films, his understanding that less is often more.

Many of the film's best gags are wordless ones that could not have been executed onstage or expressed verbally, but demand movie visualizations: Woody, the cello player, carrying his chair along as he accompanies a marching band in a parade; Woody firing a pistol at pursuing police, only to discover it's actually a cigarette lighter; Woody escaping from prison with a pistol carved out of a soap bar, only to have the rain turn it to suds; Woody robbing a sweet little old lady's purse and finding S&M chains inside. All these gags "work" because Woody was able to take his existing comic sensibility and effectively transfer it to the movie medium.

One very good gag which is possible only in a film occurs early, when Virgil's grandfather "becomes convinced he's Kaiser Wilhelm"; we are then treated to rare film footage of the grandfather, which turns out to be historic news footage of the Kaiser. Likewise, the fact that a camera cannot show us everything is a defect of the movie medium that inventive directors turn into a plus; Woody demonstrates his abilities when Virgil slowly, carefully dresses for his first big date with Louise: we see the entire proceeding only in medium shot, and feel he looks rather suave as he saunters out the door. Then, as he glumly re-enters, the camera pulls back to show us he forgot to put on his pants.

At other moments, Woody will effectively play verbal comedy on one level and visual comedy on

Sex and death: Virgil romances the blackmailer, Miss Blair (Jacqueline Hyde)...

another, thereby conveying two separate gags simultaneously, with the verbal punch-line and visual resolution hitting the audience at the same second. For instance, at one point we see Virgil/Woody cutting a square out of a jewelry store window, then (instead of reaching in and, as expected, taking the jewels) running away with the piece of glass; at the same time, we hear him talk about being so hard up that he "robbed a butcher store...got away with 116 veal cutlets...then I had to go out and steal a tremendous amount of breading...."

The veal-cutlet gag reminds one of the "enormous restaurant" theme, which is further developed in this film through the proliferation of gags (verbal and visual) related to eating. "I could watch you *eat* all night," Virgil tells Louise on their first dinner date, though the look in his eyes actually suggests lust, immediately establishing a parallel between his sexual interest and his obsession with food. Throughout the film, then, food imagery will substitute for sexual

...and then attempts to murder her.

Virgil perfects his technique with a switch-blade.

motivations. When arrested, Virgil does not speak of his problem at being sexually separated from Louise, but that is clearly implied in his complaint that the worst thing about prison life is the bad food. Sex may be impossible, but as we hear Louise explain to an interviewer about bringing him good home-cooked meals, we see an image of her forcing a single hard-boiled egg through the wire separating them. Her serious verbal tone is contradicted but the comic image, which makes a lie out of what she remembers.

In fact, the long-awaited sex with Louise may be a bit more hardboiled than Virgil expected. This is suggested (as food continues to visually tell us what's happening sexually) when, after his escape, she serves him a meal consisting of black toast, coffee poured over a tea bag, and meat cooked with the cellophane still on. That the food imagery is meant to represent Virgil's other appetite, sex, is

made even clearer when an attractive blackmailer (Jacqueline Hyde) is constantly seen not in bed with Virgil (though she is definitely forcing him into an illicit sexual relationship, as well as demanding money) but eating with her; the food she cooks is noticeably more appetizing than what Louise offers, suggesting that sex with her also has an allure Virgil did not find at home.

Finally, food becomes tied in with Woody's death obsession, as well as with sex, when Virgil tries to kill the blackmailer with a carving knife and pummels her instead with a turkey drumstick he's grabbed by mistake. Ultimately, the lack of available food conveys the lack of psychological or sexual warmth experienced by the characters: When we see Virgil and Louise share one sad slice of bologna at a picnic, the brief image—drawing on all the other food associations that preceded it—conveys much more

90

A would-be romantic: Virgil romances Louise, at first platonically...

...and then physically.

in terms of emotion and idea than one would expect from such a seemingly simple gag. Later, Virgil shows a film of a proposed robbery site to his fellow cons, insisting they then eat the film to eliminate the evidence: "buffet style...help yourself...take plates...plenty of potato salad...my wife made some coffee." And when Virgil ends up on a chain gang, we are told the food is scarce: "The men got one hot meal a day: a bowl of steam."

In a similar vein, the running gag of Virgil's glasses being broken is repeated with such regularity and intensity that it eventually transcends the level of "joke" altogether and transforms into a theme. Indeed, the film's very first gag is an image of Virgil's glasses being broken by other little boys, and then moments later by an ice-delivery man: both his peers and even a seeming protector figure victimize him, as does a judge who later tries him. Eventually, then, the chain of broken glasses gags adds up to a statement, wordlessly conveyed through the humor, about Virgil/Allen having his sight limited by the young and the old, by fellow outsiders and by the Establishment. *Money*, like most Woody films, is about sight—psychological as well as physical—and the way a person's vision will be limited by the society around him, if he lets them get away with it. Thus, when Virgil

continues trying to live up to the ideal of the perfect criminal and continues failing to do so, yet never rejects the act of trying, we laugh in the most emotionally involving way: like most of us, Virgil never learns to see for himself, never gets beyond believing in the false gods society creates for us. By consistently showing us this—and by making us laugh at it—Allen educates his audience about the foolishness of allowing one's perceptions to be so limited.

A related theme, and one which will grow in importance in future Allen films, is the inability of people to communicate through language. That concept makes for a good gag here when Virgil tries to rob a bank and cannot carry it off because he has written the word "gun" so that it looks like "gub." The way in which language, invented to make communication possible, actually gets in the way of communication will be a recurring Allen theme. Meanwhile, in writing "gub" for "gun" Virgil becomes yet another of Woody's heroes who are inept at most everything they do, but especially so when they try to conform to the norms of people around them. Other poor boys can shine shoes and spit on the leather to add a high gloss, but when Virgil tries it, he misses and hits the customer's pantleg. Excellent sight gags soon establish him as incompetent whenever he tries to conform to his contemporaries, be it their violent use of switchblade knives or the relaxation of a pool game.

"He wanted only to belong," an expert tells us, and this is what Virgil (and perhaps Woody) can never achieve. "He was unable to fit in with any aspect of his environment," another witness insists. But as the typical Woody Allen hero, he is most inept with machines. In prison, he cannot make a shirt-folding machine function properly, and when it seemingly attacks him, he suffers extra embarrassment knowing his love Louise is a former laundress; Virgil is even inept at those things his woman has mastered. Out of this sense of ineptness and inability to fit in comes another key recurring concern: the hero's pervasive sense of failure. Virgil was "an immediate failure" as a criminal, the narrator says. Worst of all, he never made the ten most wanted list. "The voting's very unfair," Louise whines in an interview. "It's who you know," and her words not only re-establish Virgil's sense of failure, but add a paradoxically comic element by describing a life of crime as though it were a career in show business: she could just as easily (indeed, more easily) be talking about the Academy Awards.

Thus, despite its crime-parody quality, *Money* actually sets the stage for the autobiographical (or at the very least highly personal) projects that reach a head with *Annie Hall*. After the script for *Money* was completed, but before the cameras began to role, Woody told interviewer A. H. Weiler: "It is fairly autobiographical and is based on my inclination toward crime." In a 1968 *TV Guide* article, Woody had confessed to "an obsession with violence," adding: "Not that I could ever be violent. If I had gone into boxing, I'm sure I would have ended with a very bad record. Still, being a crook seems an ideal way of life.... If I'm restless at night, I fantasize pulling a necklace job at the Plaza." At the same time, Woody's first wife Louise Lasser told reporter Robert Higgins that "there is a great deal of fury in Woody," noticing in him "an attraction to the element of danger, the unpredictability of the situation. And crime is a rebellion against the Establishment—like robbing the Banks of America. It's rebellious—and Woody's a rebel." Meanwhile, when considering the mundane lives most people slip into, Woody quipped: "To consign one's life to a meaningless round of subway rides, to do that hot and cold for 40 years, is not being alive at all. There's no comparison between that and a life of crime."

But Woody's fascination with crime is not his only point of comparison with Virgil. Much like Allen, Virgil as a young student scored well on I.Q. tests but demonstrated an attitude that disturbed teachers; unable to concentrate on schoolwork, he soon dropped out. The tough street kid Virgil plays a musical instrument (cello instead of woodwind) and loves baseball. Virgil's wife, like Woody's at the time, is named Louise; Virgil has parents who debate the value of what he has accomplished. The narrator tell us Virgil was born December 1, 1935, which is Woody Allen's birthday. That Virgil is a version of Woody is clear when Virgil plans a robbery so original that the other convicts regard it as "a work of art." The clincher is that this particular heist involves pulling off a bank robbery by staging it as though Virgil and his co-horts were making a film (they even bring in an aged Fritz Lang-type director!), further emphasizing the parallel between Virgil's "career" and Woody's. Essentially, though nothing in the film actually happened, all of it is (in a sense) true. *Money* is "the road not taken," an autobiographical study of what might have been.

So Virgil is a perfectly appropriate figure to express Woody's theme of sexuality and marriage. That Virgil is sexually obsessed is made clear when early on he's asked to look at the simple ink blot and tells the analyst it's "two elephants making love to a men's glee club." Later, one of his psychiatrists asks Virgil if he thinks sex is dirty, to which he replies with one of Allen's greatest lines: "It is if you do it right." Despite the fact that he's a nebbish, Virgil is one of those recurring Allen losers who unaccountably win the undying love of a beautiful woman, like Axel Magee before him and a dozen others to follow. But after Virgil and Louise marry and have the baby, domestication (even for criminals) does not augment sexuality but replaces it. Their post marital fights even include an incident in which they argue in front of chain gang members Virgil is still bound to. Critic Diane Jacobs finds fault with the love story element: "Virgil's relationship with Louise fluctuates between too-sweet Chaplinesque romance and too-snide marital bickering." But she misses the point: the true romantic views marriage as an attempt to incarnate the ideal which is doomed to fail. After all, the "too-sweet" images are all depictions of their pre-marital state, while the "too-snide" bickering is what happens after the formalization of their love. What we see is not a fluctuation at all, but a stark contrast between the love that can precede marriage and the abrupt change after the ceremony.

Woody's romantic sensibility, his negative attitude toward marriage, and his tendency to drift into movie parody are all brilliantly blended, then transformed into a totally cinematic treatment, in the two beach scenes; here, he demonstrates clearly the control he will achieve over the movie medium. In prison, Virgil lies in his bunk, dreaming about Louise, and we see his mental musings visualized in the style of an *Elvira Madigan/A Man and a Woman*-type romanticization of what it would be like to meet

The film spoofs such movies as the classic I Am a Fugitive
From a Chain Gang...   *...and the then-contemporary* Cool Hand Luke.

Louise on a deserted beach, as the camera captures their tryst in a single continuous shot during which it encircles them langorously, through soft photography and sweet music turning the moment into an ideal—which, being part of Virgil's fantasizing, it of course is. Importantly, though, the audience viewing the film in 1969 would immediately notice that the fantasy is derivative of those two earlier hit love stories, implying our ideals come not from our own individual imaginations but from currently popular films. Thus, when Virgil manages to escape and rejoins Louise, he immediately takes her not to a hideout but to a beach: being a romantic, Virgil desperately believes the fantasy can be lived out, the ideal incarnated. However, Woody wordlessly tells us through the visual language of the cinema that he (Allen the writer-director) "knows" more than Virgil does; the artist, unlike the character, realizes the ideal can never be incarnated. There are two Woody's: the Virgil/Woody, who is a person trying to live out the romantic ideal, and the artist/Woody, who knows better. Woody the artist communicates the charming foolishness of what Woody/Virgil hopes to do by shooting the *real* beach idyll from a stationary (and unlovely) camera set-up, then edits it into a number of short takes in which none of the kisses or embraces are ever completed onscreen, and finally, when Virgil tries to lift Louise up in his arms, she falls on top of him and both are hurt. The visual contrast between the abruptness and awkwardness of the "real" as opposed to the loveliness and languidness of the "ideal" cinematically communicate Allen's subscription to Keats' romantic attitude: "Heard melodies are sweet, but those unheard sweeter still..." Being a filmmaker, though, Woody communicates that idea wordlessly.

Woody's understanding of the movie medium's properties leads him to satirize past movies, and *Money* demonstrates his fascination with the documentary form, which will reach its zenith in *Zelig*. *Money*, narrated by Jackson Beck (of Paramount Newsreel fame) takes an ultra-serious tone toward some very funny material. Woody cleverly pokes fun at the tendency of documentary films to create a strained sense of the subject's relationship to the world around him, which often seems forced and facile: "1956 was a good year for most Americans," Beck ponderously tells us, as we see film footage showing various "typical" citizens (including Ike and Nixon!) at work and play, then shows us Virgil in the doldrums. Of course, what is happening to Virgil has absolutely nothing to do with the lives of those other people. In addition, there is an underlying serious concern in *Money* based on the paradox between the word-of-God style sense of truth communicated to us by any films that assume a documentary approach, and the fantasy images of the film itself. For the adventures of Virgil Starkwell are all variations on Woody's movie parody theme, all based on clichés from movies old and new: the bank robberies are out of Warner Brothers crime dramas, the chain-gang scenes by way of films as classic as *I Am a Fugitive from a Chain Gang* and as (then) recent as *Cool Hand Luke*.

But to these patent images of the underworld life, Woody grafts on the solemn perspective of a documentary. The way in which a documentary style conditions us to accept any material as factual will be an underlying theme in most of Woody's movies; Woody's parody of it, and of Hollywood genres, is more than just a gentle affectation, a clever way to achieve laughs. The combination of the two seemingly polar, diametrical approaches to filmmaking—documentary realism and Hollywood hokum—lends this film its unspoken theme, that *all* movies are myths. Myth and reality run together, in our perceptions and in Allen's pictures. Through the paradox principle, Allen creates humor by running a Hollywood cliché up against a sober documentary angle, suggesting that all movies—the fantasy and the real—become part of a single great ongoing movie that runs forever in the American public's mind.

Money can be seen not so much as a parody of gangster films or documentaries as a satire on the audience, and its complex but misconceived way of viewing criminals—the way in which, without most of us ever having experienced "the real thing," we assume a knowledgeability that is an amalgam of (mis)information absorbed from watching the various kinds of movies on the subject and getting them confused in our minds. Woody makes us aware of our

So near and yet so far: Louise visits Virgil in jail.

Incarcerated again: Virgil returns to jail.

own confusion by running them together on his screen.

So like most of Woody's films, *Money* is a movie *about* movies. Significantly, the character played by Louise Lasser finds Virgil a total "nothing" until she learns that the movie we are watching is being made; at that moment, her opinion changes. After all, anyone worthy of having his life turned into a film, no matter how inconsequential he may have seemed, necessitates a second consideration. The ultimate American dream is to become a subject of Hollywood, and Virgil manages this. At one point, the criminals in the film actually become symbols for the audience watching them. When Virgil shows his men the film of a heist site, it's preceded by "Trout Fishing in Quebec." "Ah, there's always a boring short," one of the cons mutters. *Money* is actually more closely related to *Play It Again, Sam* than might at first be obvious; there, film critic Allan Felix fails to live up to the ideal of Bogie, and here "real-life" criminal Virgil Starkwell fails to live up to the ideal of the famous past gangsters, most of them played onscreen by Humphrey Bogart. The Woody Allen character is an idealist who wants to make his mental vision real, and thus is a true romantic. But he is a typically twentieth-century American romantic in that his idealized misconception of the way things ought to be comes directly from Hollywood motion pictures. This is made clear in the film by having Virgil emerge, like all of us, as a product of the media: he cannot experience a job interview without turning it into a TV game show, cannot rob a bank without interviewing the victims as though he were a TV talk show host. Virgil is another of those Woody Allen characters who experience anhedonia largely because they have false idols to live up to and, of course, can never in real life come close to the ideal they naïvely assume is in the realm of the possible.

Meanwhile, the paradox principle pervades the film. *Money* is, paradoxically, a movie done in the style of a TV documentary; the parents (masked for anonymity) take paradoxical attitudes toward Virgil, the mother insisting he was a good boy, the father saying he was a bum. Mostly, though, the paradoxical quality grows out of everyday, mundane situations being played out in the context of a most un-mundane life of crime. Just as in *Water*, where the comedy grew out of normal Americans reacting in normal ways to an abnormal situation ("You never take me anywhere," Mrs. Hollander complained), so does Virgil approach his life of crime as though it were a normal career. When the prison guards want to torture him, they isolate Virgil with an insurance salesman; Louise's concern that their child does not have enough schooling and needs her tutorial guidance is rendered humorous by having them sit studying together in the getaway car, as Virgil desperately drives, and a police car, with cops firing guns, closes in. When Virgil tries to rob a bank and is told to get a vice president's initials on his request, or gets up in the morning to go rob a bank and is late because his wife is in the bathroom, it's yet another variation on this key theme. "I don't regret a minute of it," Virgil says of his life of crime as though he were Allen or any other show biz personality talking about a more conventional career. "The hours are good...you travel a lot...meet interesting people."

True, there are some very bad gags: bad visual gags (Virgil attempting to rob a pet store and being chased out by a gorilla) and bad verbal gags (a man arrested for "illegal possession of a wart") which are on the Jerry Lewis level. But that there are so few of these, and so many clever gags organized around themes, attests to the important filmmaker who would emerge. It's worth noting that in his book *When the Shooting Stops*, editor Ralph Rosenblum writes that he acted as a kind of Maxwell Perkins to Woody's Thomas Wolfe, insisting that the "grotesque and offensive ending" in which Virgil is shot down (in bloody and graphic *Bonnie and Clyde* style) be eliminated. Rosenblum takes credit for the gun/cigarette lighter gag being removed from the movie's middle and placed as a pre-title sequence; the early bit about rival gangs holding up the same bank moved to the middle, where a strong "set-piece" was needed; the long interview with Virgil's parents cut up and instead used as a transitional device. All this tightened the film and turned a flop into a hit.

Even if Rosenblum is correct in remembering it all this way (almost everyone who has ever worked on a film set envisions himself as the one who saved the picture), it should in no way diminish the impressiveness of what Woody accomplished. If he had not shot good material to begin with, Rosenblum could not have done anything to help, and it would be naïve to expect that Woody could not only write, direct, and star in his first film, but also perfectly organize it. Knowing about Perkins's important impact on Wolfe's *Look Homeward, Angel* does not make Wolfe seem less a genius, only a genius who (early on at least) could not list organizational abilities as a strong point. Wolfe would learn to do just that from Perkins, and perhaps Allen did indeed learn it from Rosenblum. Unlike other writer-directors, Woody has always been quick to set aside ego, eager to pick up what a strong craftsman can teach him. In future films, he would not need anyone to tell him how to organize his creation.

Woody Allen as Fielding Mellish.

Start the Revolution Without Me:

BANANAS

A United Artists Release (1971)

CAST:

Woody Allen *(Fielding Mellish)*; Louise Lasser *(Nancy)*; Carlos Montalban *(General Vargas)*; Natividad Abascal *(Yolanda)*; Jacobo Morales *(Esposito)*; Miguel Suarez *(Luis)*; David Ortiz *(Sanchez)*; Rene Enriquez *(Diaz)*; Jack Axelrod *(Arroyo)*; Howard Cosell *(Himself)*; Roger Grimsby *(Himself)*; Don Dunphy *(Himself)*; Charlotte Rae *(Mrs. Mellish)*; Stanley Ackerman *(Dr. Mellish)*; Dan Frazer *(Priest)*; Martha Greenhouse *(Dr. Feigen)*; Axel Anderson *(Tortured Man)*; Dorthi Fox *(J. Edgar Hoover)*; Dagne Crane *(Sharon)*; Conrad Bain *(Semple)*; Allen Garfield *(Man on Cross)*; Princess Fatosh *(Snakebite Lady)*; Hy Anzel *(Patient)*; Sylvester Stallone *(Street Hood)*.

Products tester Fielding grasps at basketballs in the "execusizor"...

CREDITS:

Producer, Jack Grossberg; executive producer, Charles H. Joffe; production designer, Ed Wittstein; associate producer, Ralph Rosenblum; set decorator, Herbert Mulligan; direction, Woody Allen; script, Woody Allen and Mickey Rose; photography, Andrew M. Costikyan; special effects, Don B. Courtney; editor, Ron Kalish; music, Marvin Hamlisch; casting: Marion Dougherty Associates; color, Deluxe; 81 minutes, Rating, PG.

Originally to have been called *El Weirdo*, the film eventually titled *Bananas* tells the story of Fielding Mellish (Allen), a native New Yorker (and the first of Woody's persona-figures to be so identified) whose self-interested and relatively oblivious life is changed when he falls for a pretty political activist named Nancy (Louise Lasser) and, after she breaks up with him owing to his lack of commitment, flies off to San Marcos to prove himself. There, Fielding becomes the pawn in a plan by the military dictator Vargas (Carlos Montalban) to kill Fielding, blaming the death on the leftist rebels, thereby winning sympathy and aid from the American government. But Fielding escapes, joins the rebels, and eventually helps their leader Esposito

...finds himself trying out the stereo system in a deluxe coffin...

(Jacobo Morales) overthrow the Vargas government. Sadly, Esposito quickly proves even more dictatorial than his predecessor, and Mellish is persuaded to become the new leader, journeying (incognito, behind a red beard) to America to beg for help, discovering Nancy is in love with his assumed alter-ego, and ultimately being arrested and tried when the American government discovers his true identity.

If the subject is Marxist politics, Woody wanly chose another form of Marxism for the style: the revolution may have been inspired by Karl, but Woody's approach comes directly from three brothers. "The wildest piece of comic insanity since Harpo, Groucho, and Chico climbed Mount Dumont," Paul D. Zimmerman wrote in *Newsweek*. "Allen shares their anarchic impulse to subordinate everything—plot, plausibility and people—to the imperatives of a good joke." Certainly, when Fielding reads a dinner invitation from Vargas and we hear harp music, it serves as a sly reference to Harpo; when he

cross-examines himself at the climactic trial, leaping back and forth from the floor to the witness chair, he resembles Groucho in similar situations; even the title carries connotations of *Cocoanuts*, and like *Animal Crackers*, *Bananas* rates as a classic example of the comic sub-genre known as "political travesty."

Not all critics were so kind. Stanley Kauffmann of *The New Republic* wrote the first of a succession of reviews which would find fault with Woody's attempts to establish himself as a total filmmaker: "*Bananas* is full of hilarious comic ideas and lines, supplied by Allen and his collaborator Mickey Rose; then Allen, the director and actor, murders them....With Dustin Hoffman or Robert Morse, directed by any run-of-the-mill sitcom director from the Disney stable, this might have been a knockout. But (Allen) confuses the ability to write comedy with the ability to perform it....On the rocks of his acting and direction, *Bananas* splits." Of course, many critics would take almost the opposite approach, claiming that even though Allen's writing, directing, and acting gifts may sometimes falter, what makes him so significant is his insistence on doing all three, on being a total filmmaker, an *auteur* of the antic.

...and on the streets is at the mercy of modern society...

That Woody was our counterpart to the classic comic clowns who conceived and created their own works was apparently enough for most critics, who overlooked the number of failed gags as part of the price one has to pay for an inventive and topical satirist, and accepted the overall vision as an important one: essentially, we needed Woody, and if he hadn't come along when he did, we would have had to create him. "*Bananas* is a cornucopia of nonsense," Bridget Byrne wrote in the Los Angeles *Herald-Examiner*, while *Variety* tagged it "the latest Woody Allen zany foray into the improbable."

But William Wolf of *Cue* asked: "How many of Woody Allen's bum gags can you take along with the brilliance? The question of balance hovers over the latest irreverent comedy caper from a brainy, creative man." This line would dominate future criticism of Allen's comic epics, dividing the fans from the foes. Woody's detractors note the large amount of failed humor as proof that he is overacclaimed, while his defenders insist there are more failed gags than people realize in both Chaplin and Marx Brothers films, their

greatness (like Woody's) residing more in the overall impact, as well as in those gags that *do* work, than in the misfires that must be expected from an inventive and experimental artist. "*Bananas* is a more uneven film than *Take the Money*, but it's more of a film, an adventurous exploration of comic possibilities," Stephen Mamber wrote. Only rarely does Woody make the mistake of using his camera to "follow" a verbal gag, as when the dictator mistakenly cuts a deal with the U.J.A. instead of the C.I.A.; after hearing xargas's admission of this, the audience then sees Hasidic Jews joining in the rebellion. What's impressive, though, is that on the whole, Woody took not only further baby steps toward maturity as a filmmaker, but giant leaps. In *Take the Money*, the clumsiness of the camerawork actually added to the effectiveness, because it fit in with the mock-documentary, cinema-verité approach, while serving as a reminder that this was indeed a first film, a rough-edged work of art in an age of superslick products. In comparison, *Bananas* is a satisfyingly sophisticated work, continuously demonstrating Woody's growing ability to use a camera to communicate his ideas.

For instance, Woody has verbally commented

. . .where he tries to avoid "getting involved" as thugs (including Sylvester Stallone) accost an old lady on the subway.

that he is "at two with nature," and his later film *A Midsummer Night's Sex Comedy* would offer an elongated variation of that theme, playing off his total discomfort with natural settings. As early as *Bananas*, though, he was able to wordlessly communicate this concept. Whenever a situation in the story turns out well for Fielding, filmmaker Allen consistently begins the sequence with the camera relatively tight on the characters. But whenever a situation eventually proves difficult for Mellish, the filmmaker visually clues us in on the trauma to come by having the sequence begin in long shot, with some aspect of nature (trees, flowers, foliage, etc.) framing the edges of the image, then zooming past this frame into the characters' confrontation. When Fielding meets Nancy in the park for a date, the foliage that frames them clues us in that she will break up with him; when Fielding has dinner with Vargas, the flowers that frame him hint at the darker

motivations behind the invitation; when Fielding makes love to the rebel girl (Natividad Abascal), the swamp-like scenery that initially frames them indicates that she will prove too much for him. Woody's remarkable growth as a filmmaker is evidenced by his ever lessening need to make verbal statements within the film and, conversely, his ever enlarging ability to make visual statements. Various gags scattered throughout the film attest to both this growing mastery and the simultaneous continuation of key themes, suggested earlier and now crystallized here. His theme of sight and insight is visualized when, trying to take Nancy's value system as his own, Fielding joins a leftist picketing and has his glasses knocked off, symbolizing his willingness to abandon his own unique way of seeing for Nancy's vision. Later, when his character gains insight, we initially see the rebel camp through his glasses; Allen the director allows us to perceive events as they appear to his persona, and subsequent events will suggest that he (and we) are finally seeing things as they really are.

102

Fielding romances the bright political activist Nancy (Louise Lasser)...

...until she utters those fateful words, ''Something's missing!''

Woody also introduces a religious element that will become more predominant in later films, through a dream sequence in which medieval monks, looking like the ones in Ingmar Bergman's *The Seventh Seal* (the germination point for the many such Bergman homages to follow) carry Mellish on a cross down a modern city street, though a similar group with another crucified man (Allen Garfield) fights for the space. In *Manhattan*, Woody's Isaac Davis will admit to envisioning himself as a kind of saviour ("I've got to model myself on someone"), though, as he learns here, he's not the only guy who sees himself in messianic terms. Later, in a satire on TV commercials, a priest will convince a coughing parishioner that it's easier to take a wafer if one smokes New Testament cigarettes.

In both these instances, the religious elements are introduced through media parody. Also included, during the battle on the San Marcos palace steps, is an image of a baby carriage tumbling down that elicits laughs from movie buffs who recognize it as a homage to Eisenstein's *Potemkin*, the 1925 Russian classic which contains a similar image in a similar situation. Implied in the image is the notion that we perceive reality through our preconditioned media backlogs of knowledge: it's impossible, for anyone who has ever seen *Potemkin*, to think of a revolution without remembering the way Eisenstein perfectly portrayed it. Allen also makes us self-conscious that we're watching a movie by summoning up cinematic tricks only to smash them. When Mellish receives a dinner invitation, we hear harp music playing, which we assume is merely music on the soundtrack that (according to the accepted cinematic convention) audibly tells us how to interpret Mellish's mood. But Fielding goes to the closet and discovers a harp player there. Later, at his trial, much of the humor grows from the fact that it turns into a travesty of *all* movie trials ("Does the codename 'Saphire' mean anything to you?"; "You have no compunction about teaching evolution?"). Like all Allen's work, this is essentially a movie about movies in particular, media in general.

If Woody's parody of films like *Potemkin* or Bergman classics is essentially loving satire, his attitude toward television is savage. Just as the entirety of *Money* was structured as a satire on "in-depth" TV documentaries, so is *Bananas* framed by a brilliant but angry attack on the dehumanization of events by TV

Fielding wins Nancy's heart by returning to the U.S. as a Third World revolutionary and defending himself at his own trial.

WA-12

coverage. "This is *Wide World of Sports*," Don Dunphy tells us, looking as though he really is about to introduce another normal example of the agony of defeat, only this time he continues, "We're going to bring you a live, on-the-spot assassination." Howard Cosell soon joins him, insisting, "This is tremendous," and after the president is shot, Cosell arrogantly pushes his way through for an interview with the dying man: "Would you people let me by? This is American television!" Considering TV's live (if accidental) coverage of Jack Ruby's killing of Lee Harvey Oswald, the sequence is not quite so absurd as it at first seems. Still, Woody uses the incongruity of the terrible event, as compared to (in McLuhan's term) the "cool" quality of television, to make us more aware of the dangerousness of getting our perceptions of the world from this medium: "When did you know it was all over?" Cosell casually asks the dying man. It's no accident that the shot which kills the president comes from the precise position from which the TV camera is filming the event; that is, an assassin's bullet and the camera's point-of-view are one. There is a deadly side, Woody implies by the very positioning of his camera, to the media's exploitation of events and individuals.

Naturally, Woody brings this back to sandwich his film through a perfect framing device, as Cosell is once again on hand, this time to similarly comment, with glib shallowness, on the Fielding/Nancy wedding night, suggesting (as a prelude to both *Stardust Memories* and *Zelig*) that when someone lives out his life's intents successfully (as Fielding has done, as Sandy Bates and Zelig will do), he automatically becomes a celebrity and therefore his every move (however intimate) is considered fair game. In addition to asserting media exploitation as a key theme, the TV framing device (which comments first on death and then on sex) sets up an immediate parallel between the two subjects—a parallel which will underscore this film and, as the later title *Love and Death* suggests, Woody's other work as well.

Money was structured, from beginning to end, as a TV documentary, so Virgil Starkwell never emerged as a real character, only as a media-projected image; the same will be true years later with *Zelig*. In *Bananas*, though, Woody limits the TV coverage to the opening and closing shots, freeing him to take a notable step toward the kind of "character comedy" that would be widely recognized and applauded in *Annie Hall*, wherein he gives us real people living in what is clearly the real world. Before he could make his world more real, Allen had first to make his central characters more believable. Thus, Fielding and Nancy are three-dimensional people existing in a cartoon universe. That their world still exists on a cartoon level can be clearly seen by the unrealistic way in which things work: Fielding

An undercover agent sees through Fielding's flimsy disguise.

has a grenade go off in his hand but is not seriously hurt, or can put on a silly red beard and know no one will recognize him. But that he himself is "real" becomes clear through the well-rounded, three-dimensional characterization.

Fielding is truly terrified of the hoodlums on the New York subways (including a pre-*Rocky* Sylvester Stallone), and appears to be an "I don't want to get involved" type when he pretends to ignore them beating up a crippled lady. But he demonstrates he's truly plucky a moment later when he tries to trick them into getting off at a sudden stop. Like most of us, he bounces back and forth from cowardice to courage, and we can completely understand his typical 1970's urban paranoia when we notice three and a half locks on his apartment door. When Nancy breaks up with him, Fielding's emotions run deep: his troubles enlist our empathy, whereas Virgil's only elicited laughter. Fielding can be oblivious, as when he steps out of his car and into a manhole. But he is not a simple sentimentalization of a sweet innocent alone in an uncaring world. In fact, he is sensitive mainly in a self-

105

The absurdity of death: Fielding helps organize the executions.

interested way, and can be remarkably cruel and careless when it comes to others, as when in New York he slams a locker shut on a co-worker's hand and, instead of apologizing, only insists that proves he's right about the world being hostile. Similarly, when he checks into a San Marcos hotel, he signs in after squirting ink on the innkeeper and barely flashing an apologetic look.

While Fielding is more rounded than previous Allen personas, he is also more dynamic: Fielding grows during the course of the story, from the unnoticed nebbish who goes into politics only to impress a pretty girl, to a man who reaches heights of power he would have never dreamed possible, and even wins the woman. Nancy, meanwhile, is a cameo representative of the emerging modern woman (feminist, political activist, independently minded) who goes beyond the cliché level, serving as a fine pencil sketch for the more complete canvas of such a woman that will emerge in *Annie Hall*. When Nancy breaks up with Fielding because "some-

thing is missing," we take this as more than a plot device, necessary to get Fielding into San Marcos. We react to the couple emotionally, as we would to any couple experiencing painful difficulties in their relationship in a realistic comedy, despite the fact that the backdrop here is always cartoonish—giving us yet another example of the paradox principle at work.

Indeed, Woody's attitude toward women and his theme of romantic love are both taken further than in previous pictures. Fielding finds his ideal woman in the impersonal images offered by the sex magazines that stare at him from newsstands, and has troubles only with a modern, liberated woman like Nancy. "Women's rights do not automatically mean castration," she tries to convince him, but despite Nancy's "enlightenment" she is as much an idealist/ romantic as he when it comes to sex. When they are about to go to bed for the first time, Fielding does a desperate little dance of pathetic preparation, throwing on talcum powder to make himself as near-perfect as possible, but it is not enough: she complains about the lighting and most everything else. "I love you," he tells her. "Please say it in French," she answers.

Always at the mercy of strong-arm characters, Fielding attempts to learn self-defense from the guerillas.

Director Allen steps from behind the cameras to tell Natividad Abascal how to play a scene...

...then turns actor, confronting the beautiful guerrilla...

In fact, it is her romanticism that destroys their initial relationship: they get along well together, but she keeps insisting "something is missing" and destroys a working relationship rather than accept something less than the ideal. What is missing is, of course, the unattainable, the impossible. Then, like that other great male romantic hero of our century, Fitzgerald's Gatsby (who attempted to become what he believed his Daisy wanted in order to win her), Fielding tries to become the political activist Nancy apparently wants. Like Gatsby, though, Fielding becomes something of a tragic figure when he realizes that although he has won the woman's love, she does not actually love *him*. (Daisy Buchanan fell in love with the image of Jay Gatsby the suave millionaire, but not the farm boy James Gatz). No wonder then that, like Gatsby, Mellish feels only frustration when he has accomplished what he set out to do, becoming a political power not because it is desirable to be one, but because it appears to be the only way to win the woman.

"You remind me of a boy," Nancy tells the bearded president of San Marcos, "a real idiot... would you mind if I kissed you?" They go to bed together, and so long as the woman can believe she has made love to her ideal man, she is happy: "That was practically a religious experience," she sighs. But when Fielding pulls off the fake beard and she must face the real man who exists under the image, she turns away: "I *knew* something was missing," she sighs upon recognizing him. When the two finally marry at the end, their sex, so good before marriage, is never quite the same after the formalization of the relationship ("It wasn't the worst I've had," Nancy tells Cosell).

Finally, marital bickering replaces the idyllic love-making of the earlier scenes, reminding us of the O'Toole/Schneider situation with which *Pussycat* ended. All the images of marriage that precede this final one suggest that only unpleasantness can come of it. Even the seemingly perfectly matched (and surgically masked!) parents of Fielding Mellish, who perform operations together, are less happy than we would assume, as they take opposite sides of any issue, just as Virgil Starkwell's parents did. Indeed, if one looks to his parents for a prediction of his own upcoming marriage, Fielding has reason to worry. As Dr. Mellish says to his wife: "We've been married 27 years...my name isn't Martin...it's Al!" Marriage, Allen holds, does not bring people closer together but only turns them into intimate strangers.

A number of elements are clearly autobiographical. "Why did I quit college?" Fielding complains at one point. Like Woody himself, Mellish left formal education after only a short stay and, like the young Woody, becomes interested in Existential philosophers less for their inherent value than to impress uptown girls like Nancy. He tries tossing out the name Kierkegaard to impress her, but when she mentions that the man was Danish, the best reply

...and proving himself quite adept at lovemaking.

Fielding can come up with is, "He'd be the first to admit that." Importantly, Mellish goes to see an analyst, a theme first introduced in *Pussycat* when psychiatrist Sellers turned out to be crazier than his patient, and continued in *Money*, when an off-center analyst seemed convinced all Virgil's problems stemmed from playing the cello. The analyst Mellish/Allen goes to here says nothing, but only writes away at a pad, presumably taking notes that have something to do with the patient. Paradoxically, Allen continues to satirize the analysis he has been attending with dedication for nearly two decades.

Woody's problem with machines is also in ample

evidence. The first time we see Fielding, he is working as a products tester and is at the helm of an "Execusizor," a new gadget developed to allow busy corporate v.p.'s to get their daily exercise without leaving their desks: among other devices, there are phones on spring-like coils that exercise the arm muscles, and basketballs occasionally fly out of the walls. While Woody may claim to resent comparisons to Chaplin, it's impossible not to assume this sequence was inspired by Chaplin's similar one in *Modern Times*, in which The Tramp was forced to test a feeding machine which allows assembly-line workers to lunch while continuing work. Woody even sports a similar jaunty smile when things initially go well, then breaks into a comparable look of anguish when everything goes haywire.

109

Chaplin's gag is not only imitated, but effectively updated for the seventies. "Machines hate me," Fielding later tells a friend, and he speaks not only for himself but for all Woody Allen characters and, presumably, for Woody. Fielding's most significant machine—his Volkswagen—is banged up, suggesting he's not any better with everyday machines than he is with experimental ones. He has as much trouble when serving as a guerilla: his gun falls apart in his hands; he throws away the pin and hangs onto the grenade.

Even more than *Money*, *Bananas* is a film about communication, the way in which words impede rather than help it. When Nancy breaks up with Fielding, the camera holds on them as each talks about his or her needs, while failing to listen to the words of the other. Their dialogue "overlaps"—at times we literally hear both speaking at the same time to convey that language does little to accomplish what it was developed for. If anything, language is not so much a sword with which to cut through to one another but a shield to hide behind, as when, after the breakup, Fielding makes sure that Nancy, walking away, hears him yell, "Don't worry about me, baby," when we see his face (unobserved by her) revealing the anguish he experiences. When Fielding (in disguise) later returns to America, a translator is on hand to help the "foreigner" communicate with the American dignitary who receives him. All three men speak English, and none really says anything.

Bananas (and Woody's films in general) is about the breakdown of language into jargon, about the debasement of language by many factors but especially by television—giving an additional layer of meaning to the upsettingly blithe sports-style coverage of a political assassination or a sexual consummation. Woody continues to tell us that TV desensitizes us, but now he's more specific: it's the way TV desensitizes language ("I will try to make my way through this large and demonstrative crowd," Cosell says, telling us nothing we couldn't observe for ourselves). Most of television makes us too lazy to look carefully, since some superficial boob will explain it to us anyway. This especially angers Allen, the artist who loves (and carefully labors over) his words, honing them perfectly and employing them at their hottest (again, in McLuhan terms) ability to make us think and feel and respond. When one of the TV reporters blandly declares that strife-torn San Marcos is "a land of colorful riots," he serves as Woody's ultimate satirical statement on the way in which quick, easy, facile and deadening media-speak silently bludgeons us every time we turn on the tube.

Woody also furthers his death obsession here. Though he was unable to end *Money* in the bloody death scene he had originally planned, he was able to begin *Bananas* with just such a scene. His films are dark comedies even when they are brightly lit; in fact, the contrast between the bright sunlight that physically pervades this film and the dark death obsession that philosophically underscores it adds yet another perfectly paradoxical element. Like Little Jimmy Bond, Fielding displays a low threshold for death; he is almost killed by the dictator's men disguised as rebels, then joins the rebels only to further avoid death. Later, when the rebels take over and turn out to be even worse than the dictators, they execute everyone connected with the old regime. To show the absurdity of death, filmmaker Allen has Fielding get a job calling out the numbers of those to be executed next, as though he were servicing customers at a supermarket sale; then he almost gets shot himself when he takes a second too long slipping a blindfold onto the next victim. But Fielding's nonchalant acceptance of the madness around him should not be taken at face-value, or as Allen's ultimate statement. Rather, Woody shows us his modern and fallible Everyman accepting it, making the audience laugh at its own dehumanizing acceptance of death's absurdity.

The "enormous restaurant" theme is driven home by the preponderance of jokes related to eating, which are in turn related, implicitly and subliminally, to sex and death. When Nancy first arrives at his apartment, soliciting signatures for a leftist political petition, Fielding's obviously sexual/romantic interest in her takes the form of verbalization about food ("Are you hungry? I could open a can of ribs!") and his invitation is for a dinner date, not a movie or a concert. "Do you like Chinese food?" he asks suggestively, and we know he is actually talking about going to bed. We don't see them in bed together, but we do see them after dinner, smoking, and it's of course a variation on the old movie cliché about people smoking after great sex. Indeed, Woody will make that very clear when, after Fielding later makes love to a rebel girl, we see her in precisely that stereotype image of smoking afterwards, retroactively reminding us that the image of Fielding and Nancy smoking should be taken as an indication that their meal together was only a cinematic substitute for the satisfaction of their other appetite. Even while expressing his sexual interest in Nancy through food imagery, Fielding can find ways to drag in the subject of death. "City College," he says after learning her alma mater, "a great school. I ate in the cafeteria once. Got trichinosis." Later, when someone tries to poison the dictator of San Marcos, Vargas survives (having built up an immunity), though over his shoulder we paradoxically see his food taster falling down in agony, while Fielding looks uncomfortably at the plate in front of him. At

Fielding finds himself menaced by one more enemy.

the rebel camp, he stands in line for his helping of lizard mush, but admits he would prefer poached eggs and cinnamon toast. When Fielding and the pretty rebel girl reveal their sexual attraction for each other, it's during an elongated eating sequence which owes much to the classic one in *Tom Jones*. Finally, the film's greatest gag sequence derives from the notion of hunger, and all the sexual-death connotations evoked by it. When the rebel camp runs out of food, Fielding is forced to go to a diner and casually order some take-out: "A thousand grilled cheese sandwiches, three hundred tuna fish, 200 b.l.t. (one on a roll) and cole slaw for a thousand, mayo on the side…"

The humor here is clearly based on the paradox principle of an everyday situation (ordering takeout) being placed into an absurdly inappropriate context (a Third World revolution). Throughout the film, Allen effectively employs just such an approach. In New York, Nancy casually tells Fielding she'll meet him for a dinner date if she's not off bombing an office building. The paradox of her normal social life and her radical political life is something she remains oblivious to, but which is the source of humor for the viewer. After a formal dinner party in San Marcos's lavish palace, Fielding is handed a check, and everyone immediately begins bickering about who owes how much. The dictator's men, disguised as guerillas, complain about the lousy tailoring of their costumes ("He made cuffs on my pants!") as though they were Madison Avenue businessmen. And of course the *Wide World of Sports* framing device is paradoxically inappropriate for the assassination and wedding night it comments on.

Woody would insist that *Bananas* was only "coincidentally political," but he is perhaps not the best judge of that. *Bananas* is not political in one sense: It refuses to verbally take the expected leftish stance. But Woody is careful to visualize his values. When Fielding looks through the pornographic magazines at a newsstand (*Orgasm*, *Screw*, etc.), the staid right-wing journal *National Review* is in the middle of them, making it clear through the gag that Woody considers the conservative ideas in that publication to be just as obscene.

Besides, to carefully and thoroughly demolish all political positions is to make a movie that is itself a political statement, not in the narrowest definition of that term (pro or con, one side or the other) but in the broadest and most valuable. The dictator is abhorrent, but when the idealistic revolutionaries take over, they're even worse. And what a cynical vision of U.S. intervention! The C.I.A. takes no chances this time, sending in men to fight (and die) on both sides. When Mellish returns to America as San Marcos's leader, he's picked up and put on trial by up-tight bureaucrats who claim "this man is attempting to overthrow the U.S. government from without and within." They are not so different from the paranoid Joe McCarthy henchmen who will go after Howard Prince in *The Front*. And they remind us of the similar government man in *Money* who had written a book, *Mother Was a Red*, and insists Virgil Starkwell's robbing of banks is not just his means of surviving but an insidious attempt to tear down the entire American structure. Woody's political burlesque reaches classic proportions when, toward the end of *Bananas*, J. Edgar Hoover appears in the guise of a black woman ("I have many enemies"). As *Sleeper* would soon prove, Woody is a more political filmmaker than he himself perhaps understands.

111

The Bogeyman Will Get You:

PLAY IT AGAIN, SAM

A Paramount Picture (1972)

CAST:

Woody Allen *(Allan Felix)*; Diane Keaton *(Linda Christie)*; Tony Roberts *(Dick Christie)*; Jerry Lacy *(Bogey)*; Susan Anspach *(Nancy)*; Jennifer Salt *(Sharon)*; Joy Bang *(Julie)*; Viva *(Jennifer the Nymphomaniac)*; Suzanne Zenor *(Disco Girl)*; Diana Davila *(Suicidal Museum Girl)*; Mari Fletcher *(Fantasy Sharon)*; Michael Green and Ted Markland *(Motorcycle Hoods)*.

CREDITS:

Producer, Arthur P. Jacobs; associate producer, Frank Capra, Jr.; executive producer, Charles Joffe; director, Herb Ross; screenplay by Woody Allen, based on his play; director of photography, Owen Roizman; film editor, Marion Rothman; music, Billy Goldenberg; production designer, Ed Wittstein; costume designer, Anna Hill Johnstone; An Apjac Picture, color by Technicolor; running time, 85 minutes; Rating, PG.

Play It Again, Sam opened at the Broadhurst Theater on February 11, 1969. There seemed little question that the character Woody portrayed was a fictionalized version of himself. Allen incarnated Allan, a bespectacled, intellectual nebbish who holes up in his New York apartment, mourning the departure of his wife Nancy, who has left him because (as a highbrow film critic) he is only an observer, not a doer. His best friends, Dick and Linda Christie, attempt to get him dates, but Allan turns each encounter into a disaster by going into his "act"—trying to be like the suave movie heroes he

Woody Allen as Allan Felix, film critic.

idolizes. In particular, Humphrey Bogart appears to him in his fantasies, offering terse tough-guy advice on how to handle women.

The only woman Allan is not affected around is Linda, who looks like a superficial fashion model but is in fact a deep, insecure, neurotic woman. Her psyche, if not her façade, is identical to Felix's. Understandably, then, when the glib, money-minded Dick is off on one of his endless business trips, "pals" Allan and Linda realize they are actually in love.

Most critics were seduced by the play's charms, but not to the point where they lost all perspective. Clive Barnes of *The New York Times* claimed that "The play is so nearly so very good that you wish Mr. Allen had aimed a little more accurately for a serious comedy of manners rather than just a situation farce." Then Barnes happily suggested: "But when you play it next time, Woody, how about transposing it into a slightly sadder key?" That was advice Woody would, for better or worse, take: His comedies grow progressively sadder, darker, and more emotional, with the film *Annie Hall* standing as precisely the kind of project Barnes had called for.

In the meantime, though, Woody's ambitions were more modest. Still, he was not without the need to do something beyond escapist entertainment. "The so-called point of a play," he told interviewer Peter Hellman, "has to be inherent in the characters. In my play it is nothing weighty like saying that all men are brothers, but I do think there is a point beyond the mere diversion of the thing."

Intriguingly, his own presence was almost omitted. Woody told an interviewer from *B.A.D.* that "I wrote *Sam* for me but then I didn't want to do it. I tried to get Dick Benjamin and Paula Prentiss to play it but other projects were tying them down. Then I tried to get Dustin Hoffman but he was wrapped up in contracts for films and *Jimmy Shine*. So...I was the only one who was available."

Walter Kerr was one of the few critics who felt that Woody had not yet mastered the conventions of stage writing. "In this sort of 'seven-year-itch' fantasia," he complained, "plot doesn't matter. Scenes do. But Allen hasn't turned around to look at the stage as a stage yet. He's still out front right down there at the footlights or the mike, telling us about this funny thing that is rumored to have happened to him. It's all hearsay, never the happening itself." The notion that Woody merely borrowed the old George Axelrod situation of a man alone in his apartment, fantasizing about beautiful women, and used it as an excuse to hang together night club one-liners haunts Kerr's criticism: "Indeed," he continues, "we may have come upon a possible test here for determining

Allan ogles a beautiful blonde (Suzanne Zenor) at a disco.

whether or not a comedian's imagination is particularly suited to the stage. Can the joke be acted? When Allen, who has been living on TV dinners, remarks that he doesn't bother to cook them, he just sucks them frozen, are we dealing with a giddy grotesquerie that has got to be treated as a one-liner because it would be neither clear nor very amusing if it were played out? Does any of this matter, so long as enough laughs are got? It does, it does. Unless at least some of the gags are performing gags, the stage won't fill up. The evening, for all of its verbal

113

The classic Allen plight: torn between his intellectual duties as a writer and the lure of a pair of lovely legs.

invention, will seem skimpy, undimensioned, literally paper thin—as this one does."

Kerr's approach is intriguing, though finally too harsh. He can complain that Woody's humor exists solely in the words and can't be acted out (when Woody describes his problems with pot, claiming it caused him to try to take his pants off over his head, the laugh line is funny, and funnily delivered by Allen, but of course it could not be acted onstage), but a similar charge could be levelled against, say, George Bernard Shaw's *Don Juan in Hell*, which has almost no "acting" (in the sense of physical movement about the stage) for the performers, and is often done in reader's-theater style. If Woody is not truly theatrical, then neither is Shaw, and of course he is considered the grand old man of twentieth-century theatre. Besides, in the classic Greek drama, all important action took place off stage. By making his plays so verbal, Woody was then working in the general tradition of live theatre. But this created a problem when it came time to adapt *Sam* as a film. "He'll never do it," Woody's manager-producer Charles Joffe told me when, in Autumn 1969, we had lunch just before the release of *Take the Money*. He explained that many people in Hollywood wanted Woody to do a film version, but that as with *Water* he refused and instead sold the rights for a handsome sum. Woody is uninterested in filming his own plays because he's intent on creating art, not mere entertainment. Despite criticism like Kerr's, Woody conceives of a project for a particular medium—the essay form, the short story, the play, the film—knowing that to transform a project uniquely suited to one medium into the very different conventions of another will always diminish the impact of the piece. As such, it becomes a commercial commodity rather than a work of art; a filmed play is not necessarily a film.

Several years later, though, *Sam* was released as a film, with Woody Allen as Allan Felix. I called Joffe in California and asked what caused Woody to change his mind. "Nothing," he insisted. "Woody *didn't* change his mind. He didn't 'do' it. Herb Ross did."

In *Sam*, the idea of "Bogey" could be suggested in the live theatre, where from ten rows back, a man lurking in the shadows who looks kind of like Bogart and sounds similar to him can indeed successfully suggest the Bogart ethos. But in the larger-than-life medium of movies, with the actor blown up twenty times life-size so we can clearly see every feature, he is obviously an actor pretending to be Bogart, not Bogart himself.

So Woody deferred as director; he had, after all, already established his initial directorial style: free-wheeling and improvisational. *Sam*, based on a single set play, would need a far more conventional structure. So a more conventional director was hired, Herb Ross, whose finest films—*The Turning Point*, *The Seven Per Cent Solution*, *The Goodbye Girl*—are excellent in an antithetical way to a film like *Bananas*. Ross offered what was needed for *Sam*: a solid, craftsmanlike approach resembling the one taken in the Hollywood studio system days by Michael Curtiz, director of such diverse films as *Captain Blood*, *Yankee Doodle Dandy* and, not coincidentally, *Casablanca*. After all, this Bogart classic is only fleetingly referred to in Woody's play *Sam*, but in the film version, it is the framing device which opens and closes the picture. If Michael Curtiz is Herb Ross's stylistic predecessor from the studio days, then it is perhaps more accurate to see the film version of *Sam* as Ross's tribute to Curtiz than as Woody's tribute to Bogart.

In . . . *But We Need the Eggs*, Diane Jacobs claims that "Differences between the play and the movie version . . . are slight." In point of fact, they are enormous. Onstage, *Sam* opened with Allan watching *The Maltese Falcon* and ended with Allan talking about *The African Queen*; the effect was a homage to the career of Humphrey Bogart. But in the film, references to both those pictures are eliminated in favor of *Casablanca*; the movie becomes a study of how one particular film (which happened to star Humphrey Bogart) ended up having an unfathomable effect on the romantic views of our culture. Working from Woody's screenplay, Ross makes this statement "cinematic" (that is, he "says" all this in his images and editing rather than in words) by precisely imitating the *Casablanca* airport scene in his own final scene featuring Allan, Linda, and Dick instead of Humphrey Bogart, Ingrid Bergman, and Paul Henreid. In the play, there is no airport scene, and though Allan does quote from *Casablanca* when he tells Linda to go with her husband, it has the effect of a gag when he immediately confesses where he got the words. But in the film, having observed that remarkable sequence and heard those words being spoken, there is a sense of inexorability created: a feeling that it was this man's fate to live out that sequence. This provides his admission that he's been "waiting to say it all my life" with an emotional undercurrent that cannot exist in the play's throwaway approach to *Casablanca*.

Likewise, the play ends on a totally different note. Allan has completely escaped from his role playing, and is now comfortable being himself, as we see by his impressing a beautiful young woman, also interested in cinema, with his knowledgability. But in the movie, though Allan says the same words to Bogey about not needing to be like him anymore, our final image is very different. Instead of being with a lovely girl, Allan is all alone; while he may claim to not need Bogart anymore, we see him walking away into the fog, much as Bogart did at the end of *Casablanca*. Visually, then, the film tells us that although Allan Felix may on a conscious level *believe* he has escaped from the need to imitate his movie idols, he is still doing it: there is a degree to which none of us ever can (and, perhaps, never should) completely free ourselves from the role models of the movies.

Throughout, the dialogue of the play is identically duplicated in the film. But far from suggesting that

Casablanca *revisited: Allan and Linda (Diane Keaton) live out the airport sequence from his favorite movie.*

Allan Felix experiences yet another disastrous date with a pretty girl (Joy Bang).

Jerry Lacy as "Bogie."

Under Bogie's tutelage, Allan imagines a beautiful girl (Mary Fletcher) clawing at him.

A classic Allan moment, in which sexy situation comedy turns into a moral comedy of manners: Allan falls in love with the wife of his best friend, Dick (Tony Roberts).

...e art museum, Allan makes a move on a death-obsessed ...ty (Diana Davila).

While shopping, Allan fantasizes that his ex-wife Nancy (Susan Anspach) berates him while Bogie offers advice.

Diane Keaton as Linda, the first of her Allen heroines.

the differences between the two are only "slight," a closer examination reveals the lines are said in such totally altered contexts, and with such drastically different emphasis, that they are, for all intents and purposes, different lines. A key change is the locale—from Woody's beloved Manhattan, where the play seemed part and parcel with its gotham setting—to San Francisco. The shift was made owing to a strike in New York by crew members, but however incidental the decision may have been, it changes the tone completely. Shot in Manhattan, the movie would fall more easily into the canon of Woody Allen films, where he pays tribute to the city's chaotic charms. Frisco is a far more conventionally photogenic city, just the kind of locale Ross enjoys using for attractive backdrops. If Woody had directed, he might have included a sense of being at odds with such a gorgeous place, but Ross makes the Woody Allen hero seem comfortable amid all the gorgeous locales and lovely people.

In the time-honored tradition of adapting single set plays to the film medium, Ross continuously "opens up" the play, taking interchanges of dialogue originally set in Allan's apartment and restaging

As Dick watches, Allan disrupts a beachside conversation to try and make a date with a pretty girl (Joy Bang).

Food and sex: Allan's dinner date with Sharon (Jennifer Salt) turns out to be a disaster.

He lost it at the movies: After a night of lovemaking, Allan and Linda seem dwarfed by omnipresent images of Bogart.

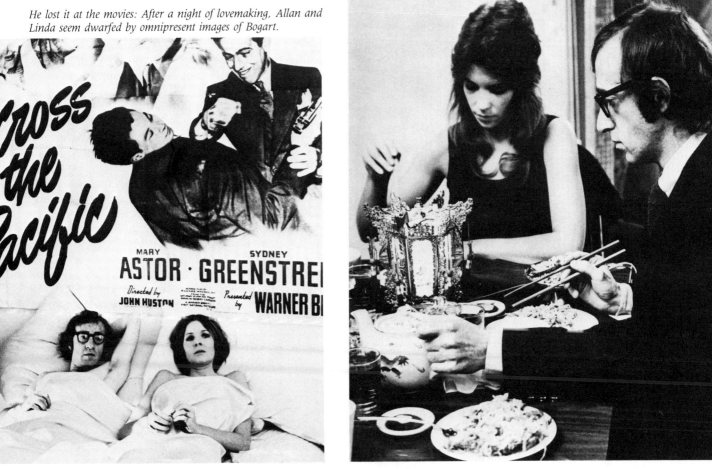

Allan's inability to understand women and their true motivations becomes clear when he dates the nymphomaniac Jennifer (Viva).

Allan longs for the lovely Linda, despite his friendship with Dick.

Linda and Allan finally succumb to their feelings...

them in various settings—at restaurants and bars, the beach, and so on. It's worth noting, though, that the play itself often moved in the direction of cinema by offering Allan's imaginative visions of such places right there in the middle of his living room. The film,

then, does not violate the spirit of the play but rather moves further in the same direction. Another clear indication of the difference between the two is that in the play we never see Allan's ex-wife Nancy except in his grotesque, dehumanizing fantasies about her. In the film, though, he runs into her in an antique shop, and though his mental musings about her were as monstrous as in the play, here they are contradicted by her low-key and pleasant presence; we are allowed to see the reality of Nancy, and realize that the vision we previously had of her was nothing more than Allan Felix's nightmare image of a real woman.

Even the placement of this added scene is significant. It happens after Allan has made love to Linda, at that point when he is clearly developing from a frustrated dreamer into the kind of doer that Nancy always wanted him to become. The play rushes toward its conclusion after the lovemaking scene, but the movie takes this unexpected but satisfying sidetrip. In the non-comic encounter between Allan and Nancy there is a poignancy: She seems to sense he has changed for the better, and appears to want to grope toward the relationship she had always hoped for with him, but then realizes it's too late now and awkwardly rushes away. The emotional impact of this scene has an effective carry-over to the following airport confrontation. Allan's courageous talk with Dick appears to grow less out of the fact that he knows Bogart is leaning over his shoulder, or that he has just achieved a wonderful sexual satisfaction with Linda and the understandable growth in self-esteem, and more (in some way) out of that fateful meeting with Nancy.

...though they are riddled with guilt afterwards.

In a movie-inspired fantasy, Allan pictures himself as a pizza chef.

A true Woody Allen film (or at least one from this early period) is characterized by a self-conscious use of the camera. Allen the director constantly reminds us, through visual homages to other great films or direct address to the audience, as well as by his fragmented editing with its freewheeling pace, that we are indeed watching a movie. Ross, on the other hand, mainly tries to make us forget this. Instead of having Woody the star say his intimate lines as direct address to the audience, they are included on the soundtrack as voice-overs, allowing us to hear what he's thinking and cutting back on the audience involvement. Instead of making his camera a clear and noticeable presence in the storytelling process (as Woody would probably have done), Ross instead uses his camera to subtly though effectively convey ideas.

For instance, whenever Dick and Linda (whose marriage is slipping into trouble) have a conversation, Ross will immediately establish that they are standing very close together, then film the ensuing conversation in a number of close shots that alternate back and forth, from Dick's face to Linda's and back again; even though the characters inhabit a close physical proximity, Ross refuses to allow us to

Susan Anspach as Allan's ex-wife Nancy. Is it any coincidence that in the previous film, Louise Lasser (his real-life ex-wife) played a woman named Nancy, or that in the film before that, Janet Margolin played a wife named Louise?

He left his heart in San Francisco.

see them "together." On the other hand, Allan and Linda enjoy an emotional closeness though they dwell apart, and to convey this Ross shoots the Allan/Linda conversations in such a manner that he first makes us aware that the two are standing at some distance from one another, and then positions his camera at such an angle as to frame both of them in a single shot, "telling" us, through his camera placement, that they are closer than they might seem.

Understandably, the critical reaction to the film was intriguingly mixed. Many reviewers who had not been comfortable with Woody's earlier anarchic experiments hailed *Sam* as the kind of film they had been hoping for from Woody, while those who had appreciated his previous combination of visual wit and aesthetic wildness complained that the new film was undeniably charming but far too conventional. Richard Cuskelly of the L. A. *Herald-Examiner* admitted that he missed "the inventive anarchy" of the earlier pictures but admired "the tighter reins of plot and characterization" which allowed Allen to "broaden his appeal, to catch an audience which has never before been able to latch onto Allen's peculiar, highly personal comic wave length." Charles Champlin of the L. A. *Times* agreed, arguing that the comedy in *Sam* "flows out of *character*, and for my dough it is immeasurably rounder, richer, more satisfying" than comic films in which the humor comes merely from situations.

"It is perhaps symbolic of Allen's broader comic constituency," Paul D. Zimmerman wrote in *Newsweek*, "that *Sam* opens in New York at the Radio City Music Hall, that mecca of Middle American taste. For *Sam* is...a very good, very funny situation-comedy in the ultimately safe Broadway tradition—well-made, consistently absurd, lacking only the anarchic, wild jazz of his Marxian movies." Only *Time*, in the person of Jay Cocks, took a totally negative approach. Ross, he insisted, "continues to direct as if he were dressing a window at Bloomingdale's. Everything looks terribly fussy and sterile."

In fact, everything looks vital and alive. There is a joie-de-vivre about the Herb Ross world that threatens to pull the Woody Allen hero, who has apparently slipped through the twilight zone from his own special and bleak universe into Ross's more easygoing one, out of his anhedonia. Never has Allen seemed so happy at the end of one of his own vehicles as he does at the end of this one. Before that upbeat fade-out, though, Woody has managed to slip in some of his key themes.

The fascination with marriage and what it does to relationships is basic to the project. When Nancy leaves Allan, she complains that since the formalization of their relationship, things have gone wrong. "During courtship, things are different," he tries to explain, but to no avail. Nancy is a romantic who wants to keep the spark of excitement alive even after the wedding ceremony; she is the one who will not settle for the mundane reality of an average marriage, but runs off to ski and motorcycle her way into a romantic adventure. Likewise, the Dick-Linda

Andy Warhol's superstar Viva as the nymphomaniac, Jennifer.

marriage suggests that not just the outwardly neurotic people like Allan have problems. In every marriage, Allen implies, there is "something missing" (as Louise Lasser told him in *Bananas*); that something is, of course, the romantic ideal.

Allen once again establishes life as an enormous restaurant in which food connects with love in the cafeteria line of our psyches. When we first see him accepting the fact that his wife has just left him, he is throwing away a plate of eggs, and the two elements—lost love and lost food—become inseparable. Whenever he takes a woman out, it is to dinner, and his sexual hunger for the first date, Sharon, is symbolized in his desperate wolfing down of a Chinese meal.

Woody's problems with machines is as pronounced as ever. He cannot put a record on the phonograph without scratching it, cannot use a hair dryer without having it attack him. Even the telephone becomes a major problem for him; he is constantly seen trying to call Linda, though often unable to make the connection. Indeed, in *Sam* phones become a key metaphor for the characters' inability to communicate. There is, of course, Dick's constant leaving of phone numbers with his answering service, which in the play was merely a cute running gag but in the film metamorphoses into something more. In the mechanized world, everyone is trying to reach and break through to other human beings by phone, and some of the most fragmented sequences in the film reveal either Allan or Dick trying to reach Linda by telephone and being disappointed. It is the machinery of our age that makes communication impossible; ironically, those machines developed to aid communication are the ones which cause the most trouble.

Woody's death obsession is in evidence: there is the suicidal girl he tries to pick up in an art museum ("What are you doing Saturday?" "Commiting suicide!" "How about Friday?") and Allan himself is

123

"killed" by Dick during one of his movie-parody nightmares in which he imagines the disclosure of the affair as if it took place in an earthy Italian neorealist film. Elsewhere, he pictures Dick taking the news calmly, as though it were a stiff-upper lip British drawing room comedy. The theme of people's envisioning possible occurrences in the forms of old movies they have been exposed to is basic to the film. *Sam*, of course, offers Allen's clearest vision of an ordinary man trying to live up to a movie myth, and if this theme decreases in subsequent Allen outings, that's mainly because it found its perfect expression in *Sam*.

Allen's continuing problem in understanding the female psyche is also in evidence. The nymphomaniac Jennifer (Viva) tells him at length that she thinks sex is something that should happen "as often and freely as possible," but when he tries to take her up on that offer, she screams and stalks away, muttering, "What do you take me for?" When he sits with Linda, alone in the apartment, trying to understand whether she wants him to come on to her or not, his plight represents that of every man who has ever wondered whether he will fulfill the woman's wishes by coming on or keeping his distance; the key, of course, is that Linda herself is unsure as to whether she wants Allan or not, at first rejecting his advances, then running back to him after she has escaped them.

The concept of role playing is one that is important in early Woody Allen films. The Hollanders in *Water* must pretend to be other people in order to escape the embassy; Virgil must assume many identities to escape detection in *Money*; Fielding must pretend to be someone he is not in order to save his country and win the girl in *Bananas*. In *Sam*, the Woody Allen hero is constantly playing a role—trying to be something he is not—but only messes up his chances to score with one of the pretty girls; he wins Linda when he learns to relax and just be himself. It makes sense, then, that the theme of role playing diminishes immediately after *Sam*. After all, at the end of this film, the character learns to relax and be himself; and if the character is Woody's persona, then it makes sense that this will be less of a problem for the artist after his alter ego learns to accept himself for what he is. The irony, of course, is that he has actually experienced the romantic ideal, however briefly: for one fabulous moment at the airport, he literally became Bogart. And that is perhaps the key to this movie's enduring popularity: In learning to be ourselves, we also learn there's a little bit of Bogart in each of us.

Woody Allen as The Fool.

124

"R" for Rabelaisian:

EVERYTHING YOU ALWAYS WANTED TO KNOW ABOUT SEX* (*BUT WERE AFRAID TO ASK)

A United Artists Release (1972)

CAST:

Woody Allen *(Fool, Fabrizio, Victor, Cowardly Sperm)*; John Carradine *(Dr. Bernardo)*; Lou Jacobi *(Sam)*; Louise Lasser *(Gina)*; Anthony Quayle *(King)*; Tony Randall *(Operator)*; Lynn Redgrave *(Queen)*; Burt Reynolds *(Switchboard)*; Gene Wilder *(Dr. Ross)*; Jack Barry *(Himself)*; Erin Fleming *(The Gorgeous Girl)*; Elaine Giftos *(Mrs. Ross)*; Toni Holt *(Herself)*; Robert Q. Lewis *(Himself)*; Heather McRae *(Helen)*; Pamela Mason *(Herself)*; Regis Philbin *(Himself)*; Titos Vandis *(Milos)*; Stanley Adams *(Stomach Operator)*; Oscar Beregi *(Brain Controller)*; Alan Caillou *(Fool's Father)*; Geoffrey Holder *(The Sorcerer)*; Jay Robinson *(Priest)*; Ref Sanchez *(Igor)*; Baruch Lumet *(Rabbi Baumel)*; Robert Walden *(Sperm)*.

CREDITS:

Producer, Charles H. Joffe; executive producer, Jack Brodsky; associate producer, Jack Grossberg; production design, Dale Hennesy; director, Woody Allen; writer, Woody Allen, from the book by Dr. David Reuben; photography, David M. Walsh; editor, Eric Albertson; supervising film editor, James T. Heckert; music, Mundell Lowe; title design, Norman Gorbat; color, DeLuxe; Rating: R; 87 minutes.

At about the same time that Dr. David Reuben's self-help sex manual was enjoying immense popularity in the social battlegrounds of the late 1960's, actor Elliott Gould was experiencing a run as silver-screen superstar for a generation. No wonder then that when *Time* magazine did a major story on the counter-culture's emergence into the mainstream, they chose Gould's face for their cover. No wonder also that when producer Jack Brodsky bought the screen rights to Reuben's book for Paramount Pictures, he envisioned it as the perfect vehicle for Gould.

But what Alvin Toffler labelled Future Shock created a problem, since society's rapid changes outstripped Hollywood's ability to keep pace with them. Before the book could be transferred to the screen, manners and morality had already undergone such a metamorphosis that the idea of asking cute, obvious questions and then answering them in pat, reassuring ways seemed hopelessly out of date, while Gould's star had meanwhile lost its lustre. So he was dropped, as was the idea of doing the screen version as a relatively "straight" situation comedy. The only approach that could work, it seemed, would be to satirize the very premise of the book, and who better to do that than Woody Allen?

Sex was the first Charles Joffe/Jack Rollins production to be done completely in a Hollywood studio, though United Artists gave them (and Woody) the necessary freedom so long as he kept within the tight $2,000,000 budget. "Dr. Reuben didn't intend his book to be one of sensationalism and our film won't," Joffe told *Variety*, be "a nudie or a lewdie." Instead, sex would be treated through the eyes of "an irreverent comic." But when the movie premiered, Dr. Reuben expressed only dissatisfaction. "I didn't enjoy the movie," he told the L. A. *Herald-Examiner*, "because it

The Fool cannot make the King (Anthony Quayle) laugh...

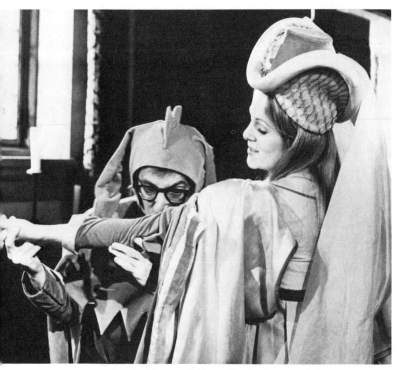

...but he likes to nibble on the tender arm of the Queen (Lynn Redgrave)...

...until he finds himself trapped...

impressed me as a sexual tragedy. Every episode in the picture was a chronicle of sexual failure, which was the converse of everything in the book." The film, then, is not so much an adaptation of the book as an undermining of it, a paradoxical reversal of Reuben's values that makes his notion "sex can be simplified" look silly.

In fact, at the time of the film's release, Woody told interviewer Joyce Haber that the film's R rating was not for sexual content but "R for Rabelaisian." On the eve of the film's release, he also told Mel Gussow: "I don't think everybody conceives of sex the way I do—surrealistic and rich with humor....I've treated it as if I were making a movie about cattle ranching." Not everybody appreciated that. "On the whole," Andrew Sarris would write, "Allen's approach is based on the pseudo-sophisticated notion...that once sex is verbalized it no longer has to be visualized. Say a dirty word and you're striking a blow for freedom of speech, but show a dirty picture and you're peddling pornography." Taking the exact opposite approach of Sarris, Mark Rowland wrote favorably that Woody "has a knack for exploring sexual attitudes without seeming either prurient or lurid."

Its theme aside, Woody clearly intended his third feature as a director to take even more significant steps toward aesthetic and technical maturity. The film's concept called for seven individual vignettes, each a visualized answer to one of Dr. Reuben's questions. He would, to succeed, necessarily have to perfect not one style (which is difficult enough) but seven, a serious challenge for a highly experienced director, not to mention one with only two previous pictures behind him. He told *Cinema* magazine shortly thereafter: "I'm giving myself a double problem, in trying to make it funny and visually arresting. I don't know if it's going to work. It's going to look great. I hope I haven't screwed up the jokes."

Here, Woody articulated what would become a paradoxical problem for him as a filmmaker: the danger that growth in aesthetic control would be paralleled by a converse lessening of his comedic impact. If *Money* and *Bananas* had received mixed but mostly popular reviews, *Sex* was his first film to be almost universally damned. "His weakest screen effort to date," *Variety* announced; "disastrously unfunny," critic William Paul concurred. Charles Champlin of the L. A. *Times*, often a Woody fan, this time cast himself as foe: "Allen often finds it impossible to sense where irreverence stops and an insulting cruelty begins or where ribaldry becomes a stale, sour ranchiness," he wrote, adding that Woody "has written words on fences or lavatory walls." More specifically, Paul D. Zimmerman of *Newsweek* wrote: "This is one of those rare films that is funnier to write about than to watch. The idea of a breast as a marauding monster may be hilarious. But the sight of a large balloon impersonating a breast kills the joke....In the end, the movie fails because it cannot survive the leap from pen to screen. Every segment fades after the statement of its initial premise."

To be fair, some critics praised the picture: "Perhaps Woody's most scathingly funny film," Jack Kroll commented. William Wolf of *Cue* argued that Woody "masterfully satirizes movies, TV, and literature while having fun with sex." Certainly, Woody's media theme is in evidence, only this time it is "how to" books and pop sociology, two equally questionable concepts that came together for an awkward marriage in Reuben's treatise. Once again, though, the banality with which the mass media covers a subject of uniqueness and interest, reducing it to an empty stereotype in the process, is the source of Allen's humor. This tendency of the media is spoofed not only by following the basic pattern of Reuben's book, with its question-answer approach, but also be the use of movie parodies for most of the sketches, again reminding us that we see real-life situations as the movies have conditioned us to see them. The key point of the movie is that none of the questions are answered by the individual sketches at all. The film, then, is a paradox: a movie that flatly rejects the book it's based on. And the paradox principle is clear from the title sequence, in which the natural innocence of white rabbits, so famous for their "performance," is offset by what we hear on the soundtrack: the wonderfully wicked sophistication of Cole Porter's "Let's Misbehave."

DO APHRODISIACS WORK?

The first sketch is one of the best, a charmingly bawdy tale of a medieval court jester (Woody) who is instructed by his father's ghost to seduce the lovely queen (Lynn Redgrave), and goes to the sorcerer (Geoffrey Holder) for a love potion which would work were it not for the unexpected arrival of the king (Anthony Quayle). One key reason this sketch works is because Allen paradoxically combines the antithetical qualities of Shakespeare's *Hamlet* with one of *Playboy*'s "Ribald Classics"; the blending of one of the world's most profound works with the passingly

. . .and then clearly illustrates the obsession with death that haunts so many Allen films.

Victor courageously struggles with Dr. Bernardo (John Carradine).

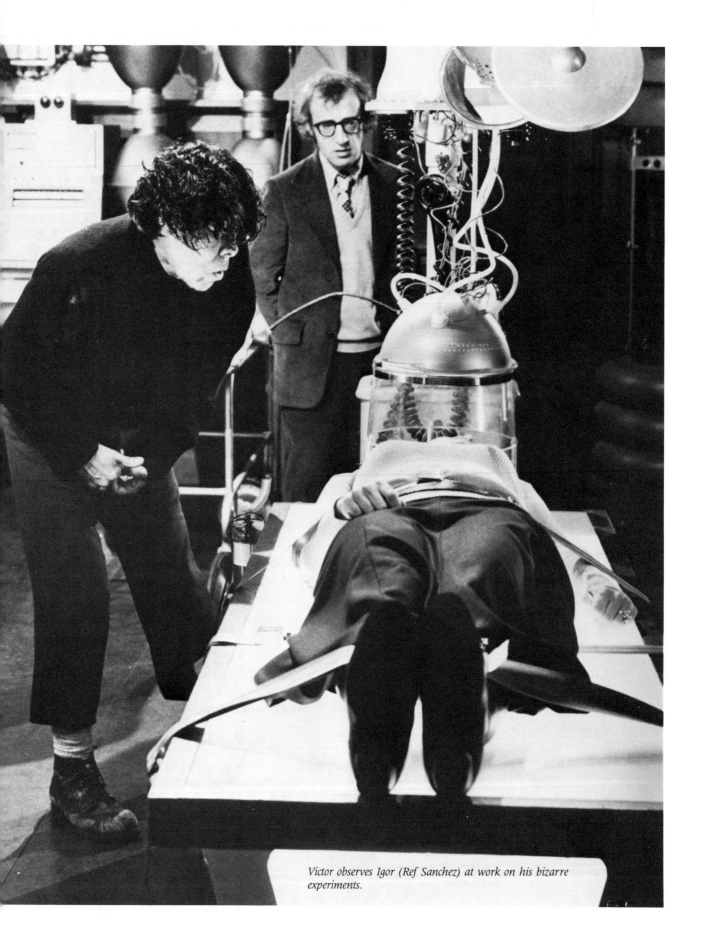

Victor observes Igor (Ref Sanchez) at work on his bizarre
experiments.

Igor makes Victor a prisoner.

Gene Wilder as Dr. Ross, who finds himself obsessed with a beautiful sheep.

amusing is a marvelous conception. Important too is that the execution clicks; shot in the rich, vivid style of a classic costume picture, this vignette has precisely the right look to it, and the paradox works as high-art language is thrust into low-comedy situations.

The sequence also makes use of Allen's food themes. It begins as the court finishes eating: "A most excellent feast," the king proclaims, "and now we will retire to the royal bedchamber," not to sleep but to make love with the queen, immediately establishing the telling link between food and sex. "I would never lay hands on the royal tomatoes," the jester later lyingly tells the queen, further establishing the connection between a woman's body and food. Even as the aphrodisiac is boiling, the jester tells the sorcerer this sex potion reminds him of food: "I think your eggs are done," and the potion itself is fed to the queen with her orange juice: sexual conquest will follow consuming of food.

The sequence also makes use of some marvelously paradoxical anachronisms, like the jester being played as a modern stand-up comic ("Ladies and germs..."), while Allen is once again cast in his role of the sexual nebbish pursuing a woman out of his class. Direct address to the audience is important ("Did you like the way I fooled these guys?" he says to us after tricking the guards), reminding us that this is a movie about movies, while some of the very best gag-lines make much of the fact that the jester is aware that he's a character in an historical film ("I must hurry, because soon the Renaissance will be here, and we'll all be painting"). Finally, his problems with the queen's chastity belt can be seen as an historical version of Allen's endless problems with machines and gadgets. The physical comedy, in which the jester has to pretend his legs are the queen's when she sits atop him, is delightful, though the sketch ends on a dark note: The jester's humorous beheading follows, in the pattern of Little Jimmy Bond from *Casino Royale*, as the comic story ends on a rather grim note.

WHAT IS SODOMY?

A superstraight Jewish doctor (Gene Wilder) finds himself obsessed with a sheep, and begins carrying on a long affair in which they check into hotels together—the sheep is even seen in daring lingerie at one point. The doctor's wife gets wise, divorces him, and when he then loses the sheep, he ends in the

Lou Jacobi as Sam, a transvestite-compulsive.

gutter—drinking Woolite. The sketch fails for a variety of reasons, first and foremost because it would probably work better as a comic monologue. Actually seeing the doctor with the sheep is too ''specific,'' making the gag seem tasteless.

Another problem is that, in conception, the story is a spoof of *The Blue Angel/Miss Sadie Thompson*-type moral melodramas in which an educated man falls from grace as a result of an irresistibly sluttish woman; had Woody shot it in the black-and-white style of those hokum films, it might have had a better chance of working. For reasons unknown, he instead filmed it in a rather bland, contemporary manner, which cuts the connection to the genre being satirized and lessens the impact. Besides, Gene Wilder is simply too good an actor for the sketch. Wilder is completely ''realistic'' in his approach, which contrasts with the cartoonish quality of the segment. Woody himself, who at that point had not yet progressed much beyond cartoon-

level acting, should have been cast by Allen the filmmaker, for with him in the role the audience could comfortably laugh at the character's plight rather than get emotionally involved, as it tended to do with Wilder.

The most interesting aspect of the sketch is its connection to the food theme: When Wilder crawls home after illicit trysts with the sheep, his wife complains that he ''smells like lambchops''; he is, in essence, making love to a dinner. We see him ordering food in the hotel room (''caviar…and grass''), though we know it's sex, not eating, they have arrived for; in contrast, the dinner scenes between the doctor and his wife look extremely sterile, suggesting their sexual problems. After the doctor and Daisy the sheep move in together, we see them eating a humble meal together, suggesting that sexual troubles are beginning for them. After the doctor loses his license, the only job he can get is as a waiter, delivering food (and all the other satisfactions it symbolizes) to other people, though now denied it himself.

130

WHY DO SOME WOMEN HAVE TROUBLE REACHING AN ORGASM?

This vignette is a so-so spoof of Antonioni-type films that goes nowhere, a joke without a punch line. A suave, sophisticated Marcello Mastroianni-like Italian (Woody) and his ultra-chic wife (Louise Lasser) suffer from existential ennui, especially in the bedroom. She cannot respond in bed, though they discover by accident that she can reach orgasm if they make love in public places. Woody's production values are good here: he really does capture the look of a European art film, with characters posing distractedly against white backgrounds or walking and talking in parallel lines as though they existed on different planes altogether, while the subtitles add to the overall effect. Some key themes are present: it is since their marriage six weeks earlier that the problem has set in, once again suggesting that marriage and good sex are antithetical; the fear of machines is suggested in his attempt to use a vibrator on her, only to have it explode in his hands; and the food theme is in evidence when they reach their greatest climax under the table at a restaurant, while everyone else is dining. She even bites the leg of another woman by mistake, as the confusion of hunger and passion reaches its extreme. But there is no verbal or visual climax to the sequnce; it's polished but ponderous, as though Woody—in his desire to get the look just right—forgot that a comic vignette is supposed to lead to a comic clincher.

ARE TRANSVESTITES HOMOSEXUALS?

Sam (Lou Jacobi) and his wife Tess drive to the parents of their daughter's fiancé for dinner. While there, Sam excuses himself to go to the bathroom, instead slipping into the hosts' bedroom, where he dresses in the woman's clothes. When he is almost caught, Sam jumps out the window and is attacked by a purse snatcher. This causes a scene, the police arrive, and both his wife and the hosts hear the ruckus outside; coming to see what's happening, they realize it's Sam. This is perhaps the most disappointing sequence in the film, despite several very funny moments provided by Jacobi in drag. The biggest problem is that it does not fit in with the film's overall concept. In *Loser Take All*, Maurice Yacowar makes a desperate attempt to classify it as a genre parody, however peripherally, claiming that "the element of film parody is not as obvious in this episode…because what is parodied is not so much a matter of genre conventions as of tone," arguing that

In a sequence never shown in America, Woody plays a spider who wants sex with his mate (Louise Lasser) but knows that she will devour him during orgasm.

it's a comic cross-comment on films like *Guess Who's Coming to Dinner?* In fact, there is no element of film parody in the vignette at all, and the audience has already accepted *Sex* as a succession of different film and media parodies. An anthology of skits has to be tied together by a collective concept, and this sketch does not fit in. In addition, it fails in much the same way that the previous one did, sucking us into a gag that appears to be leading up to a visual or verbal punch-line, then doesn't provide it. It's like listening to a comic storyteller weave a joke in detail, then finally admit he has no finish.

The vignette does have thematic resonances for Allen's work, though. The mere fact that this is a dinner date, and Sam gets up to excuse himself in the middle of a meal and go exercise his sexual fetish, is indicative of the food-sex relationship. Also, if one interprets Sam and his wife as Jews, and the other couple as WASPs, then Allen is here playing off a theme that grows more prevalent in *Annie Hall* and *Interiors*: the crude but lively and life-affirming Jews as compared to the cool, genteel, dehumanized

131

WASPs. On the other hand, if both couples are interpreted as Jewish, then the assimilation theme is in evidence: Jews who still have their clear cultural identities are going to visit Jews who have become identical to suburban WASPs, and while the guests are impressed at the cultivated life their hosts lead, they feel the need to grow vulgar as a reaction against the assimilation.

WHAT ARE SEX PERVERTS?

In terms of a "look" being properly created, this sequence goes far beyond most of the others in effectiveness. Woody persuaded Jack Barry to play himself in a black-and-white satire of a TV quiz show like *What's My Line?*, only it's a sexual show, *What's My Perversion?* In addition to clever media satire, this also employs the paradox principle of the sexless, antiseptic television style imposed on a totally sexual subject. Ironically, then, it loses some of its satiric bite today, because there indeed *are* shows (*The Love Connection* and its ilk) that are not so different from the show Woody envisioned here.

The big problem (in addition to the overt vulgarity) is that while Woody's precise duplication of a

TV game show is aesthetically remarkable, he conversely took a step backward in terms of executing cinematic comedy. The sequence is burdened by the problem of image-following-the-verbal-gag, as when we hear the announcer say that the rabbi's secret fantasy is to be bound and whipped by a shiksa goddess while his wife is forced to eat pork. The line is undeniably funny (if in a cruel and, for a Jew, self-despising kind of way), but when we then see all this enacted, it adds no humor at all to the line as spoken. If anything, it diminishes it by ineffectively repeating what was comically effective when only heard. The writing may, on a vulgar level, be funny, but it is not specifically *film* writing. However, the Jewish issue, which will grow stronger in future films, is raised; the image of the rabbi experiencing forbidden sexual pleasure while his wife experiences forbidden cuisine pleasure simultaneously furthers the tie between food and sex.

ARE THE FINDINGS OF DOCTORS AND CLINICS WHO DO SEXUAL RESEARCH ACCURATE?

Once again playing Victor Shakapopolis (Woody's character in *Pussycat*), Allen joins a pretty young reporter (Heather MacRae) going to do a story on a sex

Tony Randall as the brain operator and Burt Reynolds as the switchboard man clown on the set between takes.

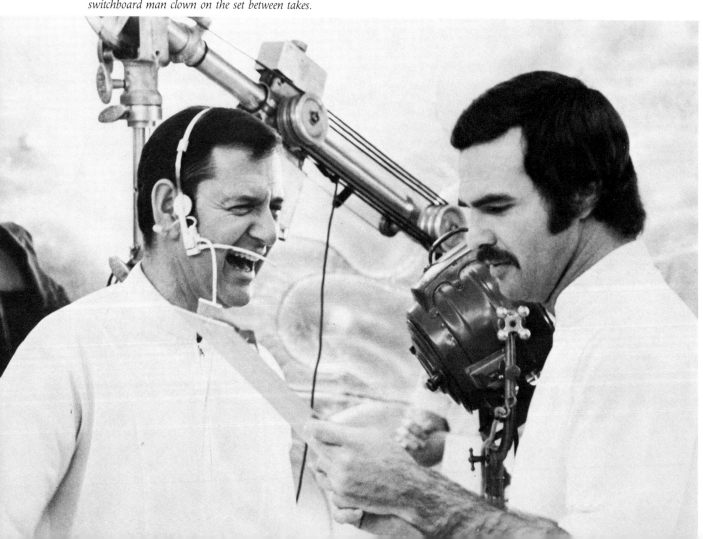

research clinic, only to discover that Dr. Bernardo (John Carradine) is a raving lunatic of the mad doctor variety (even accompanied by a hunchback called Igor). After escaping, the couple discover that a giant breast has escaped and is menacing the countryside. This sketch could have been the high point of the film, if Woody had carefully worked to give the first half the look of a Universal horror film of the 1930s (on the order of *The Mad Doctor of Market Street*), and then, in the middle, suddenly shifted to the look of a Universal giant-monster-on-the-loose film of the 1950s (*Tarantula, The Deadly Mantis*, etc.). Sadly, the sequence has none of the texture or atmosphere of either, and like the Gene Wilder sequence, fails because it's blandly realistic, never identifying its genre through an effective parody of style.

Indeed, much of it is shot in what appears to be a hand-held camera technique, all wrong for the material. However, food is a thematic key to the sequence: ''I hear you're famous for your potato pancakes,'' Victor immediately tells the mad doctor. When, at dinner, Bernardo explains his bizarre plans, Victor can still only think of his stomach: ''Are we having dessert?'' he asks when we expect a moral or philosophical retort to the doctor's ideas.

Most of the doctor's crazed experiments involve a blending of food and sex: He tells us he's studying premature ejaculation of hippos, but the hippo we see is busily eating; in another cell, a man is having sex with a large rye bread. Even when the heroes escape, Victor thinks immediately of food: ''Now we owe them a dinner.'' In fact, this sequence leads to the single line that perhaps best summarizes the food and sex theme: Victor tells his girlfriend that he had a traumatic childhood because ''I was breastfed through falsies.'' The giant breast, which kills by squirting milk, serves as a perfect symbol of sex, death, and food all together.

WHAT HAPPENS DURING EJACULATION?

The final sequence is the best, but that's putting it mildly: This is the one time in the movie when Woody's writing is completely cinematic, when he's in control of the visual texture and atmosphere he's after, and when the two blend together for a comic sketch that is brilliant both in its sense of technical control and effective humor. As a man and a woman date for dinner, then have sex in the car afterwards (immediately establishing the sex and food link), we are treated to a fanciful vision of the inside of the

Woody as the reluctant sperm cell.

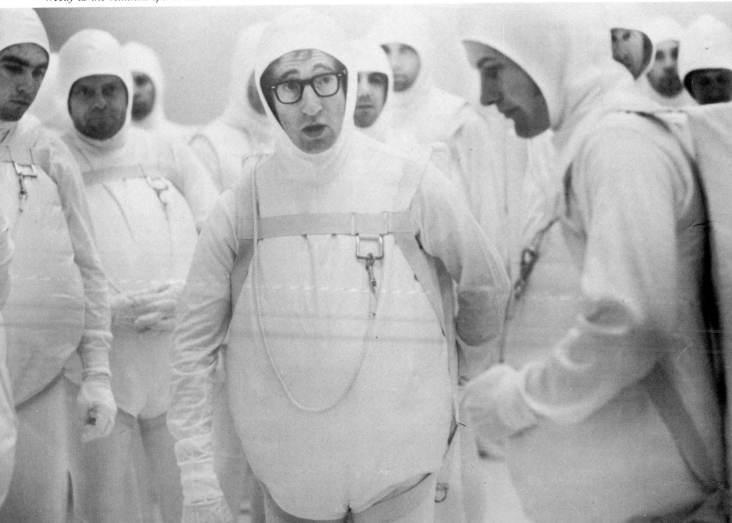

man's body, portrayed as though it were a mission control center, as the brain cells relay messages to the stomach, the heart, the sex organs. In each of these spots, actors play technicians getting the operation going.

Though the specific target for the parody may be *Fantastic Voyage*, in which people reduced to microscopic size took a trip through the blood stream, the film also takes perfect jibes at science-fiction and fantasy films, and even the clichés of old World War II movies as Woody, playing a reluctant sperm afraid to be released ("What if it's a homosexual encounter?" he grimaces) finds the courage to make the parachute jump as though this were *Thirty Seconds Over Tokyo*. When the man goes to kiss the woman, we see workers in the mouth scurrying to roll out a giant tongue; when the characters are eating in the restaurant, we see the stomach maintenance men shovelling fettucini. This is a brilliant idea, brilliantly executed; each new image of another part of the body adds to the humor, topping the previous bit. Meanwhile, the treatment of the body as a machine adds the favorite Allen theme of fear of anything mechanical, which here extends to the human body itself. Best of all, this is one vignette that does end with the anticipated punch line: As the various workers inside the body (Tony Randall, Burt Reynolds, etc.) celebrate the seduction with champagne, they hear the woman ask the man to do it again, and must stop their party to start all over.

THE MISSING VIGNETTE: WHAT MAKES A MAN A HOMOSEXUAL?

Removed before the film went into American release, this sketch featured Woody as a spider being made love to, then devoured by, fellow spider Louise Lasser. Playing off the "deadlier than the male" theme of women who destroy men while sexually satisfying them, it might have offered an intriguing aspect of the depiction of women in Woody's films. In addition, since Woody would have for once been literally, as well as figuratively, eaten by his mate during the sex act, the sequence would have offered the most graphic visualization of the food-as-sex theme.

All of this was to be observed by a homosexual scientist (played by Woody) who sees these goings on as a confirmation of his fears of women. The sketch would thus have contained a commentary on the act of observing, how one sees in something not necessarily what is there but rather a confirmation of what he hoped to find.

An Unequivocal Transition:

SLEEPER

United Artists (1973)

CAST:

Woody Allen *(Miles Monroe)*; Diane Keaton *(Luna Schlosser)*; John Beck *(Erno Windt)*; Mary Gregory *(Dr. Melik)*; Don Keefer *(Dr. Tryon)*; John McLiam *(Dr. Agon)*; Bartlett Robinson *(Dr. Orva)*; Chris Forbes *(Rainer Krebs)*; Marya Small *(Dr. Nero)*; Susan Miller *(Ellen Pogrebin)*; Lou Picetti *(Master of Ceremonies)*; Jessica Rains *(Woman in Mirror)*; Spencer Milligan *(Jeb Hrmthmg)*.

CREDITS:

Producer, Jack Grossberg; associate producers, Marshall Brickman and Ralph Rosenblum; executive producer, Charles H. Joffe; director, Woody Allen; original screenplay, Woody Allen and Marshall Brickman; director of photography, David M. Walsh; editor, Ralph Rosenblum; set designer, Dianne Wager; stunt coordinator, M. James Arnett; special effects, A. D. Flowers; title design, Norman Gorbaty; music by Woody Allen with the Preservation Hall Band and the New Orleans Funeral Ragtime Orchestra; casting, Lynn Stalmaster; a Rollins-Joffe production; color by DeLuxe; running time, 88 minutes; rating, PG.

In the late 1960's, many of the old Hollywood film genres fell by the wayside as such innovative movies as *Easy Rider* created a new era of socially relevant cinema for an audience that had either outgrown or overdosed on the formula films. Very quickly, though, audiences and moviemakers began to yearn for the good old days of those bygone but beloved genre movies, the result being that in the early seventies, our most significant comic filmmakers turned to genre parody. From Woody, there had already been a parody of Warner Brothers crime films (*Money*) and, from Mel Brooks, a surprisingly popular spoof of the seemingly dead form of the western (*Blazing Saddles*). While Woody would shortly move away from such genre parody in order to forge his own more unique comic form in *Annie Hall* and *Manhattan*, he was at the time still working within this format.

Sleeper is his satire on science-fiction films, a Rip Van Winkle-type fable of a New York health food store proprietor named Miles Monroe who goes into St.

Vincent's hospital for a minor ulcer operation, is the recipient of much malpractice, and is then frozen by the doctors. Two hundred years later, he's unfrozen by scientists living in a police state; very shortly, Miles finds himself pursued around the futuristic world by agents of a fascist dictator. He escapes only by pretending to be a servile robot working for the hedonist-poetess Luna (Diane Keaton), eventually enlightening her as to the death-in-life quality of her shallow existence. But just as she joins the rebel-underground and falls in love with the leader, Erno (John Beck), Miles is captured and ''reprogrammed'' by the Establishment. Now it is Luna's turn to deprogram him, as the two try to kidnap the leader's nose (the only part of him left after an assassination attempt) before the other fascists can reconstruct him through cloning.

Sleeper contains precise recreations of science-fiction hardware and fantasy thriller software as it appeared in the films from *Metropolis* (1927) to *2001: A Space Odyssey* (1967), but at the same time exhibits Woody's continual and impressive growth as a filmmaker, and was

The ''enormous restaurant'' theme made totally visual: Miles makes off with an oversized banana.

135

Miles rises from the ground after inhaling too much plant food at the futuristic farm.

the most complete and concise expression of his "world view" to appear thus far.

Understandably, then, *Sleeper* received the most unanimously positive reviews of Woody's film career to that point. Even Pauline Kael, usually quick to knock any Allen films, was impressed: "Physically, Woody Allen is much more graceful in *Sleeper*," she wrote in *The New Yorker*. "He's turning into that rarity, a verbal comedian who also knows how to use his body. And his acting has developed: he can register more emotions now." In *Life*, Richard Schickel heartily agreed: "The simplest measure of *Sleeper*'s success is perhaps the fact that one recalls it not by quoting Allen's one-liners but by trying to describe—inadequately—his beautifully built visual gags." Despite the fact that *Sleeper* does contain some of Allen's funniest verbal barbs yet, Schickel is correct in arguing that they are totally subservient to the visual context. Woody trying to fly with a machine strapped to his back or running off with oversized vegetables; Woody and Diane zipping across a lake as his hydro suit loses air

and propels them forward; Woody running amuck with the robots; Woody leading the police on a merry chase; Woody pretending to be a doctor and clumsily beginning a delicate operation…the visual moments are such gems that they take precedence in the memory over the verbal bits.

A pronounced relationship to the silent film tradition, as compared to Woody's tendency (up to that point) to fall back on night club mannerisms, was noted by most critics: "He strives consciously for Chaplinesque poignancy," Paul D. Zimmerman wrote in *Newsweek*, "sacrificing the funny line of the writer for the funnier mime of the actor. This conversion from cabaret comedian to silent clown often works splendidly…." Whether Woody consciously listened to those earlier critics who told him to get more filmic or whether he was only following his own instincts is difficult to say. Unquestionably, though, he was moving in the right direction. "The two aspects of Allen (character comedy and broad gags) meshed beautifully," David Ehrenstein wrote in the L. A. *Herald-Examiner*. "Allen was able to both let fly personally with his special brand of self-deprecating character humor, *and* fill up the movie landscape with baroque

In one of his fantasies, Miles imagines that he's an entrant in a beauty contest.

Miles disguises himself as a robot and serves the guests at Luna's party.

visual and verbal asides." Indeed, this total sense of balance—slapstick comedy and character development, a unique look for his film and a clever verbal wit—explains why *Sleeper* was, quite rightly, so well received.

With *Sleeper*, Allen proved himself a true comic *auteur* rather than just a comic entertainer working a bit awkwardly in the film medium. Vincent Canby noted in his *New York Times* review that *Sleeper* was "not only his most ambitious but also his best," and as a result "the stand-up comedian has at last made an unequivocal transition to the screen."

Sleeper is a cautionary fable, satirizing everything wrong with our world by projecting it into the future and exaggerating each element to be criticized for comic effect. In essence, only by distorting reality can Allen force us to see its absurdity clearly. By operating in such a manner, Allen establishes himself not only as a satirist but also a surrealist. To achieve this, Woody seizes on his most significant theme—the "enormous restaurant" concept—and employs it in a new way. First, he makes his hero a former health food store proprietor. Then he has Miles discover, in the future, the menus he offered at "The Happy Carrot" are obsolete. When the revived Miles (who himself looked like a lobster being served in aluminum foil when we see him unwrapped) requests wheat germ, organic honey, and tiger's milk for breakfast, the scientists are shocked. "You mean no deep fat, cream pies, hot fudge?" they ask—all those foods mistakenly thought

In a sequence reminiscent of Harold Lloyd, Miles dangles from a computer tape as he tries to climb a skyscraper.

Miles and Luna (Diane Keaton) try to escape in a futuristic car.

Realizing Miles and Luna are not doctors, the security guards pursue them in a slapstick chase.

Disguised as doctors, Miles and Luna operate on the dictator's nose.

of as unhealthy in the past, "precisely the opposite of what we now know as true." Miles can't believe his friends are all gone ("But they all ate organic rice!") and, when the scientists feed him, he insists "This stuff tastes awful—I could have made a fortune selling it in my health food store."

Throughout the film, Miles will find himself dealing with other people in terms of their food orientation. Disguised as a robot, he must help Luna prepare a meal for her party guests, with disastrous results when creating the machine-made concoctions as ingredients rise unaccountably in the pan, spreading over the floor like some crawling fungus. But if the Allen hero is at odds with society, he is not any more at home in natural settings; if the machine-prepared foods of today reach a point of extreme unpleasantness in the future, the same is true of natural foods. When he and Luna escape together and must forage for food, they steal oversized vegetables while a giant chicken threatens to peck them to death. Of course, Woody's revisionism goes far beyond the food gags: His scientist-hosts try to get him to smoke. "Tobacco," they insist, "one of the healthiest things for your body."

Anything which can be conveyed without reliance on words is communicated to us in a visual manner. One fine example occurs early on in the film, when Miles learns from the scientists what has happened to him. We hear none of the dialogue, only view them outdoors in a stationary long shot which reveals Allen's confidence as a filmmaker: He no longer needs to fragment the shot in order to keep the action moving, but can more subtly and effectively convey a sense of action through economical and evocative movement within the shot. Miles's body movements reveal that he thinks the scientist is joking about his having slept for 200 years, but we see his movements growing progressively more hysterical as he realizes it is no joke and then, as the capper (the visual rather than verbal "punch line"), Miles faints dead away.

140

In describing Allen's remarkable growth as a physical comedian trusting in both his own camera (as director) and his own body (as actor), critics have ventured numerous comparisons: Diane Jacobs compares him to Buster Keaton, Vincent Canby to Laurel and Hardy, David Brudnoy to Chaplin. In fact, the film comic Allen has the most in common with is Harold Lloyd. The obvious point of comparison is, of course, the glasses, which could be written off as nothing but coincidence were it not that in *Sleeper* Woody employs his glasses in much the same manner that Lloyd always did. In previous films, Allen's glasses served to heighten his aura of intellectuality. But in *Sleeper*, when Woody dons whiteface in order to make himself appear like one of the robots, he looks, behind those glasses, like the Harold Lloyd silent movie clown, a comparison heightened when Woody literally finds himself hanging onto the edge of a very high building—a direct point of comparison to Lloyd's most famous moment.

Even more than the sentimental Chaplin or the cynical Keaton, Lloyd was the comic who portrayed himself as an agreeable, easygoing man in conflict with the existing social structure, but who mounted its barricades with a good-natured sense of challenge. Woody's assaults on the negative-utopia he encounters have a similarly lackadaisical quality. But if Allen and Lloyd have more in common in terms of physicality than has thus far been pointed out, they differ in their politics. Lloyd celebrated the concept of "rugged individualism"—the notion that only a few will reach the top of the heap. For him, the monolithic social structure seemed a marvelous challenge, and his character operated out of delight in scaling the walls.

Allen, on the other hand, sees every aspect of that monolith as a possible enemy: "What kind of a government do you have?" Miles asks the scientists in disbelief of their police state. "This is worse than California!" is a reference to then-governor Ronald Reagan. In *Bananas*, we saw an idealistic revolutionary turn into an arch dictator the moment he achieved power. *Sleeper* also gives us a complex political vision: though Miles works in conjunction with the rebels, he is totally negative about the possibilities for achieving any lasting good through their hoped-for takeover. "Political situations don't work," Miles tells Luna. "In six months, we'll be stealing Erno's nose. It doesn't matter who's up there—they're all terrible."

While Woody may scoff at the attempts to read autobiography into his work, there's little doubt that in the film, Miles expresses Allen's own view: Thus, we can better understand why Woody would ardently support the "revolutionary" approaches of a George McGovern while at the same time stating

Wearing a hydro-vac suit, Miles tries to help Luna cross the river to escape the Nazi-like guards of the future.

Miles's hydro-vac suit becomes overinflated, carrying him off into the sky.

Woody Allen's physical comedy took a giant stride forward with his Harold Lloyd-like antics.

Dr. Melik (Mary Gregory) and Dr. Agon (John McLiam) help Miles face the fact that he has slept his way into the future.

that he is essentially unpolitical. There is certainly in Allen's view an anti-revolutionary approach, despite the fact that his hero begrudgingly works with and for the revolutionaries. When Miles suggests to Luna that they not worry who's in power, and merely run off by themselves, he is taking what borders on a ''rugged individualist'' attitude. The difference between Allen and Lloyd is that Lloyd appears to mindlessly take such an approach—without questioning anything—while the Woody Allen character arrives at a similar position after questioning absolutely everything.

Early in the film, Allen announced his indebtedness to Lloyd, Chaplin, and Keaton by throwing a pie in the face of one of the guards. Pie-in-the-face is an alternate term for physical slapstick of the silent period, and by immediately including such an image, Allen acknowledges this film will reveal his growing indebtedness to the work of that era. But what's remarkable is that *Sleeper* further forwards his interest in ''character-comedy'': Miles Monroe is not just a cartoon figure, even though some of his more outlandish physical actions are the closest Allen has come to creating live-action equivalents of animation.

Miles is a neatly rounded and truly dynamic character. If in *Sam* we saw the Woody Allen persona leave his insecurity behind, in *Sleeper* we see the results of his new self-confidence. Upon learning that Luna, like all future women, is frigid, he tells her, "I've cured women of frigidity—that's my specialty," and it's not a laugh line; he sounds serious, and we believe him. At one point, he even pulls out his clarinet; this marks the first time the Woody Allen persona admits onscreen his interest in anything artistic (in *Pussycat*, it was Peter O'Toole's character who had a novel in him); the clarinet stands as a symbol for the filmmaker's camera or the author's pen, representing the author's tool (whatever his medium) for self-expression. Other Allen heroes will take this theme considerably further.

One of the great paradoxes of the movie, of course, is that Miles is not really the title character; though he wakes from a two-hundred-year sleep in the opening sequence, it is actually Luna, the seemingly wide-awake woman, who is sleepwalking her way through life, as is almost everyone else in the futureworld. Miles is the one with the potential to wake them up, though he is less interested in reforming society as a whole than he is in shaking Luna into an awareness of the suffocating mindset she previously accepted at face value. The Allen theme of male-female relationships is then present, and Woody introduces this early when Miles is shown some vestiges of life in his times. "This is (a picture of) some girls burning a brassiere," he explains, adding caustically, "You can see it's a very small fire." The gag seems intended to raise the ire of feminists, though in fact the complexity and paradoxical nature of his attitude towards women becomes clear in the structure of *Sleeper*'s storyline. Early in the Miles-Luna relationship, he helps the mindless, thoughtless woman to reach a new level of consciousness. Up to this point, the movie might seem sexist doctrine: one more self-glorifying male who sees himself as the Pygmalion figure. But that is not what the film (or subsequent films) says. Instead, the woman—once sparked to intellectual activity by the intelligent man—quickly surpasses him in terms of commitment to positive change, completing the process by forcing him to rise to her new level.

The woman (Luna in the futuristic *Sleeper*, Annie in the more realistic *Annie Hall*) has been conditioned by society to live a non-thinking lifestyle; but if the male hero provides the necessary spark, serving as the catalyst to crack her cocoon of oblivion, she is then capable of first outdistancing him and then pulling him up to her level. Allen offers an image of the battle of the sexes as a gentle sparring match between equals, the kind of quality that makes the old Spencer Tracy-Katharine Hepburn classics seem so remarkably en-

Diane Keaton as the radiant Luna, who transforms from a nonthinking, nonpolitical person to a social activist owing to Miles's influence.

lightened for their time. Certainly, Allen has already gone beyond the nebbish character; it's clear from the ending that he's won Luna away from the more conventionally attractive (but rather bland) Erno. Part of what appeals to her is his refusal to subscribe to any party line; she may make the transition from being a dedicated fascist to a dedicated revolutionary, but he is able to chart his own unique course. To do that, he defends the right of every man and woman to think. Still, thought, prized as it is, must always play second fiddle to something even more significant. When someone mentions changing Miles's brain, he gasps: "My second favorite organ!"

The destruction of sexual interest is the only tragedy greater than the destruction of intellectual interest, and the futureworld has fascistically reduced both to mechanical functions. When Luna talks before her enlightenment, she sounds like one of the machines in her home; when she wants sex, she walks into a machine—the Orgasmatron—designed for that purpose. Woody's continuing theme of hatred for machines reaches its logical climax as sex is reduced to a function of the machine age.

143

Miles in a rare moment of ecstasy.

Ironically, Miles must himself pose as a machine—a robot—in order to survive. (Woody is not beyond admiring a particularly well-made machine: One of the film's greatest gags features him finding a two-hundred year-old Volkswagen, and the audience roars when he turns the key and it immediately starts up.) But the reduction of sex to a machine-like routine is unforgivable, and with his negative attitude toward formal education it's also understandable that he pokes fun at Luna for having a degree in "Cosmetic Sexual Technique and Poetry."

"Meaningful relationships between men and women don't last," Luna warns him. "There's a chemical in our bodies that makes it so we get on each other's nerves sooner or later." In *Annie Hall*, that statement—which concludes *Sleeper*—will form the basis for what happens. Here, though, love can still charmingly conquer all. Unable to listen to any more of Luna's bad poetry (an imitation of Rod McKuen's), he

nonetheless kisses her, and everything is all right; it's a bit like Buster Keaton kissing his girlfriend in *The General* after he has come to understand, and accept, all her faults, but loves her anyway. What he tries to pull her out of is the shallow, hedonist world that becomes all-pervasive in the future, and in his more realistic contemporary films is symbolized by Southern California. Indeed, the image of the future in *Sleeper* can be interpreted as Woody's exaggerated nightmare vision of the L. A. lifestyle: beautiful, superficial people who think they are deep, who elevate kitsch to the level of high art ("It's Keane...no, it's more than Keane...it's Cugat!" someone admiringly says of Luna's worst poem) and immerse themselves in immediate pleasures. When one of the hedonists is seen wearing a swastika, there can be little doubt about Allen's feelings toward mindless escapism: It's just one step before fascism.

Woody cannot resist including other key themes, at least in passing. There is the theme of marriage, and what it does to sexuality. When someone mentions that coming out of his sleep state he has been without sex for 200 years, he quickly adds "204, if you count my marriage." The concept of life imitating art, rather than the other way around, here has Miles and Luna communicating by playing out a scene from *Streetcar Named Desire*—only with the roles reversed. Allen's theme of Jewishness and assimilation is forwarded, with Allen's paradoxical attitude toward his own Jewishness revealed in two key scenes. One involves Ginsberg and Cohen, the Jewish robots who run a tailor shop; in the bland, banal world of sameness that we see, they are at first charmingly ethnic, then depressingly vulgar. In a later scene, involving rebels acting out a Jewish family dinner in order to stir Miles's memory of his pre-programmed identity, the WASPs attempt to portray "typical" American Jews, even as Miles is experiencing anxiety attacks from his "assimilation" into their society.

There are some homages to the Marx Brothers: When Allen tries shaving and cannot trust his mirror image, the sequence stirs memories of Harpo in *Duck Soup*; when Luna lists all Erno's attributes and Miles replies, "Yeah, but can he do this?" and dances around ridiculously, it's Groucho from *Animal Crackers*. But the look of the film is Allen's own, and he announces his growing romantic vision early on, when the scientists show him pictures of important twentieth century personages, asking him to identify them. Woody supplies marvelous misinformation on some, identifying Charles deGaulle as a French chef, parodying the way our historians misinterpret the past; then, in a brilliant pre-Watergate prediction, he describes Richard Nixon as a former president who did something so horrible all trace of him had to be eliminated. Finally, though, he stops at F. Scott Fitzgerald—the great American romantic, and a writer with whom Woody shares a common view—and in all seriousness says, "A very romantic writer, very big with college girls." Shortly, the growing romantic strain in Woody's films would reach the surface, making him very big with college girls, too.

The paradox principle, as well as the ability to use the soundtrack of a film to contrapuntal effect, is brilliantly employed. Here, the music is the meaning. The improvisational charms of Dixieland jazz aurally represent the opposite of the sterile "perfection" that's been achieved in the visual scheme of the futureworld. By movie's end, Woody has established himself firmly enough as a master of the visual medium that he can relax and allow a dialogue interchange to close out the film. When Luna scoffs that he believes in nothing, he corrects her: "Sex and death," he insists, "the two things that occur once in my life." More than a gag, though, this is an affirmation of the two great, even existential, concerns—ones which would fittingly form the title, and the basic theme, of his next film.

The Russians Are Coming, The Russians Are Coming:

LOVE AND DEATH

A United Artists Film (1975)

CAST:

Woody Allen *(Boris)*; Diane Keaton *(Sonia)*; Frank Adu *(Drill Sergeant)*; Lloyd Battista *(Don Francisco)*; Olga Georges-Picot *(Countess Alexandrovna)*; Harold Gould *(Count Anton)*; Jessica Harper *(Natasha)*; Jack Lenoir *(Krapotkin)*; James Tolkan *(Napoleon)*; C. A. R. Smith *(Father Nikolai)*; Georges Adet *(Old Nehamken)*; Patricia Crown *(Cheerleader)*; Harry Hankin *(Uncle Sasha)*; Alfred Lutter III *(Young Boris)*; Denise Peron *(Spanish Countess)*; Zvee Scooler *(Father)*; Beth Porter *(Anna)*; Henry Czarniak *(Ivan)*; Despo Diamantidou *(Mother)*; Florian *(Uncle Nicolai)*; Brian Coburn *(Dmitri)*; Luce Fabiole *(Grandmother)*.

CREDITS:

Producer, Charles H. Joffe; associate producer, Fred T. Gallo; executive producer, Martin Poll; director, Woody Allen; screenplay, Woody Allen; editing, Ralph Rosenblum, Ron Kalish; special effects, Kit West, Peter Dawson; costume designer, Gladys De-Segonzao; music, S. Prokofiev; photography, Ghislain Cloquet; art director, Willy Holt; DeLuxe color; 85 minutes.

Love and Death finds Woody halfway between *Sleeper* and *Annie Hall*, between being the maker of delightful genre parodies and the creator of dark auto-biographical comedies. Though there were hints aplenty in even his earliest work of the thoughtful, demanding style of comedy fighting to emerge from beneath his charming clown's facade, it is in *Annie Hall* that the bittersweet tone will at last break though. *Love and Death* is a brilliant bridge between the two styles, a film that maintains a marvelous balance between the crowd-pleasing sight-gags of his former frolics and the serious social issues of his later philosophic works. In retrospect, the darker aspects of *Love and Death* take precedence over the plentiful comic bits, but at the time of the film's release, Allen was disturbed when audiences walked out happy and critics recommended the film as a good time. "People don't connect with the

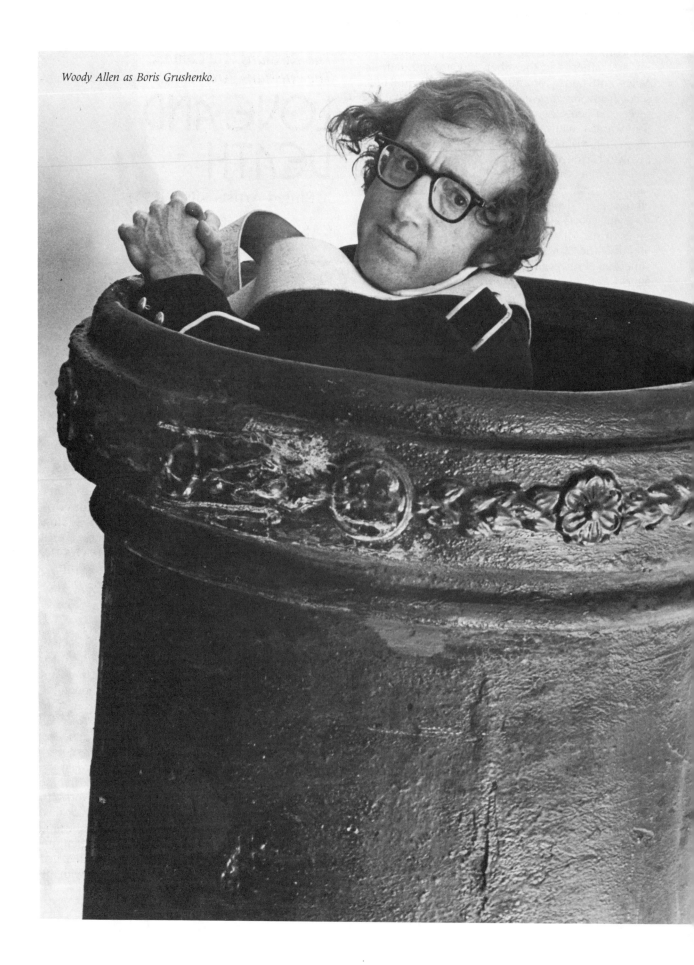

Woody Allen as Boris Grushenko.

seriousness of that picture because of the [comic] tone," he would observe sadly.

In fact, though, the key to *L & D*'s brilliance comes in the way that serious issues are expressed mimetically, through the gags. On the surface, the film seems little more than a likable genre parody, only with somewhat more intellectual ambitions (because of its loftier target) than *Sleeper*. In the latter film the conventions of sci-fi/fantasy were being lovingly parodied; in *L & D* it's the great Russian films of Sergei Eisenstein, as well as the masterpieces of Russian literature (especially Tolstoy's *War and Peace*) that are warmly laughed at. The key to Allen's technique, though, is his ability to take a pop culture approach to high art. His story is about an inveterate coward named Boris (Woody) who doesn't want to join the fight against Napoleon but, after being forced into doing so, becomes an inadvertent hero. Boris at last wins the hand of his great love, his cousin Sonia (Diane Keaton), who then convinces him they must assassinate Napoleon. This has as much in common with a diverting Bob Hope costume film (especially *Monsieur Beaucaire*) as it does with the loftier works Woody pokes fun at.

The paradox of Woody playing a flippant character like Bob Hope's in the context of a Tolstoy epic that takes on the tone of Dostoyevskian existential angst creates the humor. But it also sets up a statement for the more than casual viewer; the duality of the entire project is not only what makes it funny, but also what makes it a meaningful expression of Woody Allen's psyche, for the film represents the remarkable tension between Woody, the expert popular entertainer, and Allen, the closet intellectual-existentialist who would, in *Interiors*, loudly come out. In many ways, *L & D* still stands as one of his best films, because it is the one that most perfectly conveys the duality of his nature through the tension in the work itself.

No wonder, then, that the film is literally suffused with dualities. The title itself can, on one level, be taken as a preliminary statement of the duality of both man's existence and Allen's vision: The most pleasurable aspect of the here and now as compared to the most terrifying element of the unknown. Boris himself has a double nature: coward and hero, nebbish and stud; it goes even further, because he is (in terms of "character") a Russian, and one who occasionally comments about the Jews, while at the same time he is clearly (as an "actor") a Jew himself. So Boris unaccountably makes comments that come from a Jewish outlook: he refers to one unpleasant woman as a "meskite," asks for some sign from God like a burning bush "or my Uncle Sasha picking up a check." The duality extends beyond race to the

Boris proves a misfit when he joins the army.

Boris loves his cousin Sonia (Diane Keaton), who has eyes only for his brother Ivan.

concept of time: Though he wears the costume of a nineteenth-century Russian, he also sports his own twentieth-century horn-rims; he will dance in the old Russian style, then casually admit there are worse things than death: "If you've ever spent an evening with an insurance salesman, you know what I mean."

In fact, the film's finest gags result from such a duality. Onscreen, Woody Allen is simultaneously Boris, the central figure in the story, and Woody

The many faces of Boris Grushenko.

Allen, the public persona who is playing Boris yet can constantly wink at us. The same is true for the antagonist: There are two Napoleons, the real dictator and his stand-in who is killed by mistake. When Sonia seduces Napoleon so Boris can kill him, there is a noise. "I heard *two* voices," Napoleon insists. Earlier, when Boris angers the lover of a beautiful countess, the man challenges him to a duel and calls for seconds. "Seconds?" Boris explains. "I never gave her seconds." Sonia admits to being two people, half angel and half whore. There is even a duality in the derivativeness of Boris's character. At one moment, he is the Bob Hope of *Beaucaire* and the other such period-piece pleasantries, licking his lips at the countess but fearing her lover-protector: "We could run a check on your crogenous zones, but what about the dybbuk?" A moment later, he is Groucho Marx, as he introduces himself to the Spanish nobleman: "No, it's a greater honor for me …" Hope and Marx are the antithetical aspects of American film comedy: Hope is the ultimate reactionary, embodying all the smarmy self-satisfaction of the leech on society, while Marx was the consummate anarchist, making merry mayhem of that very social structure. Allen is, paradoxically, as influenced by the one as he is by the other.

This, of course, leads to the contrary quality of Allen's own humor. At his best (as in *L & D*) he fuses the extreme opposites and comes up with a paradoxical vision. By incorporating aspects of diverse (even antithetical) comic approaches into his own unique outlook, Allen establishes himself as the end-product of the various styles that preceded him, all yoked together in one movie and one man. For this reason, we can accept the Allen hero's going from Chaplin style little-guy sentiment to a Buster Keatonish sense of stoicism, from Bob Hope flashiness to Groucho Marx fanaticism, from broad Mack Sennett slapstick to Ernst Lubitsch sophisticated wordplay without experiencing a sense of strain. No wonder, then, that most film critics felt that even the splendid *Sleeper* had been surpassed. Penelope Gilliatt spoke for many colleagues when, in *The New Yorker*, she called the film "imperially funny," adding "we turn out to be not really so much in Russia as in Russian literature. It is a literature seen through Woody Allen's unique prism … as if it were being read by a student racked by anxieties about both the afterlife and the common cold."

That last phrase perfectly captures the paradox not only of this film, but of Woody Allen in general: equally weighty concern with the Large Questions and with the most common everyday occurrences. She also implies that *L & D* is essentially an extension of Allen's earlier fascination with the way our vision of the world is taken not so much from experience with

Boris and Sonia are finally together, but even after getting the girl of his dreams, he finds he's still unhappy.

Boris enjoys a romantic interlude with the nyphomaniacal Countess Alexandrovna (Olga Georges-Picot).

Goaded by Sonia, Boris attempts to assassinate Napoleon
(James Tolkan).

A rare moment of bliss for Boris and Sonia.

The threat of death: Boris duels with Count Anton (Harold Gould)...

...and winks at the audience after sparing the man's life.

Sonia, in a placid mood.

Boris and Sonia in their wedding bed: ''No, not here!''

Boris confronts death . . .

. . . is taken by the grim reaper . . .

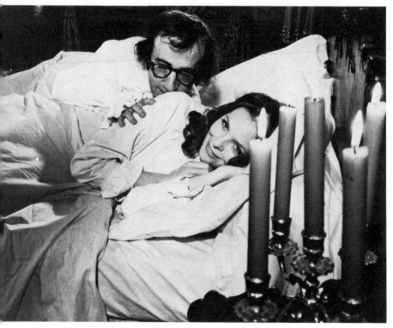

the world, but with media representations of the world, which we (often incorrectly) assume is the same thing. The difference between this and, say, *Money* is that there he was spoofing the shallowness of television, whereas here he takes on the depth of great literature and cinema, which helps explain why the tone of *L & D* is loving satire, whereas the tone of *Money* was savage satire. Judith Crist, calling the film ''a wonderfully funny and eclectic distillation of the Russian literary soul and style,'' also noted in her *New York* review that ''Allen goes for the character rather than the cartoon, the situation rather than the set-up, the underlying madness rather than the surface craziness.''

Critics also noted Allen's humor was growing ever darker. Paul D. Zimmerman of *Newsweek* commented that "we catch him at his best—more nervous, desperate and inspired than ever before. If there is a jittery edge to our laughter, it is because Allen, in this comic response to the angst of death, is treating something of a common problem," adding that the film "bristles with Allen's private terrors, which connect with our own." Allen's ability to make us laugh loudly at our own deepest fears testifies to the great value of comedy and the catharsis, every bit as effective as that in tragedy, which it can provide, making Allen's own negative comments about the comic form untenable.

Some reviews were less enthusiastic. Stanley Kauffmann, a near-constant Allen critic, used the film as an excuse to raise an issue which would come to the forefront with subsequent films: the increasing problem of give-and-take between Woody's growing technical control over his medium and his diminishing comic punch. "His performing improves," the *New Republic* review insists, "and so does his directing—at least he now puts the camera in the right place most of the time. However … much of the photography, by Ghislain Cloquet, is just too beautiful. The picture was shot in France and Hungary, and some of it is gorgeous. None of it should be. For instance, the sweeping mountain background for the recruits' drill is utterly incongruous with Allen's horseplay."

In fact, the "incongruous" quality Kauffmann notes is not a problem at all, but an aspect of Allen's vision and his humor. It is the visual paradox between the soldiers' horseplay and the elegant surroundings that causes the comic reaction; without that discrepancy, the sight gag would be routine. Ironically enough, whereas Kauffmann complained that Allen's ever-increasing technical control diminished the emotional-comic element in his films, *Time*'s Stefan Kanfer made the incredible statement that "Allen has not altered in technique since his earliest films. The only plot that ever concerns him is the one in which he will be buried." Here, of course, truth about the film and the filmmaker is sacrificed for the sake of a glib gag. And while the theme of death does continue to haunt Allen's films, this is part of his substance, not his style. "His persona," Kanfer added, "is still the kind of man whose profile should not be painted but wallpapered." But in addition to being a flat and unfunny gag, that statement is also totally incorrect: any close inspection of what Boris goes through shows him to be anything but the nebbish character. The earlier Allen desperately tried to get into bed with beautiful women and struck out; Boris is himself seduced by a breathtaking countess, who tells

. . .and dances off with him, in a lighthearted sequence that nonetheless has deep, dark resonances.

Director Allen coaches actor James Tolkan for an upcoming scene.

him (straight-faced) that "You were the best lover I ever had." Such men are painted, not wallpapered, whatever their physical profile may be.

In *Sleeper*, Allen's parting comment to Diane Keaton (and his audience) was about "sex and death, two things that occur once in my lifetime." That gag was

Unpleasant parents: though they do not wear masks, Boris's mother (Despo Diamantidou) and father (Zvee Scooler) hardly comprise the ideal family.

the germination for the next film, a key theme that had already been suggested in the earlier pictures and which would grow in significance with each successive film. The relationship of love to death is what the cinema of Woody Allen is really about: the way in which the seemingly diametrically opposed forces are actually the positive and negative sides of the same coin. Certainly, this is not a new concept, and has been the source of much comic thinking even in the classics: whenever one of Shakespeare's characters speaks of dying, there is almost always a double entendre, since in addition to the state of moribundity, the word also colloquially referred to a man's exhaustion after sex. Woody's own modern variations on this ancient theme paradoxically establish both his uniqueness (his variations are very much the products of his own imagination) and his universality (he is a part of the ongoing tradition of popular comic thought).

Death haunts the film. In Boris's opening voice-over, he tells us he's about to be executed for a crime he didn't commit, then takes his specific problem and makes it universal: "Isn't all mankind ultimately executed for a crime it never committed?" Characteristically, he then deflates such pretensions by quickly adding a gag line about his being the one to go the next morning, and this will be his consistent technique throughout: undercutting big issues with little gags. When as a child he meets Death, though, he quickly establishes the serious love (sex) and death theme, not by didactically speaking outside the humor, but (far more effectively) by turning the theme into a gag. "What happens after we die?" the young Boris asks. "Heaven? Hell? God?" Then he asks the key question: "Are there girls?" His gag is a variation on the Is-there-sex-after-death? routine, while in Boris's life, girls (the potential for sex) will often cause potential death. When Sonia (angry at being rejected by the man she loves, Boris's boorish brother) announces she will marry the elderly Minskov, the man is so happy at the thought of possessing her that he immediately drops dead; later, when she marries the herring dealer, she

154

Though he will eventually enter into The Dance of Death, Boris early on performs a dance of life.

inadvertently causes his death by forcing him to prepare for a duel over her honor. Boris has to fight just such a duel after dallying with the countess. If not death itself, then certainly the threat of death always accompanies a sexual encounter. Indeed, it is Boris's love for Sonia that causes him to try and kill Napoleon (though the idea for the assassination is all Sonia's, who gleefully and innocently announces, ''Let's assassinate Napoleon!'' as if she were suggesting a party game, forwarding the Allen theme that the female of the species is deadlier than the male). When Boris is executed at the end, it is not because he had any strong political convictions (he opposed the assassination idea throughout) but only because he wanted to ''satisfy'' his woman.

Sex and death is continued in diverse gags, be it the ''hygiene play'' the soldiers witness (which reminds them, as in a contemporary training film, that a casual sexual encounter can prove fatal) or the simple slapstick sight gags, as when upon meeting

the countess, Boris immediately takes the sword he has been busily killing people with and playfully thrusts it at her, turning it into a phallic symbol that carries fatal overtones. Boris is told by a friend that the countess's husband died in her arms trying to satisfy her, the clearest example in the entire film of the sex-as-death imagery. What's important, though, is Boris/Allen's attitude upon learning this. ''Died smiling, no doubt,'' he jokingly says. The serious point underlying his gag is that the old notion of a fatal attraction toward a femme fatale is very complex indeed: As in the sadly unseen sequence in *Sex* involving Woody and Louise Lasser as spiders, there's a certain perverse appeal to being devoured or destroyed during the process of making love with a beautiful woman.

Since sex and death are intricately interwoven, it makes perfect sense that food is tied in equally with each of them; this is indeed the film that contains the ''enormous restaurant'' line, the work that most clearly identifies food as Allen's symbol for both our sexual appetite and our death fears. Every creature, Boris tell us near the beginning, is part of a vast food

155

All does not go well in bed for Boris and Sonia.

Diane Keaton, quite radiant as Sonia.

chain, devouring something smaller and about to be devoured by something larger. When Sonia reveals her dual nature to Boris, telling him she's half angel, half whore, he revealingly responds: "Let's hope I get the half that *eats!*" This line has usually been written off as just a silly, absurd, bizarre gag that sounds funny but doesn't really mean anything. In fact, it's basic to Allen's concept of food as consistently portrayed in this movie and in the body of his work. The husband who Sonia can't stand is, after all, a herring dealer; the fact that she is sexually disgusted with him is reflected in the rather unpleasant pickled foodstuff he is seen caressing, at times almost sexually. In fact, her sexual rejection of her husband because of a too-strong identification with food provides an important means of understanding Sonia. After all, when a potential lover goes to kiss her, she stops him (despite her attraction to him), insisting: "Don't—we just ate!"

Indeed, food has implications for everyone's well-being. When an officer tries to explain to the men how terrible it would be for their families to live under Napoleon, instead of the expected warnings about rape and abuse, he asks: "Do you want them to eat that rich food and heavy sauces?" Later, Napoleon himself is seen at a moment of crisis, trying to perfect the dessert that would bear his name before his old enemy can create Beef Wellington: "The future of Europe hangs in the balance," he shrieks. Absurdist comedy, to be certain; but if it be madness, there is method in it—Woody Allen's unique method.

When the Countess invites Boris to join her for tea, there is no question (considering the look in her eyes) that she's actually interested in sex; conversely, when Sonia invites Boris to her room for sex, he responds by referring to food: "I'll bring the soy sauce." When the subject is death rather than sex, it's Sonia who falls into food imagery; as soon as her husband passes on, she turns to the fellow grievers and says, "Where do you want to eat?" Even when Boris faces his own imminent death by firing squad, he is surrounded by food, telling us that the French prisons at least had good cuisine, as an elegant pastry wagon is wheeled into his glum cell.

When Boris returns to speak to Sonia one last time, she asks him what existence-after-death is like; naturally, he answers with a food simile: "You know the chicken at Treskie's Restaurant? It's *worse!*" Before he dances off, though, we understand that he and Sonia have communicated in a more complex way than earlier Allen men and women managed to do. Essentially, their relationship is a replay of the Miles-Luna one from *Sleeper*; once again, the intellectual man radicalizes the airhead woman; once again, after igniting her spark, he watches as she goes far beyond him in terms of her commitment and dedication.

In previous Allen films, though, one of the lovers was a romantic, the other a realist. In *Money*, it was Virgil who qualified as the romantic; in *Bananas*, Louise Lasser's character senses "something is missing." The interesting innovation in *L & D* is that each member of the couple is a romantic or a realist, but at different times, so they are never in synch—and never happy. In the film's first half, Sonia is the romantic, idealizing Boris's brother in her mind (we see him as a lout), mainly because she cannot have him, then wrecking her life because she can't have the "perfection" she knows (actually incorrectly believes) would be hers if only they were together; Boris, meanwhile, wants only the happy reality of a working relationship.

However, when Boris finally wins Sonia and they find simple, normal, everyday happiness in their relationship, *he* is the one who in the film's second half echoes the words previous women said to him: "Something was missing," he tells us. He actually falls into an anhedonic state, depressed without reason to be so, and even attempts suicide. The film provides a dry run for *Annie Hall* (despite the costume film trappings and period decor): an image of the modern relationship and why it fails. The shiksa goddess wants a man with a perfect balance of the mental, spiritual, and sensual; her inability to find such a man (and her romantic belief, however unfounded, that the one man she can't have must surely possess all these qualities) frustrates her. The Jewish male wants the woman who is a perfect physical specimen who can prove she is bright by absorbing his world-view and not going beyond it. Neither can have what he or she wants.

Allen makes clear that he is really talking about a modern relationship by infusing the film with anachronisms. The black drill sergeant who swaggeringly instructs the Russian soldiers, the cheerleaders at the battle scene, even Boris's glasses and overall manner constantly comment on contemporary styles by being comically imposed on the past. But when Allen turns again and again to the theme of marriage, it is modern marriage that he speaks of. When someone mentions the Jews, he wryly comments: "I hear their women don't believe in sex after marriage." If marriage is supposed to make romance permanent, it in fact does the opposite: "I'm not in love with you," his wife tells him; and, in their wedding bed, when he tries to touch her she says, "Don't—not here." "I don't want to get married," Sonia's friend Natasha insists. "I just want

A true romantic: Boris sees Sonia as the woman of his dreams.

to get divorced." Indeed, no marriage in the film is successful: not Sonia's first, not Boris's parents', not even Napoleon's, for he tells Sonia that if he had a woman like her for his wife, he would have already conquered Europe.

Boris's politics are identical to Miles's in *Sleeper*: He scoffs at both war and revolution, since the only difference between living under the czar or Napoleon is that one is taller, but he ends up performing the ultimate existential/revolutionary act for the love of a woman. And, of course, there are plenty of machines for him to run afoul of, from muzzle loading guns to sabers that fold up at awkward moments. Allen's references to other movies here tend, understandably, to be mainly to Eisenstein's: the Prokofiev score for the battle scenes, identical to the one in *Alexander Nevsky*; the "montage" use of sheep running across the battlefield to tell us, through a cross-cut that at first seems jarring, the metaphorical comparison of soldiers to sheep (Chaplin had earlier borrowed such a technique for the opening of *Modern Times*); the statues of lions that, through editing, appear to be one lion falling asleep, reversing the lions "waking" in *Potemkin*; the shattered eyeglasses, again a reference to *Potemkin*. But Allen begins the film with white-on-black titles that resemble a typical Ingmar Bergman opening, and ends on a shot of Diane Keaton in profile and Jessica Harper in shadowy full-face that precisely mimics the best-remembered image of that Swedish director's *Persona*. Even the death figure who appears and dances off with Boris resembles the one in *The Seventh Seal*.

The death figure also introduces Allen's growing concern with metaphysics and the spirit world; after all, Boris as a child had a concept of himself visually communicated to us as a crucifixion, picking up on Fielding's crucifixion dream in *Bananas* and leading to Isaac's messianic self-image in *Manhattan*. A dead man with a bullet in his head comes back to converse with Boris, and later he comes back from the dead to talk with Sonia, all the while suggesting that there may not be anything but a void beyond the understood world. In *A Midsummer Night's Sex Comedy*, Allen will stage the conflict that is germinated here.

A final theme is language, and its tendency to destroy, rather than aid, communication. Sometimes, this takes the form of a Marx Brothers gag; as when challenged to a duel by a man who plans on sending over his seconds, Boris insists, "If my seconds are out, call on my thirds." The real target, though, is the ready-made phrase. When he and Sonia have a political discussion, it breaks down in lines like "Violence only leads to violence," after which he admits, "I'm all out of clichés." Shortly thereafter, when he meets the Spanish Don and entourage, they swap mindless expressions ("No news is good news"; "News travels fast") until he mouths another such meaningless phrase as though it were profound, turns to the person next to him, and says, "your turn." Language grows stale and degenerates into jargon. In this world, true communication seems impossible; looking into the next, Boris sees evidence that God is not wicked, only an underachiever. And he sees, once again, that love, sex, and death are connected. In that Bergmanesque ending, the word that Sonia and Natasha keep repeating is "Wheat!" (the staff of life and, thus, the most basic of man's foods). They are, of course, the women Boris finds sexually appealing; and he comes back from the dead to visit them one last time.

Woody Allen as Howard Prince, functional illiterate.

158

Moonlighting:

THE FRONT

Columbia Pictures (1976)

CAST:

Woody Allen *(Howard Prince)*; Zero Mostel *(Hecky Brown)*; Herschel Bernardi *(Phil Sussman)*; Michael Murphy *(Al Miller)*; Andrea Marcovicci *(Florence Barrett)*; Marvin Lichterman *(Myer Prince)*; Lloyd Gough *(Delaney)*; David Margulies *(Phelps)*; Norman Rose *(Howard's Attorney)*; Charles Kimbrough *(Committee Counselor)*; M. Josef Sommer *(Committee Chairman)*; Danny Aiello *(Danny La Gattuta)*; Marilyn Sokol *(Sandy)*; John "Jack" Slater *(TV Director)*.

CREDITS:

Producer, Martin Ritt; executive producer, Charles H. Joffe; associate producer, Robert Greenhut; director, Martin Ritt; photography, Michael Chapman; art director, Charles Bailey; writer, Walter Bernstein; music, Dave Grusin; editor, Sidney Levin; costume designer, Ruth Morley; casting, Juliet Taylor; 94 minutes, Print, Metrocolor; Rating, R.

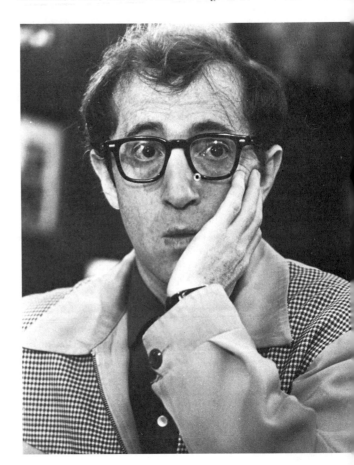

When Howard becomes a front for blacklisted scriptwriters, he meets the lovely script editor Florence Barrett (Andrea Marcovicci).

The Front tells the story of Howard Prince (Woody), a lunch-counter cashier and small-time bookie who can never quite pay off his winners. Howard is constantly hitting on his older brother Myer (Marvin Lichterman) for a loan. But this is New York in the early 1950's, and one day Howard is approached by an old high school pal, Al Miller (Michael Murphy), who has achieved fame as a writer for the new medium of television. Al's career is at a deadlock: despite his enormous talent, he's been blacklisted for his liberal political attitudes. Unable to get scripts past the network watchdogs who report directly to the committee, he suggests that the unknown, non-political Howard "front" for him, handing in Al's first-rate scripts and passing himself off as the author. Phil Sussman (Herschel Bernardi), the producer of the *Grand Central* dramatic-anthology show, is so impressed with Howard's work that he makes him the series' top writer, while Phil's lovely assistant, Florence Barrett (Andrea Marcovicci) is so touched by Howard's writing that she literally falls in love with the man who (she believes) created it.

The overbearing Hecky Brown (Zero Mostel) befriends Howard.

Then, things begin to snowball: Howard starts writing for all of Al's friends as well; shortly he's considered the most prolific television writer around. But his new friend, *Grand Central*'s host and narrator Hecky Brown (Zero Mostel), has nothing but problems. Years ago, Hecky joined a May Day parade and signed some pinko petitions to get near a pretty, politicized girl; now he's the Committee's latest target. Hecky is blacklisted and unable to work on television, but the Committee agrees to reconsider Hecky's case only if he will spy on the unknown new writer Howard. When the likable boy is summoned before the Committee, Hecky's guilt at the betrayal of his friend overwhelms him, and he commits suicide.

Zero Mostel as Hecky Brown.

Florence, meanwhile, has long since dropped out of the commercial TV business in order to publish a small radical paper decrying the blacklist of her friends. Though Howard has given her money and some moral support, he has been so enjoying his newfound status and financial success that he refuses to make a strong commitment to her cause and avoids taking sides in public. Florence, unable to go on living with a compromiser, breaks off their relationship. But when Howard is finally called before the subcommittee as a "friendly witness" who, they hope, will name names of the leftist associates, Howard has been radicalized by the event of Hecky's death. Aware that he will be held in contempt for refusing to answer their questions, he tells them in no uncertain terms what they can do to themselves. Then—after kissing Florence goodbye—Howard allows himself to be led off to jail.

Much of the film's power derives from the fact that it was made by people who were themselves

Howard Prince wins Florence away from her stockbroker boyfriend thanks to his literary reputation, making him an odd variation on the theme of the Woody Allen hero whose intellect attracts fascinating, neurotic women.

blacklisted 25 years earlier. Indeed, as the final credits roll, they not only identify the producer, director, writer and cast members, but also list the year in which each was blacklisted. Naturally, this lends the film a strong sense of integrity and authenticity. The people behind the cameras are clearly making a movie not only about what they know but, beyond that, what they lived through. For instance, the scene in which Howard drives Hecky up to the Catskills so the onetime headliner can play for an embarrasing $500, and instead only receives $250, is not only one that happened, but which in fact actually happened to Mostel. "Like Woody in the movie," screenwriter Walter Bernstein would later recall, "I drove Zero up there ... His performance was filled with rage—he'd keep breaking off to curse the audience, and the more he cursed, the more they kept applauding and laughing. He was brilliant—

and frightening." Bernstein did not conceive of this as either autobiography or docudrama, though, and created a compilation of incidents which happened to various people. Hecky's suicide, for example, is based on the case of Philip Loeb, the actor who played Gertrude Berg's husband between 1949–1951 on TV's *The Goldbergs*. Like Hecky in *The Front*, Loeb swore under oath that he had never been a member of the Communist Party, but that did not end his harassment or allow him to work, and, like Hecky in the film, Loeb committed suicide in a hotel room. In Loeb's case, the event took place five years after the blacklisting and was accomplished with sleeping pills; in the film, the time span was "tightened" for the dramatic impetus it could serve in Howard's story and also made more cinematic by having Hecky walk out of the camera frame toward the hotel window. The camera then follows his path, effectively showing us the empty room and open window.

Officially, Woody's involvement with the film was only as an actor. As he told interviewer Ken Kelley in 1976, just before the film's release: "I

161

Andrea Marcovicci made her theatrical film debut as television script editor Florence Barrett, though she was already well respected for her stage and TV work.

Herschel Bernardi as Phil Sussman, the harassed TV producer who gives in to network pressures.

remember hearing about blacklisting when I was in public school, not really understanding the implications of it all. But in retrospect, what I know now historically, it was a horrible time. The script expresses me politically even though I didn't write it. … It was fun to try and act in something serious.''

In an article for *America*, critic Tom Allen described the film's impact as "The Blacklist Made Palatably Commercial," indicating the general line of attack taken by key critics, who either dismissed the film with reserved complaints or damned it with faint praise. The vast majority of observers could not help but be on the film's side, and on the side of that earnest moviemaker Martin (*Norma Rae*) Ritt, but nonetheless had to put their emotional rooting for the film aside in order to admit that *The Front* leaves much to be desired.

It is certainly a pleasant film, and that is actually part of the problem: After a quarter-century of silence, the first major movie about that black spot in post-war history turned out to be a rather bright, cheery, good-spirited comedy-drama. The intention (and it too is an admirable one) was to make a work of mainstream middlebrow entertainment that would communicate a commentary on the horrors of the blacklist, rather than fashion a political diatribe which might be more "serious" and "uncompromised" but which no one would go to see.

One thread that runs through criticism of *The Front* is its antiseptic quality. Noting the way in which Howard Prince allows himself to be carted off to jail at the end, after making a futile gesture of defiance, Colin L. Westerbeck, Jr., wrote in *Commonwealth* that he provided "a fitting image for the political wisdom our movies so often contained. To be a popular art in this country, art must be safe. It must be soothing rather than inciting. It must teach passivity rather than political action. Its message must be, as in *The Front*, that the only possible heroism is to take it in the neck." Also criticizing the ending, but from a different perspective, was William S. Pechter of *Commentary*, who found it less a realistic possibility than wish fulfillment realized onscreen: "That moment in which he tells the Committee off provides as richly satisfying a climax to the film as any one might wish for, but it is, without a doubt, pure fantasy: staircase wit—with the movie granting everyone who ever muffed the opportunity a second chance to say what (legal niceties aside) 'I-should-have-said.'"

The film seemed slight, especially considering its substantial subject. It settled for using the blacklist as a catalyst by which a Woody Allen hero is plunged into career and romantic situations he is unprepared to handle, and while that certainly made for some agreeable moments, it also led to a less than vivid depiction of the era. The focus, after all, is not on

Producer Phil Sussman (Herschel Bernardi) warns Howard Prince to keep his nose clean so far as associating with "pinko" writers.

blacklisted artists (they are all seen in supporting roles) but on a charming charlatan and his misadventures in passing himself off as a writer. Richard Schickel of *Time* concurred: "Despite many virtues...the picture seems thin and schematic." The historical incidents were not as fully digested as they ought to be, while the characters were too simplistic: the bad guys who work for the Committee never reveal the slightest indication that they are capable of any compassion or are even peripherally related to the human race, while the good guys who stand up against them are unrelentingly pure and sympathetic. "There is, in the end," Schickel wrote, "something held back about *The Front*, some strange refusal to really dig into and turn over very rich historical and psychological soil. The result is a film unworthy of its excellent intentions."

Howard Prince transforms into something of a social activist and goes up against members of the House Un-American Activities Committee.

Pauline Kael also attacked the movie along similar lines: "Almost as if by reflex, [Bernstein] has written one of those scripts about how the common man must become involved, must learn what he stands for...like the heroes of the forties wartime movies written by those who were later blacklisted....*The Front* is slightly archaic, not because it's set in the early fifties but because of its problem-play dramaturgy—craftsmanlike, careful, skimpy." The problem is not that the film takes a comic approach toward the blacklist era, but that it is a safe, sweet situation-comedy approach: how much more effective, and more appropriate for the material, if it were a scathing black comedy on the order of *Dr. Strangelove*.

To be fair, some important critics had only praise for the picture, and were impressed that instead of creating a self-serving, self-indulgent work, Ritt and Bernstein and their colleagues refused to turn bitter. "The quiet but acid laughter in *The Front* is a humane and cleansing exorcism of a frightening moment of our time," Jack Kroll wrote in *Newsweek*. Robert Hatch of *The Nation* wrote that "*The Front* is full of laughs, full of tears...It doesn't tell you how bigotry gets a hold on this country from time to time, but what it does, which more serious discussions never quite seem to do, is make you sense how it would feel to be played with by jackals....Laughter is a useful tool in the cause of virtue." Ultimately, though, the problem with *The Front* is not that it attacks the blacklist through a comic rather than dramatic mode, but that, as those other critics pointed out, the exposure of a dark era demands dark comedy.

Howard drives Hecky up to the Catskills for an ill-fated club appearance after the famous comic has been blacklisted from television.

The radiant Florence quits her lucrative TV job in order to publish a small anti-blacklisting newsletter.

In addition to discussion as to whether the film was politically substantive, another mild controversy grew over whether or not Allen was the right choice to play Howard Prince. In retrospect, Maurice Yacowar would write that the part "remains consistent with Allen's persona," citing that "Prince is a wisecracking, slightly neurotic loser who by a con seems to become a success." The question, though, is whether this typical Woody persona is the way Ritt and Bernstein originally conceived of their character, or whether Howard Prince was altered to fit Woody once he agreed to star. A number of Howard's lines are so perfect for Allen that it's difficult to believe he didn't write them himself: "Buy them off," he says of the people persecuting him and the other writers. "How expensive can they be? I mean, they're just Congressmen." When his friend Al goes into the hospital, Howard kids him: "You gotta lay off health foods." And best of all, "In my family, the biggest sin was to buy retail." Though Woody claims he was hired strictly as an actor, it would certainly seem that Woody was allowed to make a more substantive contribution. Even screenwriter Walter Bernstein admitted, "It would be very tough for Woody to act in a completely serious film...the audience comes prepared to see WOODY, and they have a response to *him*. I think the audience would have a hard time accepting him in other roles." Essentially, Bernstein admits that Woody is more of a movie star than an actor, more of a single persona introduced into various film projects than a performer who can change himself in accordance to the demands of a specific part.

And in the context of *The Front*, this strikes a viewer as either satisfying or jarring. Bea Rothenbuecher of *Christian Century* wrote: "More than any other element, it is his characterization that bridges the distance between today's audience and a time of national divisiveness that many prefer to forget." Westerbeck also noted this bridge: "In contrast to everyone else's clothes, Woody Allen's two-button suit with wide lapels is distinctly contemporary. And like his clothes, his heroism is out of place in the early fifties. It is quite right that his whole role in this story should be that of an imposter, a front, because he *is* fronting for something—for the values of our own times. He's today's culture hero."

Intriguingly, some of the critics who were roughest on Woody in his own films had the nicest things to say about him in *The Front*. Pauline Kael wrote: "Making his debut as a 'straight actor,' Woody Allen is able to fill out Howie with 'Woody.'...Allen's timing and Stan Laurel-Alec Guinness smiles bring everything possible out of the material. When you see Woody Allen in one of his own films, in a peculiar way you take him for granted; here you appreciate his skill, because you miss him so much when he's offscreen." Robert Hatch added: "A peculiarity to which I have confessed before is my inability to laugh at Woody Allen. His abrasive, wise-cracking brat seems to me a fictional creation of limited charm and his elaborate gag machines too ponderous for their inherent risibility. I have, you might say, been tone-deaf to the screen's most popular comedian. Woody Allen in *The Front*...is an entirely different matter. Not that the character is much changed; he is still the smart-aleck fraud, fast-talking his way through a pool of alligators. But this time the man-eaters are not papier-mâché props for Allen's one-liners....And this time Allen's begoggled jester, working in the context of a real catastrophe, seems a funny man even to me."

But not to Stanley Kauffmann, who criticized the film even more heatedly than any of Allen's own. "Allen makes it difficult for the people around him to work because they are trying to act and he is doing his night club stuff," he wrote, adding that "Here we get a hybrid—a role that was apparently written 'straight' but is played by Allen...a very funny writer who has lately been learning how to direct and perform his own idiosyncratic comedy,

but he has not yet begun to learn how to act, in any legitimate sense, and worse, doesn't even try. He bends almost all of this role to the Allen *schnook* persona—all the vocal and physical angularities, the wriggling, the apologetic sidewise aggressiveness. It wrecks what credibility the film might have had, and credibility is *all* it might have had." Critic Russell Davies concluded: "The problem with the picture is not that Allen has taken on a 'serious' role that is too much for him, but, on the contrary, that director Martin Ritt has made him feel too much at home. As the political climax is reached, Woody is still funny—jarringly funny—so that his final clash with the Committee is not felt to be an historical self-sacrifice, but merely the culminating gesture in a comedy performance."

In fact, though, the real problem with Woody's presence (I consciously avoid the word "performance") here is not touched on by any of the above analyses. The audience that has, since the mid-sixties, devotedly attended Woody's films does so

Screenwriter Walter Bernstein and producer-director Martin Ritt.

not only because he is funny onscreen but because they regard him as an important filmmaker: a director and, more basic still, a writer. Besides, most have read his books and followed his short pieces for *The New Yorker* and *Playboy*. Thus, they only partially perceive of the Woody persona as a schnook-schlemiel; beyond the Allen character's awkward stabs at social amenities, there is always the hint of the private man, a genius in general but, more specifically, a genius at the typewriter. The idea that Howard is near-illiterate and cannot write to save his life is never completely accepted by the audience watching *The Front*, because we're always aware that Woody Allen is playing Howard Prince.

This helps explain why one scene which ought to be uproariously funny doesn't quite work, despite being played out nicely. Howard shows up at the TV studio and is told there's an emergency: he will have to go into an adjacent room and rewrite the current script at once. If Howard Prince had been played by, say, Dustin Hoffman or Richard Dreyfuss, we would immediately experience a ripple of humorous tension: how is he going to handle this one? But because Woody plays Howard exactly the same way as he plays every other character (and therefore *is* "Woody"), we half expect the character to suddenly realize he's a born writer and knock off the script they

Hecky veers toward suicide when he realizes he can no longer work.

Screenwriter Walter Bernstein and Woody Allen discuss an upcoming dramatic sequence on the set of The Front.

need. We don't believe Howard's wriggling and worrying about what to do, not because Allen in any way plays the scene badly (he plays it very well, in that his gestures and reactions are all exactly right for the situation), but only because he's Woody—Woody the writer!

Since *The Front* is not a Woody Allen film *per se*, it would be ridiculous to analyze it in terms of his techniques. Ritt is a more conventional filmmaker, so none of Woody's cinematic daring is present here. Still, Woody was attracted to the script, agreeing to do it even as he rejected all sorts of other offers, and that suggests a certain affinity for the sensibility of Bernstein's work. For one thing, the relationship of Howard to Florence has a great deal in common with the Fielding/Nancy relationship in *Bananas*. Once more, the man with no strong political ties at all grows political in order to satisfy the highly politicized woman he loves, and then ends up becoming a political hero (and accepting some serious political reponsibilities, even becoming a leader) in order to eventually win her.

In both films, the hero faces and accepts the possibility of jail for his liberal attitudes, though in *The Front* there is none of Woody's wildly surrealistic approach. Instead of being a living cartoon, in which the filmmaker can dazzle us with editing jokes and bizarre bits of dialogue, *The Front* is essentially "realistic-comedy," in that everyday situations are exaggerated only slightly for comic effect, rather than truly distorted as in Woody's films. But as in Woody's own films, we here see the conventionally beautiful woman attracted to a homely man, giving up a more conventional lover (her unseen stockbroker) for him. When Florence learns Howard can barely write his own name, the romantic theme is introduced: Florence loved not Howard the person, but her mental image of Howard the writer. Likewise, the story chronicles Howard's gradual growth from a bum to a crusader, as a result of his various experiences. In a particularly memorable shot, we see Howard criticizing the work his writers have been handing him, chastizing their recent scripts. Eventually, like Allan Felix in *Sam*, Howard is a dynamic character who outgrows his initial self-serving attitude ("Watch out for number one!") and puts himself on the line by standing up for what he believes in. We believe Howard's change from an oblivious, callow character to a man capable of an act of courageous defiance.

In his post-*Sam* period, Allen continues to demonstrate the confidence of his newly enlarged and enhanced character. His playing of the love scenes with the beautiful Marcovicci is completely acceptable. We don't laugh at the thought of her giving up her boyfriend for him; we *believe* it. The comment on the television industry is one Woody would certainly subscribe to: It is here portrayed as a most gutless form of entertainment or communication. The finality of Hecky's death, and the remarkable effect this has on Howard's life, works as well as it does here in part because of the way Woody had previously depicted his own death obsession in films.

The Jewishness of most of the characters, and the way in which their persecution is, on an inarticulated level, tinged with anti-Semitism, fits in well with Woody's own notions, and the business of role playing—characters who turn life into theatre by playing roles for one another rather than just being themselves—is basic to Howard's ploy here, as he plays the role of a writer. "Just be yourself," Diane Keaton told Allen in *Sam*, "and some girl will love you!" Before *The Front* is over, Howard will courageously drop his front and allow Florence to see him for what he is; after an initial shock, she will indeed accept him and love him for himself. Howard literally lives out the advice Allan Felix received, and we see it was indeed good advice.

By appearing in *The Front*, Woody accustomed his built-in audience to accept him in a film that contained a real-life landscape rather than the living-cartoon setting, as well as having a plot that contained serious situations and everyday emotions as well as comic one-liners. In so doing, he (perhaps inadvertently) paved the way for the acceptance of his next film, *Annie Hall*, with its own combination of the two and its emphasis on the real over the whacky.

Boy Meets Goy:
ANNIE HALL
A United Artists Release (1977)

CAST:

Woody Allen *(Alvy Singer)*; Diane Keaton *(Annie Hall)*; Tony Roberts *(Rob)*; Carol Kane *(Allison)*; Paul Simon *(Tony Lacy)*; Shelley Duvall *(Pam)*; Janet Margolin *(Robin)*; Colleen Dewhurst *(Mom Hall)*; Christopher Walken *(Duane Hall)*; Donald Symington *(Dad Hall)*; Helen Ludlam *(Grammy Hall)*; Mordecai Lawner *(Alvy's Dad)*; Joan Newman *(Alvy's Mom)*; Jonathan Munk *(Alvy, age 9)*; Ruth Volner *(Alvy's Aunt)*; Martin Rosenblatt *(Alvy's Uncle)*; Hy Ansel *(Joey Nichols)*; Rashel Novikoff *(Aunt Tessie)*; Russell Horton *(Man in theatre line)*; Marshall McLuhan *(himself)*; John Doumanian *(Coke fiend)*; Bob Maroff and Rick Petrucelli *(Men outside theatre)*; Dick Cavett *(himself)*; Johnny Haymer *(comic)*; Lauri Bird *(Tony Lacy's girlfriend)*; Jeff Goldblum *(Party guest)*; Humphrey Davis, Veronica Radburn *(Analysts)*; Shelly Hack *(Pretty Girl on Street)*; Beverly D'Angelo *(Star of Rob's TV Show)*; Sigourney Weaver *(Alvy's date at end)*; Walter Bernstein *(Annie's date at end)*.

CREDITS:

Producer, Charles H. Joffe; associate producer, Fred T. Gallo; executive producer, Robert Greenhut; director, Woody Allen; script, Woody Allen and Marshall Brickman; photography, Gordon Willis; editing, Ralph Rosenblum; art director, Mel Bourne; animated sequence, Chris Ishii; costume design, Ruth Morley; casting, Juliet Taylor; Panavision DeLuxe; 93 minutes; Rating: PG.

When Woody woke the morning after the 1978 Academy Award ceremonies, he learned from *The New York Times* that his film *Annie Hall* had swept the

Woody Allen as Alvy Singer.

Oscars, picking up trophies for Best Actress (Diane Keaton), Best Original Screenplay (Allen and Marshall Brickman), Direction (Allen) and Best Picture of the Year. Woody himself had not bothered to fly to California to attend, but instead spent the evening playing clarinet at Michael's Pub, then later read himself to sleep with *Conversations with Carl Jung*. When asked his reaction to the awards, Woody said simply: "I was very surprised. I felt good for Diane because she wanted to win. My friend Marshall and my producers Jack Rollins and Charles Joffe (who accepted the award for Woody) had a very nice time. But I'm anhedonic."

In fact, "*Anhedonia*" had been the original title for the film that would eventually become *Annie Hall*, though he was in the end persuaded by United Artists to change it only weeks before the film's release. Anhedonia, of course, refers to the psychological situation that might be described as acute melancholia: the inability to enjoy oneself, no matter how pleasant one's circumstances. And while the thrust of the film was changed, during the writing, filming, and editing, to the relationship between Jewish night club comic Alvy Singer and his shiksa goddess Annie Hall, the theme of

anhedonia still runs through the picture, serving as the key that unlocks Alvy's characterization. Woody's collaborator, Marshall Brickman, told interviewer Susan Braudy that he and Woody wrote *Annie Hall* by "walking up and down Lexington Avenue and across to Madison and talking and talking and talking." Sometimes, they would stop long enough for ice cream. The process of working with Woody became a sort of "highly stylized conversation," and in the end it was impossible to pick out who had contributed what. "When you collaborate," Brickman said, "you are both responsible for everything. You never know when one person will make the other person think of something. The early parts are hard. You try not to make any big mistakes, to paint yourself into a corner."

For instance, in their first draft, Woody and Marshall made Diane Keaton a neurotic New York girl, but soon realized that left no room for dramatic transition. This led to their assigning her a family in Wisconsin. "You keep asking each other—who is this guy, what are his values? Face it, the movie only hints at profound issues, but we asked ourselves, 'Is it neurosis or honesty that makes the character Woody plays so pessimistic? Is it merely maladjustment, immaturity, or is it a relentless philosophical integrity?'" For his part, Woody had wanted, at least since December 1973, to write a murder mystery. While *Sleeper* was still in its Christmas release, Woody worked on just such a story with plans of beginning production that spring. However, the script did not successfully gel, and instead Woody started work on the film that would eventually become *Love and Death*. But the murder mystery would eventually be written and shot, though never seen by the public.

Annie Hall, hailed as a charming, unlikely romance, was originally filmed as that murder mystery. After it was in the can, Woody and editor Ralph Rosenblum came to feel that the murder mystery plot—which was the original incentive to do the film—appeared less interesting than the relationship which had developed between the two main characters. Whether Rosenblum is correct (as he asserts in *When the Shooting Stops*) that it was at his insistence that the murder mystery was pared down to a contemporary love story, or whether Woody had considerably more input in shaping the final work than Rosenblum chooses to remember, is difficult to say. More than four hours of film was trimmed down to two and a half hours and then, finally, to the 93-minute print. In fact, according to co-author Brickman (as quoted by Rosenblum), *Annie Hall* originally sounded more like the finished product *Manhattan*: "The first draft was a story of a guy who lived in New York and was forty years old and was examining his life. His life consisted of several strands. One was a relationship with a young woman,

Alvy, the New Yorker, falls in love with Annie Hall (Diane Keaton), a young woman with middle-American roots.

Alvy, Rob, and Annie peek through a wire fence to the schoolyard where the young Alvy grew up in Brooklyn.

another was a concern with the banality of the life we all lead, and a third was an obsession with proving himself and testing himself to find out what kind of character he had."

Woody himself described *Annie Hall* as being "sub-

169

The cast of characters includes (from upper right, clockwise) Colleen Dewhurst as Mother Hall; Carol Kane as Alvy's politically-oriented wife Allison; Tony Roberts as his best friend Rob; Shelley Duvall as his one-night stand, rock critic Pam; Janet Margolin as his social-climbing wife Robin; and Paul Simon as Tony Lacey, the man who takes Annie away.

jective and random'' in its style, while Diane Keaton noted that a key distinction between this movie and some of Allen's earliest, whackier efforts, was that here ''The jokes come out of behavior rather than absurd circumstances.'' The critics, who had long since decided Woody Allen was our great comic *auteur* and were hungry to happen upon a film which would establish him as the American Ingmar Bergman as well as the contemporary Chaplin, gushed over *Annie Hall*, paving the way for the Oscar sweep.

Ray Loynd of the Los Angeles *Herald-Examiner* hailed it as ''his wittiest, best film to date, both more socially and personally observant in its departure into the foibles and traumas of a human relationship.'' In *Saturday Review*, Judith Crist called it ''Allen's most satisfying creation and our most gratifying comedic experience in recent years.'' In *Time*, Richard Schickel wrote: ''a ruefully romantic comedy that is at least as poignant as it is funny and may be the most autobiographical film ever made by a major comic.'' In *Newsweek*, Janet Maslin heralded the film as ''bracingly adventuresome and unexpectedly successful, with laughs as satisfying as those in any of Allen's other movies and a whole new staying power.'' Even the near-constant Allen critic Stanley Kauffmann tolerantly wrote in *The New Republic* that ''the cheery news [is] he has written his best film script and he is now a competent director.'' Only a small handful of critics found anything negative to say, though Pauline Kael did call it ''the neurotic's version of *Abie's Irish Rose*,'' while M. J. Sobran, Jr., wrote in the *National Review* that ''What it finally comes to is ninety minutes of coitus interruptus, fun but fruitless. *Annie Hall* may

170

look like a comedy or a romance, but it's really a *tsuris* trap."

Critics who hailed *Annie Hall* as Woody's "breakthrough film" (and that was most everybody) failed to notice how many serious undercurrents there were in the earlier films, or the growing sense of darkness in theme. They also fail to take into account that *Annie* contains much recycled material. When Alvy performs a stand-up routine for a college audience, his line about cheating on a metaphysics test ("I looked within the soul of the boy sitting next to me!") is only one of a large number of gags taken directly from Woody's own earlier night club routines, and an awareness of this makes it impossible not to take Alvy Singer as an autobiographical figure for Allen himself. Beyond that, it helps us understand the function of this film for Woody at that point in his career: by including so much old material, he makes this a compendium of his work up to that point. Though *A.H.* was hailed as the beginning of Woody's new direction, it may be more correctly perceived as an apotheosis of his earlier work, solidifying all his material from that previous period and freeing him to start fresh in the next one. After all, *Interiors* (love it or hate it) is certainly a "new" venture in a way *A.H.* was not.

Thus, people who look back at the film today, and wonder why this relatively slight if often charming romantic-comedy could have won the Oscar for Best Picture, need to put the film in its proper context. Timing can play a devastating factor in the question of whether a film does well or poorly, both at the box-office and in the critical response it elicits. *A.H.* could not possibly have been better timed. As Diane Jacobs argues, "Social as well as artistic factors contributed to [its] immediate success." That may be an understatement! *A.H.* looks, to anyone casually catching it for the first time, like one of the most artistically overrated films in cinema history, but one must study it as a celluloid document that arrived midway through the 1970's to understand the impression it made.

Certainly, the question of feminism and its impact on the traditional male-female relationships was a significant one for people surviving the era when the sexual and social revolutionary changes of the 1960's lost their flower-power idealism and came crashing up against the brick wall of reality. The difficulty of making an old-fashioned, romantic, committed, traditional realtionship work in the new no-rules aura of adapting to constant upheavals in lifestyle weighed heavily on the minds of people who had been young in the swinging sixties and were now approaching early middle age. That "nervous romance" between Alvy and Annie may have been a combination of autobiography and imaginative invention, but a certain sector of the public saw in it a screen romance that captured the way they lived, boiling down man-woman relationships in the Me Decade to a symbol of what everyone (or, at least, everyone who counted) was going through. It spoke to them on a level Woody himself may not have even been trying to communicate; they saw in *A.H.* what they wanted to see, and that was a love story for their time, and of their time.

Which, of course, opened the film up to charges that it glorified the culture of narcissism. Some of Diane Keaton's comments (to *Time out*) indeed do

Alvy, in a fantasy sequence, confronts himself as a child (Jonathan Munk).

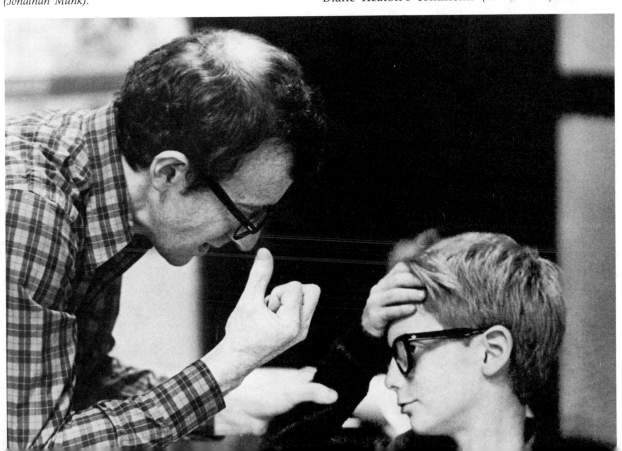

At a New York literary party, Alvy tries to get his wife to make love in the bedroom while intellectual conversations are going on in the hall.

The Paradox Principle: A split screen shows Annie and Alvy consulting their analysts, offering radically different interpretations of the same situation.

make the film sound like just such a document: "Some people have come up to me and said, there's so much of what we feel in it. It's about relationships now, and what it's like for us. I mean, obviously, there's been a change (in society at large). There's many more people who are single and not actually ready to get married....Women who are 30 and not ready and not knowing if they want to get married and who are still finding out about themselves." What's important, though, is that the film is about something more than all this: ultimately, it's about the emptiness of the culture of narcissism. Keaton describes Annie's attitudes as though they were one and the same with the attitudes of the movie itself. But the film, its title notwithstanding, actually shares Alvy's attitude, his point of view of Annie and what happens to her.

Allen's symbol for the culture of narcissism is Southern California, with its perennial sunlight, hot tubs, health food restaurants, and synthetic TV sitcoms. In contrast to all this is the island of Manhattan. "I do have an overidealized view of New York," Woody told me at the time of the film's release. "In *A.H.* I was careful to shoot on gray, overcast days so it would look moody and romantic. In Los Angeles, we shot in hot light because that is what strikes me about L.A., that bright sunlight." As Annie becomes more and more a part of the L.A. scene, Alvy senses he is losing her but, beyond that, fears even more that she is losing the wonderful quality she once had—when she was in New York. That Annie will eventually return to New York on her own, after their break-up is final, and that Alvy will run into her at a threatre where *The Sorrow and the Pity* (his favorite film, a four-hour documentary about Nazism) is playing, suggests that like Alvy, Annie is one of those radical innocents who may be temporarily tempted by hedonist pleasures but will always instinctually return to what is truly important in life. If a reconciliation between them is too much to hope for, at least there is the part of her that has not changed, that comes back if not to him then at least to his city, where rude cab drivers and dirt on the streets stand for something more basic and valuable than the antiseptic accoutrements found in Los Angeles.

The character who here stands for the culture of narcissism is Alvy's one-time best friend in New York, Rob (Tony Roberts), who surrenders to the world of sunscreens, available blonde bimbos, and phony laugh tracks to cover up bad TV material. Rob never comes back to New York ("I played Shakespeare in the park—somebody stole my leotard!"), opting instead for the pleasure of the moment and an eternity of mediocrity. For Annie, Tony Lacy (Paul Simon) is the silver-tongued devil who seduces her with promises of a lovely lotus-eating

Alvy and Annie spend a weekend on Long Island, working on their relationship.

The perfect couple for the 1970's: Diane Keaton and Woody Allen not only played Annie and Alvy, but emerged as pop-culture icons as well.

present, but despite her seeming acceptance of this world (she looks amazingly like Luna in the early scenes of *Sleeper* when Alvy visits her), Annie eventually breaks with it (for reasons never shared with us). Alvy returns to writing his serious work, trying out new relationships, even though the one he wants with Annie can no longer be. Despite the large number of laughs along the way, the ending is bittersweet.

This was, after all, the age of *Looking for Mr. Goodbar* (the movie version of which starred, intriguingly enough, Diane Keaton), the era of singles bars and swift encounters. These are the very qualities Alvy (and Allen) turns his back on; he wants a lasting relationship. Like the earlier films, *A.H.* is about marriage, only this time the theme has to be re-interpreted somewhat for the seventies. In flashbacks, we see Alvy's earlier, unsuccessful relationships with women, including his failed marriages to both Allison Porshnik (Carol Kane), a political activist who (like Louise Lasser in *Bananas*) takes the man who professes little interest in politics (though he does meet her at an Adlai Stevenson fund raiser) and makes him so political that he can't sleep with her for trying to sort out the Kennedy conspiracy possibilities, and Robin (Janet Margolin), a pretty but pretentious member of the New York literary set. We also see, in terms of the depiction of relations with woman, his least satisfying affair: with Pam (Shelley Duvall), a rock critic for *Rolling Stone* who, in her total pseudo-hipness, is a fitting symbol for the Culture of Narcissism and is quickly rejected by Alvy, following a brief and unsatisfying (for him) tryst.

Then, of course, there is Annie. In the earlier Woody Allen films, the idea of people co-habitating in an unwedded state seemed naughty and fun; it was only after they formalized their relationships that problems set in. In *A.H.*, the problems set in the moment Annie moves in with Alvy, even though marriage is not yet an issue. It's important, though, to keep in mind that unlike the earlier Allen films, *A.H.* belongs to the mid-seventies. Indeed, as compared to "swinging" (the casual pick-ups of the bar scene), a couple living together, and working at maintaining a relationship, seemed in this new decade's context to be almost old-fashioned. Although Woody and Annie never do get around to formalizing their relationship with a wedding vow, the point is that from the moment when they begin living together (and the relationship begins to fall apart!), they are spiritually if not technically married. That explains why all those terrors Woody depicted in the married states of characters in earlier films haunt Annie and Alvy in their (technically speaking) non-married state.

Once more, there are nightmare visions of frightening marriages offered by both sets of parents: Annie's cold, formal, foreboding WASP parents;

Diane Keaton as Annie Hall.

Manhattanites: Annie, Alvy, and Rob take an unexpected trip.

In a fantasy sequence, Rob, Alvy, and Annie peek into a long-ago party at Alvy's parents' house.

Alvy's vulgar, warmhearted, sloppy Jewish parents. Alvy looks at each pair and is seized with foreboding: he doesn't want to turn out like either, and resists a commitment—at least early on, when Annie is pushing for one. But Alvy/Allen's anhedonia also figures in. When Annie wants to work toward a lasting commitment, he is miserable because he fears it; when Annie begins to wander off in her own directions—emotionally, intellectually and sexually—he is horrified and wants her to move back in, even proposing marriage. He is, in the end, alone (though not without companionship, since we see him on a date with no less a beauty than Sigourney Weaver) because he did not act in time; it was the failure to commit himself at that moment when it must be done that consigns him to later being a friend, rather than a lover-husband, to Annie. Alvy begrudgingly accepts his fate: he clearly wants to maintain that freedom which Annie threatened, but

at the same time realizes there is an emptiness without commitment to the right person. For Alvy, that person could only be Annie Hall, and all relationships afterwards are likely to be letdowns.

If this makes him sound tragic rather than comic, that is a correct assessment of the movie's tone. If there is any degree to which Alvy is a member of The Me Generation, it is in his attempt to make Annie over in his own image while refusing a commitment to her. But Allen sees more than Alvy does, and by presenting his own persona as a lost, bewildered man, shell-shocked in the sexual battleground of the mid-seventies, Woody turns *A.H.* into a warning *against* the dangers of the Culture of Narcissism. Somewhat surprised by the overwhelming acceptance of the film, even outside New York City, Woody tried in 1978 to describe its universality for viewers: "I guess what everybody understood was the impossibility of sustaining relationships, because of entirely irrational elements....Later in life, you don't really know what went wrong." In fact, part of what goes wrong is the romanticism of each of the lovers. Alvy and Annie are each looking for some kind of perfection we've all been

175

led to believe we can expect from a mate; failing to find it in each other, they let a wonderful working relationship fall by the wayside. Perfection does not exist in real life, though, and, sadly, their belief that it can be found keeps them from a more realistic, if compromised, love.

That Allen the artist understands far more than Alvy the character does is made clear by his constant comparisons of life to art, and his insistence the reason we need to create art is not to achieve immortality (a notion Woody rejects) but to make things work out perfectly. Early in the film, as Alvy and Annie wait in line to see a movie, he is angered by a loudmouth pseudo-intellectual's babbling about Marshall McLuhan; Alvy then yanks McLuhan out from behind an advertising display, and the great media prophet tells the astounded professor that he knows nothing of McLuhan's work. "Boy," Alvy says, turning to the audience, "if life were only like this." Woody once more makes us self-conscious about the fact that we are watching a film; he also makes clear that such a wonderful little victory is possible only because Allen the artist is in control of what happens to Alvy.

Toward the film's end, we see Alvy turning his unpleasant California experience with Annie (she refused to resume their relationship) into art; many of the words are the same ("So this is how it ends—at a health food store on Sunset Boulevard") but with one key difference: in the play, just as the

young actor performing Alvy's role is about to leave, the young actress playing Annie decides to go back with him. "What do you want?" Alvy asks us. "It was my first play." Then he adds: "You know how you're always trying to get things to come out perfect in art because it's so difficult in life."

For most critics, Allen made things come out just right in *A.H.*; in fact, though, the film's failings, which barely seemed worth noting at the time, are quite obvious when the film is removed from its cultural context. The kindest thing one can say about the style is that it is eclectic. Woody literally tries everything imaginable, from realistic dramatic sequences to situation comedy to surrealism to dark comedy. Just when we have accepted that this is a more realistic comedy than any he had done before (taking place in the real New York other people inhabit rather than his mental, cartoonish, personal landscape), he will jarringly violate the sense of realism: when he walks out of a theatre and mutters that he wonders where Annie is, a passerby tells him "She's in California living with Tony Lacy." Woody films some sequences with subtitles telling us what the characters think as compared to what they are saying; an animated sequence depicts Annie (when Alvy is angry at her) as the evil queen in *Snow White*, even as Alvy admits to always having been attracted to dangerous women. Alvy, Annie and Rob are even able to travel back in time at one point, visiting his relatives during the war years; at another, Alvy sits in his old school, surrounded by the kids he grew up with.

The result is a kind of patchwork quilt of a film, and it contrasts remarkably with the perfectly seam-

Granny Hall (Helen Ludlum) cracks up the cast with an impromptu gag.

You Can't Go Home Again? Alvy goes, in this dream sequence that sees him revisiting his old school.

less *Manhattan*, which in fact would be the perfect realization of the kind of movie Allen was attempting in *A.H.* Here, Allen tries to alternate comedy with drama, and fails to quite pull off the delicate balance he's after; in *Manhattan*, he more wisely, more artistically blends rather than balances the two elements. *A.H.* is actually an imperfect though necessary dry-run for *Manhattan*.

In the meantime, he had produced an uncertain brew: an uneasy mixture of pleasant gags and problem melodrama, the most blatant expression thus far of Woody's key themes. The paradox principle has never been more aptly illustrated than in the use of split screen to show us Alvy and Annie visiting their shrinks at the same time, simultaneously interpreting the same facts in totally different ways. When asked if they have sex often, Annie replies, "Constantly...three times a week," while he says "Hardly ever...three times a week." This, of course, also establishes the theme of analysis, introduced earlier in the film when young Alvy is analyzed by a doctor who wants to understand why the child has stopped doing his homework. His reason is simple: he has fallen into an anhedonic state after learning that in several million years the universe will be no more. All logical attempts to

make him understand that it doesn't matter, since we will all be long dead anyway, do not help; the problem is, he has had a glimmer of the perishability and impermanence of everything, not just of individual men or man himself but the cosmos that contains us all. Why work to leave something for the future when eventually there will be no more future?

But Alvy does continue to work, so the serious art vs. hedonism theme also comes into play. Alvy may not be able to achieve any lasting sense of being through art, but he continues to try and create art for art's sake, because it is what he was meant to do. The opposite of that, of course, is commerce, and nowhere has he more heatedly attacked television and the people who create it than here. We see Alvy growing sick at the thought of giving away an award on a live TV show, becoming nauseous when he sees the pathetic non-art his friend Rob creates. As compared to the anathema of television, there is the appeal of movies: that Alvy constantly goes to see a documentary film attests to Allen's strong affinity for that form (we think of *Take the Money*...and *Zelig*); his attending Bergman's *Face to Face* allows us to realize that such heavyweight projects have assumed the role once played in his life by *Casablanca* and *The Maltese Falcon*.

Woody's death obsession is in ample evidence here: he gives Annie only books with the word

Alvy and Annie try to relate, dwarfed by pop-art backdrops.

Annie and Alvy cement their early friendship.

in an earlier film. In *Take the Money*, we heard the narrator claim a serum experimented with in prison temporarily turned Virgil into a rabbi. When we then see him looking like a Hasidic Jew, the visual gag does nothing but duplicate the verbal gag. However, in the scene in which Alvy has Easter dinner with the Hall family, Woody recycles that gag, now making it work beautifully: Grammy Hall (Helen Ludlam), already described by Alvy as "a classic Jew-hater," observes him trying pathetically to eat the ham; then we see him from her point of view, looking like that same Hasidic Jew. Here, though, the gag works because it doesn't follow a line of dialogue, but is strictly visual.

The Easter dinner sequence furthers the "enormous restaurant" theme, as Alvy's discomfort with his lover's family is expressed through food. "We'll kiss now...then go eat," Alvy tells Annie on their very first date. His initial repulsion at what she orders in the deli (pastrami on white bread with mayo and lettuce) suggests the problems that lay ahead for them, though the scene in which they prepare lobsters together paves the way for their more pleasurable moments. Woody's scorn for intellectuals is in evidence in the New York literary party sequence, where he prefers to slip into the bedroom and watch a Knicks game on TV; the body always takes precedence over the brain, though we sense he would give anything to be back at that New York literary party when he later finds himself at an insipid California party. Allen doesn't sentimentalize Alvy: his hero is downright nasty when, on their first meeting, he reduces Allison to a cultural cliché, and she effectively, if gently, puts him down for it; when Annie and Alvy sit on a bench, sarcastically commenting on the people walking by ("Here comes the winner of the Truman Capote lookalike contest," he says, and the man is played by Truman Capote), there is an air of superiority and cruelty to their banter. His attitude toward authority is clear when a policeman attempts to give him a ticket and instead of handing over his driver's license, Alvy rips it up; and his incompetence with machines is seen when he bangs his car into two others. When Alvy tries to "assimilate" into WASP culture, the results are suitably hysterical, and when he tries to associate with modern, ostensibly "hip" people, he fares no better.

In the end, he must learn to live with the notion that nothing is permanent ("Love fades!" proclaims a little old lady on the street), and in *A.H.*, the Woody persona appears to be begrudgingly accepting what the Diane Keaton character told him in *Sleeper*: that there are chemicals in our systems which eventually make us get on each others' nerves. Part of the problem stems from the inability to communicate through

"death" in the title, though he seems downright healthy in rejecting the death obsessions of the apparently normal brother of Annie, Duane (Christopher Walken), who feels a compulsion to drive directly into someone else's car. Duane and his family represent those genteel gentiles who at one moment seem so superior to the sloppier Jewish characters, then a second later look cold and uninviting compared to the loving (if less than sophisticated) Jews. In this context, it's worth mentioning that Woody here effectively revives a joke he muffed language: in the scene in which subtitles tell us what the characters are really thinking as compared to what they say (mundane cocktail-hour patter as compared to inner angst), Woody's theme of the inadequacy of language is perfectly expressed. He even touches on an issue that will grow in importance in several films such as *Stardust Memory* and *Zelig*: the concept of celebrity being both an attractive and difficult status, as when Alvy—waiting in front of a movie for Annie to join him—is surrounded by ferocious looking autograph hunters.

Most of all, though, Woody had the chance to further delineate his attitudes about women and the inability of men ever to completely comprehend them. He fluctuates, thinking of Annie at one moment as a cartoon of an evil queen (a vision of her which, significantly, he finds sexually stimulating), a gentle and rewarding friend the next. Pam may find sex with him to be "a Kafka-esque experience," but he rejects the one-night stand with the hedonist to pursue the woman whom he helped, Svengali-like, to enlighten, only to find her needing to liberate herself from the man who liberated her. He is, of course, on a search for his own identity, underlined by the fact that his friend Rob makes up a name for him ("Max") which he uses in reference to Alvy throughout the film; this only underscores Woody's own search for a new identity through the making of this daring and more demanding picture.

The Grown-Ups' Table:
INTERIORS
A United Artists Release (1978)

CAST:

Kristen Griffith *(Flynn)*; Marybeth Hurt *(Joey)*; Richard Jordan *(Frederick)*; Diane Keaton *(Renata)*; E. G. Marshall *(Arthur)*; Geraldine Page *(Eve)*; Maureen Stapleton *(Pearl)*; Sam Waterston *(Mike)*; Missy Hope *(Young Joey)*; Kerry Duffy *(Young Renata)*; Nancy Collins *(Young Flynn)*; Penny Gaston *(Young Eve)*; Roger Morden *(Young Arthur)*; Henderson Forsythe *(Judge Bartel)*.

CREDITS:

Producer, Charles H. Joffe; executive producer, Robert Greenhut; director, Woody Allen; screenplay, Woody Allen; photography, Gordon Willis; editor, Ralph Rosenblum; casting, Juliet Taylor; costume designer, Joel Schumacher; production designer, Mel Bourne; 93 minutes; Rating: PG.

During an interview on the eve of *Annie Hall's* release, Woody told me his next film would be "a totally serious one, that I won't appear in. My presence is so completely associated with comedy that when the audience sees me, they might think it's a sign for them to begin laughing." He also added that if this film were successful, and he was generally accepted as a serious filmmaker, he might at some future point feel confident enough to make a dramatic film in which he did appear. It's worth noting, though, that in reviewing Woody's earlier comedy films, Pauline Kael argued that "in his movies he's the only character, because his concept of himself keeps him alone. When we see his films, all our emotions attach to him: his fear and his fraility are what everything else revolves around. No one else in his films has a vivid presence."

Certainly, Woody had begun to move away from that problem with *Annie Hall*; no one can deny Diane Keaton's character is a fully rounded, three-dimensional woman of the 1970's. Whether or not Woody read Kael's comment (though he does have a propensity for her publication, *The New Yorker*, being one of its key fiction contributors himself) is difficult to say. Certainly, one way of looking at *Interiors* is as a reaction to the type of criticism Kael forwarded, an attempt by Woody to make a motion picture in which he's not only not the focal character but in fact not a character at all.

Interiors concerns people not unlike the ones at the Easter dinner table in *Annie Hall*. The film examines the effect on a WASP family when the father (E. G. Marshall) decides without warning to leave his icy home situation with his wife (Geraldine Page), eventually marrying a (presumably Jewish) life-loving vulgarian named Pearl (Maureen Stapleton). This causes his first wife to commit suicide by walking into the surf at their dune road home. All of this is viewed mainly from the point of view of the three daughters, a writer (Diane Keaton), an actress (Kristen Griffith), and a brilliant young woman with no discernible talent at all (Marybeth Hurt), who is ultimately the pivotal character in the storyline. More than anything else, Allen seems to be trying to analyze the plight of a person who has the ambitions and angst of an artist but, paradoxically, none of the creative gifts.

Why the burning desire to do a completely dramatic film? Woody's comments over the years help explain that. In 1976, he told Ken Kelley that "I know I could make a successful comic movie every year, and I could write a comic play that would do very well on Broadway every year. What I want to do is go to areas I'm insecure about and not too good at....I'd like to take chances—I would like to fail a little for the public." Woody has, of course, always degraded his own comic gifts, overestimating the dramatic: "I have always felt tragedy was the highest form," he would in 1979 say to Frank Rich of *Time*. "With comedy you can buy yourself out of the problems of life and diffuse them. In tragedy, you must confront them and it is painful, but I'm a real sucker for it." He is, of course, unfairly downgrading the comic mode: the works of Swift and Twain still exert their remarkable impact today, though much of the dramatic literature of their periods has been long since forgotten.

No comment of Woody's is more revealing on this subject than his classic (though controversial) statement: "When you do comedy, you're not sitting at the grownups' table, you're sitting at the children's table." Woody wanted to move to the grownups' table, and *Interiors* was to establish his move. It's worth noting, by the way, that his key metaphor for art has to do with food: like sex and death, creativity also takes its metaphor from eating, since it's a *dinner* table he's talking about!

The famous and controversial Bergmanesque final shot: Diane Keaton, Kristin Griffith, and Marybeth Hurt.

If Allen finds drama more satisfying than comedy, he finds Bergman more compelling than any other film dramatist. Indeed, when Bergman was visiting New York and requested a dinner meeting with Woody, Allen (according to a 1981 interview with Charles Champlin) found the great Swedish film-maker not at all mysterious or intimidating but rather "a charming, middle-class work-ethic film-maker." Fascinating that, in describing himself to Natalie Gittelson for a *New York Times* story two years earlier, Woody told her that "I'm a middle-class film-maker," while his subscription to the work-ethic is as well documented as his own charm is obvious. His description of Bergman, then, is in fact a description of himself. Before the film's release, Jack Kroll interviewed Allen and found Woody to be "a man at a crossroads—if you can find a crossroads in the maze that passes for his psyche. Call it rather a turning point. Woody Allen, the funniest neurotic of our time, is about to switch his comic mask for the stern visage of serious drama. His new movie...is a brooding, Bergmanesque affair without a single laugh in it. 'At least with no intentional ones,' says Allen."

Allen's gag line turned out to be amazingly prophetic, because most audiences found the film so unrelentingly serious that it finally began to look like a satire on Bergman's style. As Kroll eventually

wrote in *Newsweek*, "If Woody were to make a parody of Bergman, the perfect title would be *Interiors*, and for a while the film does seem like parody gone straight." Critic Philip Bergson, who dubbed the film "spare chamber-cinema, shot through a lens in close-ups and scenelets," ultimately argued that "it unnervingly evoked Bergman—perhaps more in parody than homage, for I suspect that underneath it is an exquisite jest," though Richard Schickel seemed more correct when he wrote in *Time* that "Despite advance word this was to be this deservedly respected writer-director's first entirely serious film, a faint hope stirs. Perhaps he is merely setting up the biggest Woody Allen joke of them all, since this kind of talk, and film making, is one of his best satirical subjects. Alas, the snapper never comes. Instead, one wades deeper into ever shallowing waters."

Understandably, then, only one year after *Annie Hall* received the most enthusiastic praise of his career, *Interiors* was almost universally panned, allowing Woody the luxury he had requested: the right to fail before the public. Schickel, usually the first to spring to Allen's defense, wrote that "One is sympathetic to Allen's problem. As great comedian to his age, he must have felt that the faintest suggestion of humor would have stirred audiences to a risibility from which he could not recover their attention. But, of course, the absence of wit does not necessarily betoken seriousness; it merely betokens the absence of wit.... Doubtless, a necessary movie for Allen, but it is both unnecessary and a minor embarrassment for his well-wishers." Peter Rainer of the L.A. *Herald-Examiner* complained that "the emotional depth Allen is trying for...doesn't jibe with his comic temperament, which, at its best, is based not on pretension but the puncturing of pretension. He's working against his own best gifts in order to be something he's not, an American Ingmar Bergman...the emotional and psychological crosscurrents are as vaporous as mist." Stanley Kauffmann scoffed that it was a "tour of the Ingmar Bergman Room at Madame Tussaud's"; Maurice Yacowar correctly labels it "A Chekhovian vision of an O'Neill family, expressed with Bergmanesque rigor"; James Monaco insisted "we have depended on Allen for more than ten years now as champion against just this particular sort of bad-faith artiness and the mid-cult sensibility from which it stems"; Pauline Kael called it "a handbook of art-film mannerisms; it's so austere and studied that it might have been directed by that icy mother herself—from the grave."

Jack Kroll expressed his disappointment with insight: "*Interiors* has the look of a Bergman film, helped by Gordon Willis's Nykvist-like cinematography, but it does not have the creative elation that triggers elation in the audience, no matter how dark

Renata (Diane Keaton) and Flynn (Kristin Griffith) talk about their parents' crumbling marriage as they walk along the beach.

Arthur (E. G. Marshall) tries to maintain a good relationship with his youngest daughter Joey, even though he realizes she's bitter about her parents' break-up.

Flynn, who symbolizes the sensuous side of life and the superficial aspect of the arts, steps out onto the terrace for a breath of sea air.

the artist's vision. Henry James insisted on the sense of 'fun' that was in his supersubtle novels, and Yeats reminded us that 'Hamlet and Lear are gay; Gaiety transfiguring all that dread.' In *Interiors*, Woody gives us his dread untransfigured and it's hard to swallow.'' Indeed, for many it was downright impossible, the film that would begin a disaffection of some former fans. After all, the mark of a major filmmaker resides in his abilities to offer themes that are uniquely his own, expressed through a technique so perfectly appropriate for his themes that we are struck with the rightness, as well as the originality, of the total vision. But from that moment when, at the beginning of *Interiors*, we see Diane Keaton standing by the window, spreading her fingers out over the pane of glass, it's clear that Allen's imagery is borrowed from Bergman. At the very end, he goes even further in aping the most obvious elements of Bergman's vision, as the three young women self-consciously line up in an overcomposed image one wishes was intended as the kind of comic cross-reference to Bergman we saw in the Diane Keaton/Jessica Harper *Persona* shot that closed out *Love*

and Death. There, though, we laughed with recognition, and here our laughter is instead uncomfortable, as we guiltily look around to see if others in the audience find this Bergmanesque posturing as embarrassing as we do. Red Skelton once put it perfectly: Imitation is *not* the sincerest form of flattery—it's *plagiarism!*

The film did have its defenders. Penelope Gilliatt claimed that this ''droll piece of work is [Woody's] most majestic so far,'' adding, ''It's as true a tragedy as any that has come out of America in my memory.'' Alexander Walker viewed it as ''the work of an artist whose potential we thought had been fully and satisfyingly realized in other kinds of films; with this one Woody Allen gives us the enormous excitement of seeing gifts in use that we never suspected he possessed.'' Understandably, several constant Allen critics praised this rather unrepresentative film. In *The Nation*, Robert Hatch wrote that ''by segregating his group from all the trivialities and casual contacts that cushion life, he has produced an…intensely vivid distillation of clashing sensibilities in a time of ambiguous moral authority.'' In *Commonweal*, Colin L. Westerbeck Jr., insisted that ''Allen has made a film which is perhaps even better than the film Bergman might have made from the same material.'' But their enthusiastic

The cast of characters includes Richard Jordan (upper left) as Frederick; Kristin Griffith (lower left) as Flynn; Marybeth Hurt (upper right) as Joey; and Sam Waterston (lower right) as Mike.

In a rare lighter moment, Mike and Joey crack a smile during a family reunion.

Eve opens her birthday gifts as various members of her family gather to watch.

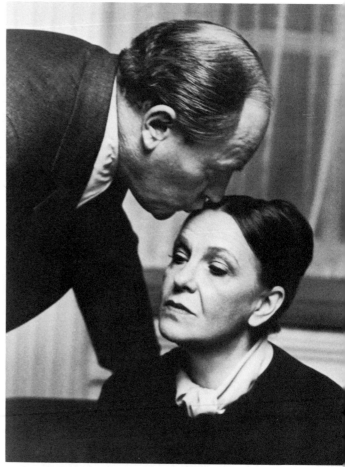

Arthur plants a wary kiss on the forehead of his ice-queen wife Eve (Geraldine Page), though he is drawn to the warmth of another woman.

responses to the film have to be tempered by the fact that neither cares for the bulk of Allen's work.

And to a fan, *Interiors* seems something of a betrayal. Essentially, it offers a Jewish intellectual's misconception of how WASPs talk and relate, a satire on Bergman unaccountably played straightfaced, a film that looks to have been made from a blueprint rather than a script. *Interiors* is not only disciplined and

controlled but overschematized and unrelentingly formal. It means to be sophisticated and is only over-refined, tries for subtlety and instead achieves slightness; it's a movie about stiff, sterile people that looks like a stilted, even silly misreading of their morals and manners.

In trying for strong emotional and intellectual effects, Allen achieves only affectation. Self-consciousness with the camera is not the same thing as self-expression; profound sounding speeches lead to the pretentious and the portentous. Instead of "high-seriousness," Woody achieves only self-indulgence and, in attempting to experiment and break new ground, he provides a film full of second-hand images, recycled themes, and stolen sensibilities. Heavyhanded where it wants to be heavyweight, *Interiors* is derivative instead of daring, suggesting that comic genius Woody Allen may be as inept at creating serious drama as that greatest of screen dramatists, Ingmar Bergman, is at creating comedy: indeed, Allen's *Interiors* rates alongside Bergman's *All Those Women* as one of the most ill-conceived movies of all time.

Some critics feared, even early in Allen's career, that his desire to technically master the film form might be accompanied by a lessening of his overall impact, and *Interiors* provides further evidence of that problem. The movie, so ineffective as an overall work, nonetheless contains some extremely intelligent choices in terms of camera and editing. In order to visually reveal to us the emotional distance between E. G. Marshall and Geraldine Page, Allen films a conversation between the two of them in such a way that, even though they are sitting near each other in the same room, we never see them onscreen together, but rather view a tight shot of one, then the other; their spiritual lack of togetherness is made visual, asserting Allen's understanding of the "plastic elements" of film. Likewise, when E. G. Marshall and Maureen Stapleton are married, we hear the entire ceremony, but do not see either of them; instead, the camera remains on the faces of the daughters, and the husbands (Sam Waterston and Richard Jordan) of two of them, making use of the contrapuntal possibilities of sound films: We receive one sort of information on the sound track and a totally different sort of information on the screen. But the best moment in the movie borders on being a gag: when Eve attempts to commit suicide by gassing herself, the entire sequence is portrayed by close-ups on her hands as she diligently seals the windows and

doors with thick black tape; but she runs out, and we see a clear uncertainty in the movement of this perfectionst's hands when she must suddenly switch to a thinner brand of white tape.

If only this potential in the plot for the most sophisticated of all comic techniques, an ironic approach toward the material, suffused the style of the film as a whole, *Interiors* might have been a truly sophisticated film instead of a sententious one. Seriousness of intent and solemnity of effect are not the same thing, and while Bergman succeeds by managing the former, Allen here fails by falling into the latter. Woody does try to use the film as a metaphor for his concern with the artistic experience. Renata is the serious artist, intent on creating subtle, lasting works of art even though she perceives the purposelessness of her efforts in an impermanent universe; Frederick is the man of talent whose work is out of tune with his times, and receives little recognition; Flynn is more a popular entertainer than an artist, creating superficial film roles enjoyed by the public but not admired by the critics; Joey is unable to transform her creative temperament into artistic works; Eve is the interior decorator who achieves a balance between her artistic sensibility and the business world by working at a practical job which calls for an artistic perspective. In part, at least, her profession leads to the film's title: the movie is about the revelations of interiors of the people and places we see.

Woody's Jewish theme, as well as his notion of assimilation, is in evidence when Pearl (whose Jewishness seems an unstated implication of the proceedings) attempts to become a part of the ice-palace family. This forms the most interesting tension in the

Renata and Frederick brace themselves for the difficult family problems they know are ahead, while also trying to resolve their own relationship.

movie: we go back and forth from perceiving Pearl as outlandishly out of her class in comparison to these cool, reserved, elegant-looking WASPs, to seeing her as a breath of fresh air (her vulgarity notwithstanding) in comparison to such lifeless types. The tragedy is that the film is every bit as lifeless as the characters, making Pearl (who at least brings a little excitement with her, just as her bright red dresses conflict with all the restrained beiges, pallid greys and sterile whites of Eve's overorganized rooms) more of a comic buffoon than Woody perhaps intended.

If Pearl brings the life force with her (she appears almost as an earth-mother when she gives artificial respiration to the nearly drowned Joey, seeming to be breathing life into the girl's frail frame), she also brings food imagery into the film. Before Pearl's arrival, we get the impression no one in the movie ever eats anything; in the perfect and rigid world Eve (the pun of her name appears intended) has created, food is as nonexistent as the sex it so often symbolizes for Allen. The characters are like scientific specimens, perfectly preserved under glass: indeed,

Woody Allen, who does not appear in the film, directs Diane Keaton as they prepare for a particularly serious scene.

when we glimpse Eve riding in a car, we see her contemptuously rolling up the window to shut out the life around her; when entering Joey's apartment, she immediately requests the window be closed to shut out the encroaching noises of the street. But when Renata invites her sisters over for *dinner*, this first acknowledgement of food also turns out to be the introductory situation for *Pearl*. And when she stops eating to talk, she *talks* about food: "That food," she says about the European vacation she and Arthur have just taken, " I could eat lamb six times a day." Eve and Pearl represent the struggle so often depicted in Allen films between brain and body. "Give me a good sirloin any day," Pearl says, happily sharing her wisdom with the girls. "Charcoal...and *blood rare*!" That is, as red as the dresses she sports.

Significantly, one of her ex-husbands was a chef; it would not be all that surprising to learn that his name was Hollander. "Would you like some more gravy?" she asks after making this announcement. Of course, food has been associated, in past films, not only with sex (the life force) but with its complement, death. Arthur immediately acknowledges this when he admits that he'd love another piece of cheesecake, but is afraid of the effect on his heart. "Have it," Pearl insists, solidifying the bridge

that food serves between life and death, making clear that to enjoy the former one must be willing to risk the latter: "You'll live to be a hundred if you give up all the things that make you want to." Importantly, he accepts the cheesecake and the enjoyment of life while risking death (but, either way, moving out of the sterility of Eve's world); then, carrying the metaphor further still, he licks some of the cheesecake off Pearl's fingers with sexual glee. When these characters later congregate again at the family's beach house, Pearl is seen serving food.

Like *Annie Hall*, *Interiors* is about the difficulty of maintaining relationships when there is something in our chemistry that makes us get on each other's nerves sooner or later. It is also about marriage, as we see three failed marriages (Eve/Arthur; Joey/Mike; Renata/Frederick). Yet it is not pessimistic, for the Pearl/Arthur marriage at the end lends the film an edge of hope that a marriage can be something other than death-in-life.

Woody also includes his own attempt to understand the female psyche. When Frederick comes on to Flynn, he is amazed that she turns him down, because it seemed so obvious that she was flirting with him, getting him to pull her boots off and touch her in the process. But perhaps she was only attempting to be friendly, totally oblivious of the powers of her own surface sensuousness, which causes her to be sincerely shocked that he so misread her signs and interpreted them as an invitation for an affair. Can a woman that sensuous be oblivious to the impact of her presence on men? Unfortunately, Allen seems less able to understand this aspect of women than any other, which is why Flynn (who symbolizes this side of the female psyche) comes across as a less fully realized character than any of the others. In *Sam*, when Woody reduced this problem to a joke (the nymphomaniac who tells Allan Felix she is always ready for sex, then screams "What do you take me for?" when he tries to touch her), it perfectly expressed his charming confusion over this aspect of womanhood. In *Interiors*, when he attempts to seriously dramatize the same syndrome, it only comes off as an artist's ineffectual stab at dramatizing something he doesn't fully understand.

Woody has said that "The questions and feelings in Bergman's films are what interest me—an investigation of spiritual values and faith." However, his own *Love and Death* is a more fitting (and uniquely Allenesque) analysis of these matters than this attempt to ape Bergman's exteriors. Before starting work on *Interiors*, he told *Esquire* that "the line between the kind of solemnity I want and comedy is very, very thin. That's why it's so easy to satirize Bergman. If you bring the drama off, you hit people at the most profound

level, but tenth-rate Bergman…is like soap opera. My biggest fear is that I'll write a mawkish and embarrassing soap opera and not know it." With *Interiors*, Woody's greatest fear was realized.

An Expedient Culture:
MANHATTAN
A United Artists Release (1979)

CAST:

Woody Allen *(Isaac Davis)*; Diane Keaton *(Mary)*; Michael Murphy *(Yale)*; Mariel Hemingway *(Tracy)*; Meryl Streep *(Jill)*; Anne Byrne *(Emily)*; Karen Ludwig *(Connie)*; Michael O'Donoghue *(Dennis)*; Victor Truro, Tisa Farrow, Helen Hanft *(Party Guests)*; Bella Abzug *(Guest of Honor)*; Gary Weiss *(TV Director)*; Karen Allen *(TV Actress)*; Damion Sheller *(Ike's son)*; Wallace Shawn *(Jeremiah)*; Mark Linn Baker *(Shakespearean actor)*; John Doumanian *(Porsche owner)*; "Waffles" trained by Dawn Animal Agency.

CREDITS:

Producer, Charles H. Joffe; executive producer, Robert Greenhut; writers, Woody Allen and Marshall Brickman; director, Woody Allen; photography, Gordon Willis; production design, Mel Bourne; costume design, Albert Wolsky; editor, Susan E. Morse; music by George Gershwin, adapted and arranged by Tom Pierson, performed by the New York Philharmonic and Buffalo Philharmonic Orchestras; casting, Juliet Taylor; Mr. Allen's wardrobe, Ralph Lauren; running time, 96 minutes; Rating: R.

With *Interiors*, Woody bottomed out. But his next film was something more than a mere return to form: *Manhattan* is Allen's masterpiece to date. It never became quite the popular favorite *Annie Hall* had been, but the film succeeds aesthetically in a way *A.H.* did not.

The improvement in *Manhattan*—proof that the accolades heaped upon *A.H.* did not go to Allen's head, and that despite the near-unanimous praise he knew what was wrong with the film and worked carefully to overcome it—can be seen throughout as comedy and drama are completely fused, creating the necessary consistent tone that marks all pictures in which a sophisticated artist is in complete control. "I think that with *Manhattan*," he told interviewer John

Woody Allen as Isaac Davis, Manhattanite.

Isaac buys Tracy (Mariel Hemingway) an ice-cream soda, while she gives him a harmonica for a gift; pointing up the essential child-like innocence of their relationship.

Fordham, "I've integrated things more,…It's like a mixture of what I was trying to do with *Annie Hall* and *Interiors*." In *Manhattan* he created a film that emotionally involves us with totally believable, fully realized, finely drawn characters, while also intellectually involving us with the deeper meaning of what happens to them. But if the old bellylaughs are gone, in their place is something better: a sly, subtle, totally sophisticated comic sensibility.

Indeed, when Woody described his intended effect to Natalie Gittelson, he said he had hoped to communicate "my subjective, romantic view of contemporary life in *Manhattan*. I like to think that, 100 years from now, if people see the picture, they will learn something about what life in the city was like in the 1970's"; in *Time*, Frank Rich labeled it "a prismatic portrait of a time and place that may be studied decades hence to see what kind of people we were." That is precisely what Jean Renoir, in his masterpeices *Grand Illusion* and *Rules of the Game*, did for the European elite. Understandably, then, *Grand Illusion* is cited several times during the course of *Manhattan* as the favorite film of the focal character, Isaac Davis. If *Interiors* failed in part because Allen made pretenses to knowledgeability of a WASP culture he had only an outsider's dimly focused understanding of, *Manhattan* rings with the authenticity of an artist who knows his subject. His sense of the language and lifestyle of a subculture he is completely familiar with allows him to depict it with a style that treads a fine line between being a celebration of that unique demi-monde and a scathing criticism of it.

With its black-and-white photography and Gershwin score (which are functional rather than

In the famous Rizzoli bookstore, Yale (Michael Murphy) argues with his best friend Isaac over values and priorities.

Jill (Meryl Streep), estranged wife of Isaac, refuses to listen to his entreaties that she not write a book about their failed relationship.

The flippant Mary Wilke (Diane Keaton) proves both amusing and aggravating when she and Isaac visit a museum.

Yale and Mary enjoy an adulterous affair.

ornamental, since they impose on modern Manhattan landscapes the sensibility of the main character, who mentally and emotionally lives in the past), *Manhattan* is a pure expression of Woody Allen. The ambiguity of Allen's attitude and the irony of his approach are the equal of Renoir's; his use of the camera and his style of writing are completely his own. One year earlier, Richard Schickel had lamented over *Interiors*, sympathetically suggesting that "We could have accepted, as a logical outgrowth of his work to date, the rue and irony of a full-scale comedy of (upper) middle-class manners"; *Manhattan* is the film he requested. "I wanted to make," Woody later explained, "a serious picture that had laughs in it." There is only one sight gag in the movie: When Isaac and Mary (Diane Keaton) go rowing in Central Park, he leisurely lets his hand drift in the water, then finds it covered with a murky pollutant. More often, though, the comedy is present in the ironic wisdom with which he observes his fellow New Yorkers. "A drama with comedy rather than a comedy with drama," producer Joffe labelled it. The film does, of course, work on a certain level as a cinematic equivalent of one of those "I Love New York" buttons Manhattanites began to chauvinistically sport at about the same time: "It was photographed so beautifully and romantically,"

Maureen Stapleton was overheard commenting at the opening night party for the film, "that it almost makes you forget all the dog poop on the streets." Certainly, Allen is the country's foremost New York chauvinist: "Of all the cities I've been to," he has said, "I like New York the best. Because it's very exciting, active....What I feel about New York is hard to say in a few words. It's really the rhythm of the city. You feel it the moment you walk down the street. There's hundreds of good restaurants, thousands of brilliant paintings, you can see all the old movies, all the new ones...It has to do with nerves, with the blood that runs through the city. It's dangerous, noisy. It's not peaceful or easy and because of it you feel more alive."

Manhattan captures the beat and the tempo of the Big Apple, beginning with the first montage sequence that cuts from one breathtaking vista to another, marvelously edited to the rhythms of the Gershwin tunes; from that moment on, it's clear *Manhattan* will serve, at least on one level, as Woody's valentine to the city he so loves. But there are other levels, and the film is less an upbeat paean to New York than it might at first seem. On the voice-over, we hear Isaac continually repeat that "he saw New York as a metaphor for the decay of contemporary culture," and the film does imply the most complex narrative form Woody had thus far attempted. Isaac is writing a novel; the unnamed narrator of his book is to Isaac what Isaac is to Allen, a fictional mouthpiece for his own attitudes. No wonder, then, that a few days after the film's release,

Mary and Isaac grow closer when they meeet at an elegant New York party.

Woody explained that he saw, as backdrop for this particular story, a society that had been "desensitized by television, drugs, fast-food chains, loud music and feelingless, mechanical sex" (that is, by the culture which had developed during the 1970's). Near the movie's end, Isaac complains into his tape recorder that "people in Manhattan are constantly creating these unnecessary neurotic problems for themselves because it keeps them from dealing with the terrible, unsolvable problems of the universe"; Woody himself insisted that "until we find a resolution for our terrors, we're going to have an expedient culture." An expedient culture is another term for a culture of narcissism; he constantly shows that under their shimmering surface, his characters are a contemporary variation on Eliot's Hollow Men.

The story concerns Isaac Davis, a successful TV writer who quits his lucrative but unsatisfying job (he knows he is turning out nothing but junk) in order to write a serious novel (and turn out, he hopes, an important work of art). He is also involved with a beautiful seventeen-year-old, Tracy (Mariel

One of Gordon Willis's magnificent black-and-white compositions that shows the sheer sophistication of the entire project: Silhouetted amid statuary in the sculpture garden of the Museum of Modern Art, Isaac and Mary chat over cocktails.

Diane Keaton as Mary Wilke, high princess of The Culture of Narcissism.

Hemingway), who must leave their dates early so she can go home and do her schoolwork. At 42, Isaac is self-conscious about their age difference, though Tracy takes it in stride. Still, when Isaac meets the pseudo-intellectual Mary (Diane Keaton), mistress of his best friend Yale (Michael Murphy), he cannot, upon learning that she and Yale have broken off their relationship, resist getting involved with the woman, though he must break up with Tracy. In time, though, Yale and Mary decide to resume their affair, Yale going so far as to move out on his wife Emily (Anne Byrne). At this point, Isaac realizes how much he misses Tracy and rushes across Manhattan to her place, hoping to stop her from moving to London, even though he previously insisted a semester studying there could only do her good.

Allen's analysis not only of these particular characters but of the larger lifestyle they represent is remarkable in its ability to distill a significant subculture: "He has closed out the decade and pinned it down like a butterfly on a board," Lloyd Rose wrote in the L.A. *Herald-Examiner*. "He touches every base in young, hip, upper-middle-class New York—Elaine's, MOMA, Zabar's, Bloomingdale's—and lays bare with irony and affection the intellectual affectations, moral shallowness and lonely confusion of his characters" as well as the broader canvas they come to symbolize.

How remarkable, then, that he could be accused of aggrandizing his subject. Peter Biskind complained that the "triumph of Tracy over Mary represented a triumph of the 1970's over the 1950's, *Playboy* over Freud, the id over the superego. *Manhattan* was a thinking man's *Porky's*"; Peter Conrad, summarizing The Me Decade for London's *Sunday Observer*, fingered Woody as basic to the problem: "Allen, stooped and balding, perpetual adolescent, has become a totem for our times, and no wonder. The nympholepsy which incites him to pound after Mariel Hemingway is another symptom of the jogger's disease. This wizened dwarf is actually in love with the remote recollection of his own youth, for the Seventies is the decade in which those who were young in the Sixties began to creak, limp, and wrinkle." Constant Allen critic Stanley Kauffmann complained that "What George M. Cohan did with the Stars and Stripes in 1919, Allen is doing with neurosis in 1979, waving it, telling us that as long as we're proud of it, we're all pretty damned OK."

In fact, though, OK is the opposite of what, in *Manhattan*, he's telling us we are. Attractive, yes; OK, no. Throughout the story, Isaac is attracted to Yale as a friend and Mary as a lover; he rejects Tracy mainly

The film's only sight gag: Boating in Central Park, Isaac drifts his hand in the water and finds it covered with pollution.

In the film's most unforgettable image, Mary and Isaac grow deeply involved with one another on a wistful New York late-night interlude.

because, in their eyes, he is involved in an infantile, embarrassing situation with a child. We sense Tracy is something else entirely—perceptive and honest. Isaac understands this. His attraction to Tracy shows that, like Holden Caulfield in J. D. Salinger's *Catcher in the Rye*, he can lose his own innocence yet still recognize it in others. He knows, as in Wordsworth's "Ode: Intimations of Immortality," that "nothing can bring back the hour of splendor in the grass, or glory in the flower," but he grieves not, and finds strength in what remains behind: the ability to perceive innocence and appreciate it. For all his romantic spirit, he is only a man, and can be temporarily seduced by the facile and the flashy. Yale and Mary, the male and female symbols of the Culture of Narcissism, are the agents of seduction.

They are willing to do what we hope Isaac will in the end refuse to: trade in integrity for expediency. She has the brains and raw talent to be a worthwhile novelist, but instead spends her time doing journeyman journalistic work or knocking out a "novelization" of a popular film, because it's easy and financially rewarding. He wants to write a book about O'Neill, and screws around instead; the money that he has saved to start a little literary magazine ends up going for a down-payment on a Porsche. But when Isaac quits his lucrative job to try his hand at serious writing, we know he will in the end reject Narcissism; he runs back to Tracy, realizing almost too late that she is what Wordsworth, Coleridge and Shelley would have called "the child as swain" ("The child," Wordsworth wrote, "is the father of the man"), the uneducated babe (and we all know what Woody thinks of formal education!) as closer to God and basic truth than adults. "I don't want the things I love about you to change," he whines. As always, she is the wiser of the two. "Not everybody gets corrupted," she reminds him.

The Culture of Narcissism is expressed in a single line—by Mary when, taking sado-masochistic delight in torturing herself with guilt over having an affair with a married man, she whimpers petulantly: "I'm beautiful, I'm bright, and I deserve better!" Certainly, Allen has drawn Mary and Yale as attractive characters, but that is not to say he aggrandizes them: Their attractiveness is what makes them so appealing and so dangerous. No wonder Yale and Mary end up together at the end: they deserve each other, and serve as the symbolic first couple of the Culture of Narcissism Isaac flees from.

194

Mary and Isaac are amused by an exhibit at the Whitney Museum.

Caught in a sudden downpour, Isaac and Mary dash for shelter: in context, the scene hints of the sudden storm Mary will cause in Isaac's life.

Even after they are sleeping together, Mary and Isaac find that they have not completely severed the ties of past relationships.

Tracy (Mariel Hemingway) and Isaac shop for groceries in one of their lighter moments, though he is even then worrying about their age difference.

Isaac may hesitate, delay, almost muff his chance; but in the end, he goes to Tracy rather than to the Narcissists. When Isaac tells Yale, "You're too easy on yourself," insisting, "It's very important to have some kind of personal integrity," we see not Woody the moralist, as some critics have tagged him for lines like this, but Woody the philosopher-artist who has created a film for a moral purpose, a story drawn along sharp and clear but never simplistic moral lines. The ending of *Manhattan* is not unlike the ending of Fitzgerald's *The Great Gatsby*, when Nick Carraway turns his back on the thoughtless, foolish lives of those friends who lived the good life in the New York of a half-century ago, making his way back to the heartlands, the midwest, back to the "garden"; Nick may have been temporarily seduced by the glamour and glitter, but in the end he wakes up and rejects it.

Isaac is a contemporary Jewish variation on that theme; the seemingly "hip" Woody Allen persona is actually a traditional, old-fashioned American romantic who clings to certain spiritual values even if, paradoxically, he is the first to call the existence of God into doubt. No wonder that when the glib Yale and the flippant Mary list F. Scott Fitzgerald on their "Academy of the Overrated," he grows furious. Tracy is his own personal "garden," and he goes back to it in the end. *Manhattan* is the film in which Woody openly acknowledges his own romantic bent: in the opening lines, he has Isaac say, "He idealized it [New York] out of all proportion...no, he *romanticized* it all out of proportion." John Simon could shriek that the "most irresponsible" thing in the film is "the implication that a thoroughly decent man of 42 can find fulfillment in love and sex only with a 17-year-old girl," while Pauline Kael could chide: "What man in his forties but Woody Allen could pass off a predilection for teen-agers as a quest for true values?" Both ignore the fact that Tracy is used not as a realistic character but as a symbol (and Hemingway's inanimate acting only adds to this quality)—a grail, an image of radical innocence and an allegorical figure of purity.

Another thing that distances Isaac from the Culture of Narcissism is the fact that he has a child; his narcissistic friend Yale throughout the film tries to convince his wife that they should not have a child, since such a responsibility would endanger their pursuit of pleasure and the principle of immediate gratification that Yale imposes on Emily. "*Manhattan*," Woody has said, "is about the problem of trying to live a decent life amidst all the junk of contemporary culture—the temptations, the seductions." But the film succeeds aesthetically as well as philosophically.

Allen's perfect control of every element can be seen in the way he uses cars, so often a metaphor for his inability to deal with machines. Here, he takes that notion beyond the level of recurring gag and turns it into a motif that suffuses every aspect of the film: imagery, dialogue, and plot. A car, of course, is what Yale is going to waste his money on; a car is what Isaac apparently used to try and kill the lesbian lover of his ex-wife (Meryl Streep), who is now writing a book about their failed relationship.

196

The cast of characters includes Michael Murphy (upper left) as Yale; Meryl Streep (upper right) as Jill; Anne Byrne (lower left) as Emily; and Mariel Hemingway (lower right) as Tracy.

Throughout the film, we see each significant set of characters try, without much luck, to cement a relationship while driving. In each successive scene, Allen's camera is behind the car, doggedly following them, as we hear their conversations in a voice-over technique. The failure of each of these affairs to amount to anything thus appears to grow from the fact that they were developed in that vehicle which has always been associated with Los Angeles, a city Allen despises, and actually seems out of place in his beloved New York: It is no small matter, then, that at one point in the film Isaac/Allen claims all cars should be banned from Manhattan. The only relationship in the film that is not developed in a car is the Isaac/Tracy one (they are always seen walking places) and significantly, when Isaac at the end wants to get to Tracy's house as quickly as he can, he cannot flag down a cab. He cannot get there by car, and is forced to make the journey on foot instead.

Other Allen themes are effectively developed, including his love for movies and hatred of television. We see the idiotic TV show Isaac works for ("Human Beings—Wow!") and the great old films he retreats to. When he and Tracy talk of breaking up, he shrugs and says, "We'll always have Paris," quoting Bogie's line to Bergman from *Casablanca*, showing that at least a touch of the old Woody is still with us. He is constantly trying to educate Tracy about the joys of the Old Hollywood, and in one particular scene makes sure that she can identify Veronica Lake from all the other film actresses of the 1940's. This conversation lends a special poignancy to the final sequence in which, as Isaac and Tracy talk about their future, her hair suddenly falls over her eye exactly as Veronica's did in her famous films; we know, at that instant, that Isaac has succeeded in instilling in her those values he cherishes. In this scene, as in all others, Tracy is lit with a brightness that makes her appear almost incandescent, like one of those lovely young earth-women who, in Bergman's early films, held out the hope of salvation for the world-weary heroes.

On the other hand, Mary—who could draw Isaac into a spiritual darkness—is kept in dark clothing and moves through shadows. Despite a nice forecast for a Sunday in New York, when Isaac tries to spend that day in Central Park with Mary, a sudden dark cloud brings on a rainstorm, sending them into the planetarium, where their blossoming love takes place amid images of intergalactic darkness; the dead surfaces of the moon suggest the deadness, and the moon madness, of their oncoming relationship. The first time they make love, the screen immediately goes dark; the second time they make love, the sequence begins in darkness. In each case, this visualization transforms the spiritual darkness of her attitudes into a visualized state. With Tracy, the lovemaking scenes were always brightly lit; and instead of watching them actually making love, we saw Isaac and Tracy eating—pizza, Chinese food, ice cream sodas. At the end, when Isaac muses about Tracy going off to England and meeting other drama students, he remains calm until he mutters, "You'll have *lunch*—and attachments form!"

Nowhere in his films has Allen so brilliantly organized his frames. Whenever Isaac or any of the other characters come close to the realization that relationships are difficult to maintain, we see the character forced into one side of the Scope-screen frame. Sometimes, the remainder of the frame is filled with objects and clutter; at other moments, the remaining half of the frame is literally turned into a visual vacuum by the placement of some object which blocks everything else from our sight. When *Manhattan* was sold to cable-TV, one stipulation was that the film could not be "reduced" to standard screen size, but would have to be broadcast with the full Scope image shown, and the top and bottom of the screen blanked out with borders. The decision was a wise one: with an "adjusted" screen size, the scenes described above would have been reduced to close-ups of the characters' faces, and the meaning of the movie would have been lost, so completely is it contained in the composition. Because here, Allen's careful and conscious craftsmanship is not (as in *Interiors*) a case of style without substance; here, the form *is* the content. Woody's vision of the emptiness of the lifestyle he chronicles can only be communicated by the wide-screen images of characters crowded into small spaces while adjacent vacuums suggest the emptiness of their lives.

Michael Murphy and Anne Byrne, who play Yale and his wife Emily, clown on the set between takes.

Trying to write on his living room couch, Isaac realizes that he desperately misses Tracy.

"I never had any trouble meeting women," Isaac says near the film's end, making clear that even if he loses both Tracy and Mary, he will soon be with another pretty girl. The earlier Allen—the nebbish of *Sam* and those other films about guys unable to get girls—is gone. He also forwards his spiritual concerns: When Yale accuses him of trying to play God, Ike simply retorts that "I've got to model myself on someone." His view of women and their own romantic preoccupations is stronger than ever. Throughout the movie, Mary talks about her ex-husband with such excitement that we expect him to have Einstein's brain, Gregory Peck's looks, and Harry Reems's staying power. But when we finally get to see him, he's played by Wally Shawn: shorter, balder, and homelier than Woody Allen. What Mary loves is not the man but her mental image of him. In fact, though, Woody looks like more of a romantic hero than ever before: as he moves and gestures with relaxation and self-confidence, he actually appears "cool" and attractive. He again shows us marriages crumbling (Yale and Emily), teachers who betray you (Mary had an affair with her teacher and he failed her anyway), and food as a metaphor for sex ("Have you got anything to eat here?" he asks Mary when he comes to her apartment hoping to make love). Life and art once more get confused: "This is shaping up like a Noel Coward play," he mutters when Mary tries for a civilized break-up. And to counter the glibness of Yale's Academy of the Overrated, he sentimentally concocts an answer to it: the Things That Make It Worthwhile, including everything from Cezanne's paintings of pears to Frank Sinatra's recordings to a pretty young woman's face...

Manhattan ties Renoir's *Rules of the Game* as the greatest high-comedy film of all time, standing as the American equivalent of that brittle, moral movie. If Allen was influenced by Renoir, he did not in any way imitate him, and there is all the difference in the world between the two. As Jack Kroll wrote in *Newsweek*, "Allen's nostalgia isn't nostalgic, it's the ironic fist in the velvet glove....The city itself seems to be remembering the Gershwin music, reaching out to its art deco grace as if supplicating relief from the dissonant New York of the 1970's, a city that's boxed in emotionally as well as architecturally." As Andrew Sarris put it in the *Village Voice*, *Manhattan* is "the only truly great American movie of the 1970's."

199

9½:
STARDUST MEMORIES

A United Artists Film (1980)

CAST:

Woody Allen *(Sandy Bates)*; Charlotte Rampling *(Dorrie)*; Jessica Harper *(Daisy)*; Marie-Christine Barrault *(Isobel)*; Tony Roberts *(Tony)*; Daniel Stern *(Actor)*; Amy Wright *(Shelley)*; Helen Hanft *(Vivian Orkin)*; John Rothman *(Jack Abel)*; Anne DeSalvo *(Sandy's Sister)*; Joan Neuman *(Sandy's Mother)*; Ken Chapin *(Sandy's Father)*; Leonardo Cimino *(Sandy's Analyst)*; Eli Mintz *(Old Man)*; David Lipman *(George, Sandy's Chauffeur)*; Robert Munk *(Sandy as a boy)*; Sharon Stone *(Pretty girl on train)*; Jack Rollins *(studio executive)*; Howard Kissel *(Sandy's manager)*; Judith Crist *(critic)*; Louise Lasser *(Sandy's Secretary)*; John Doumanian *(Armenian fan)*.

Woody Allen, who as Sandy Bates, film director, wears European-style dark sunglasses identical to those worn by Marcello Mastroianni in so many of Fellini's films...

CREDITS:

Producer, Robert Greenhut; executive producer, Jack Rollins and Charles H. Joffe; production designer, Mel Bourne; costumes, Santo Loquasto; director, Woody Allen; writer, Woody Allen; photography, Gordon Willis; piano music, arranged and performed by Dick Hyman; running time, 89 minutes; Rating: PG.

With his previous stab at a totally serious film, Woody's fans were at least willing to give him the benefit of the doubt, to pass off the failure as an interesting artist's desire to experiment in an entirely different mode. But if *Interiors* seemed a forced attempt to create a unique and original work that fell within the general style of Ingmar Bergman, *Stardust Memories* looked like a self-conscious steal of one particular film by Federico Fellini, *8½*. Moreover, Woody not only assumed Fellini's storyline and filmmaking style verbatim, but also included a depiction of his audience as a circus of grotesques that caused Woody's fans to recoil in horror: for in *Stardust Memories*, he certainly seemed to be announcing that he hated the people who loved him.

Like Fellini's *8½*, *Stardust Memories* concerns an acclaimed filmmaker who finds himself at a point of artistic block partway through his latest picture, and

who must sort out not only his film work but also his personal life (which his film is based on) as well as the past that haunts him. Both Guido (Marcello Mastroianni) and Sandy Bates (Allen) must make sense of their sex lives, for each is tempted by seductive neurotics and offered a chance at spiritual salvation by an earth-woman. In Sandy's case, the women are Dorrie (Charlotte Rampling), an elegant, insecure beauty whose sudden shifts in temperament ultimately land her in an insane asylum, where the doctors immediately fall in love with her dangerously irresistible darkness, and Isobel (Marie-Christine Barrault), a life-loving French woman whose healthy fertility is confirmed by several children in tow, and who offers Sandy a safe, sane respite from the psychologically shadowed relationship with Dorrie. He is emotionally torn apart because the two, though opposites, are equally appealing to the opposing elements within him.

Confusing all this is another girl, Daisy (Jessica Harper) he meets while the guest of honor at a film festival of his pictures held at a resort where a critic (Judith Crist) regularly holds court. Sandy is under continual pressure, from fans who want everything from autographs to contributions for varied charities to a chance to audition; from the studio heads who want to change the ending of his last film and add humor to his next one; from the women in his life, who threaten to strangle him with their diverse needs. But he finds Daisy appealing, not so much in spite of the fact that she announces ''I'm trouble!'' (which is what Dorrie said the day she met him and, not coincidentally, is what Mary warned Isaac in *Manhattan*) but, significantly *because* of it. Having screwed up his life with Dorrie (who Daisy reminds him of) he feels the urge to do it again with Daisy. His artistic side impels him toward the dangerous, which he must experience if he is to produce his best work, a record of his journey through the dark side (''I'm *fatally* attracted to you,'' he tells Dorrie the first time he meets her, introducing the relationship between sex and death that haunts Allen's films). But he is a man as

...though in Fellini's 8½, Marcello actually sported glasses that look remarkably like those Woody usually wears!

201

well as an artist, and that holds him in check by pulling in the opposite direction, causing him to be attracted to bourgeoise existence: talking about mundane matters with Isobel over a lunch with the children. He wants mutually exclusive things; wants to be an artist and an ordinary man at the same time. In wanting this, Sandy Bates expresses the angst of all artists everywhere.

At the time of the film's release, though, he was interpreted less as a universal symbol of the artist than as a stand-in for Allen himself. Woody himself refuses to admit that Sandy Bates is "really" Woody Allen. "From the time of *Annie Hall*," he told Charles Champlin in 1981, "people regard anything I do as autobiographical, so I guess they look at *Stardust Memories* and say is *that* what you think of us? I can't always sit with people and tell them to think of it as a fictional film about a filmmaker going through a crisis in his life. It's hard for them to dissociate him from me."

In fact, though, why should we? Sandy Bates, like Woody Allen, is a stand-up comic who became a famous comic filmmaker and then switched to drama, a move which did not sit well with his fans. Like Woody, Sandy divided his time as a child between playing stickball on the streets and practicing magic in the privacy of his room. Like Allen, he makes films starring Tony Roberts (here playing himself!); when an audience asks him questions about his films, he responds with lines Allen has himself used in similar situations. Like Allen, Sandy lives in Manhattan and refuses to join the Hollywood scene; like him, he worries that his films are insignificant time-killers which mean little in the context of an enormous but crumbling universe. *Stardust Memories* is about "a filmmaker-comedian who's reached a point in his life where he just doesn't find anything amusing anymore and so he's overcome with depression," Woody claims. "This is not me, but it will be perceived as me." How could it be perceived otherwise? When Woody created that human chameleon Leonard Zelig or small-time talent agent Danny Rose, nobody confused the character with the man writing and playing him; obviously, they were only roles Woody designed for his own talent to portray.

Woody could insist that he never had a French girlfriend like Isobel or one who, like Dorrie, ended

As Isobel, Marie-Christine Barrault plays the earthy, fertile woman who offers Isaac a chance for a healthy escape from his oppressive career and his neurotic lovers...

...and the chance to love a woman as healthy as the one Claudia Cardinale played in Fellini's 8½.

up in an asylum. But for once, John Simon's nastiness seems fair when he complains there is an "all-embracing dishonesty at work here. Almost everything we are told or shown about Sandy Bates is true of Woody Allen, yet with just enough deviations from strict autobiography to allow Allen to declare it presumptuous to equate him with his protagonist." For critic Peter Rainer, Woody had not grown from a maker of pleasant little comedies to an artist creating more meaningful works, but had experienced an aesthetic contrition and an emotional contraction "from what was fresh and original" to the working out of "some private inner drama the public is only partially privy to. Is it philistine to wish [his] movies were funnier these days? I don't think so—they would be better movies if they were. Gifted filmmakers should be free to experiment, of course, but there comes a time when you have to realize what your limitations are, and build on your strengths."

The most notable strength of Allen's early comedies, as well as his masterpiece *Manhattan*, is that they

Dorrie (Charlotte Rampling) is the irresistibly neurotic woman in his life; Sandy can neither control his attraction to her dangerous dark moods nor let her go...

showed Woody off as a one-of-a-kind comic; early on, he may have borrowed liberally from The Marx Brothers, Bob Hope, and Charlie Chaplin, but in time a Woody Allen vision (in terms of both style and substance) had emerged, *Manhattan* being its most sophisticated and successful expression thus far. In *S.M.*, he obviously aped the style and structure of Fellini's greatest work, and such imitativeness is ordinarily the clearest indication of a second-rate talent. As Stanley Kauffmann wrote in *The New Republic*: "Satire becomes parasitism. Allen isn't kidding Fellini or even revering: he's saying that he wishes he *were* Fellini and by the very act of persistent imitation confesses that he knows he never will be." Granted, Woody was not alone in this: Bob Fosse's *All That Jazz* is that choreographer/filmmaker's autobiography, also done in the *8½* manner. But what makes Fellini such a great artist is that he came up with a filmmaking technique that was completely original and precisely expressed himself; by adapting Fellini's format, other filmmakers only appear to be admitting they are unable to come up with unique styles to express unique visions. To copy a genius is to admit one is not a genius.

Writers usually make that mistake when they are young and naíve, then mature and go on to try and

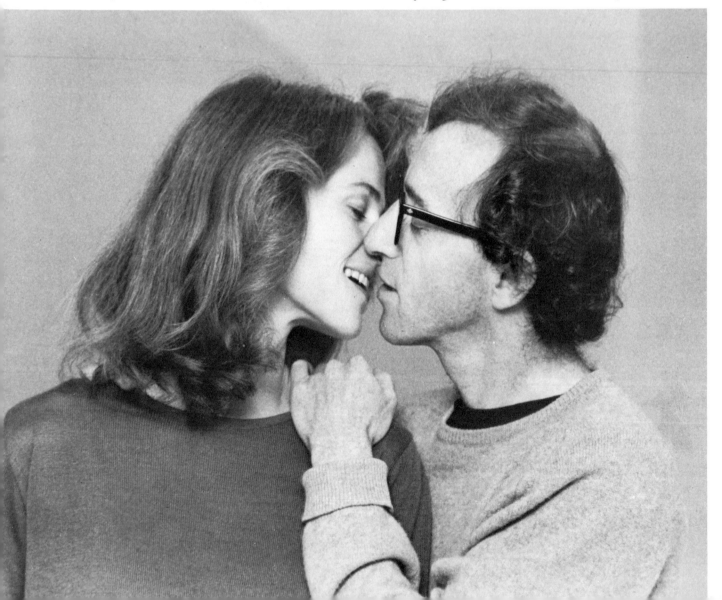

forge their own styles. For Woody to have made such a film so late in his career is more unforgivable than if he had turned out something so self-indulgent and imitative in his early days as a filmmaker.

Earlier on, in fact, he seemed to have a better grasp on the bond between a filmmaker and his audience. In 1975, at a press conference following a New York preview showing of *Love and Death*, Woody announced: "I make a deal with my audience. My contract is that there be plenty of laughs. Some directors guarantee violence, others promise sex. If I start out earning a big laugh every two minutes, I'm relentless about keeping up the pace." Perhaps the great problem with *S.M.* and *Interiors* is that Woody assumed the "deal" was off but the audience did not. His defenders would argue Woody "grew" while his audience failed to; his critics would charge that he lost touch with his audience and began to make films more interested in "consideration" than "communication." "Woody," Thomas Thompson wrote in *The Hollywood Reporter*, "postures in *Stardust Memories* as a misunderstood genius in a region of rubes."

This could stand as Allen's attitude toward his audience watching the movie, or to Sandy Bates's vision of the audience that surrounds him during the film festival. Either way, it is not a flattering portrait. They ask only the dreariest of questions ("What were you trying to say in this picture?"; "Do you find it hard to direct yourself?"; "Did you study filmmaking in school?") to which he provides pithy, droll answers, which in turn send the assembled multitude into gales of laughter at his superiority. And, physically speaking, they are every bit as grotesque as the characters who surround Guido in Fellini's *8½*; indeed, Allen even lights them with the same strange combination of brittle bleakness and harsh brightness Fellini employs, accompanied by tinny music that sounds suspiciously like Nino Rota. Perhaps when he was making *S.M.*, Woody should have been reminded of a comment he had made to *Boston After Dark* in 1969: "Fellini," he said, "is an utter magician, but he has no heart. I am knocked out by his technique but his films bore me." No wonder, then, that Allen's most Felliniesque film bored his audience.

Thomas Thompson wrote: "I departed *S.M.* drenched in the spirit of the film—mean-tempered. Maybe I took more offense than Woody intended, but it seemed a usually estimable artist had just done something petulant, i.e., kick his audience in the ass. Here was punishment for people who laughed at *Annie Hall*, but then found *Interiors* less deep and more excruciating than a root canal." Defending the film, Diane Jacobs called it more "honest and considerably less engaging than *Manhattan*," insisting *S.M.* "was almost universally misunderstood by the critical community." For Jacobs, a scholar studying Woody's films and finding a single thematic thread running through them, *S.M.* does offer a gold mine of possibilities. But for the casual viewer—and, for better or worse, most people will always be casual moviegoers, just as most critics remain barometers for that audience—*S.M.* is an insulting and angering film, as derisive as it is derivative.

After interviewing Allen at length, Charles Champlin was able to arrive at an interpretation Woody himself agreed was the correct one: a movie about "the problem of a man who on the basis of his achievements should be both fulfilled and accepted, and who finds himself spiritually bankrupt." A man who, in Woody's words, "has accomplished things,

...though perhaps he could use a whip to control her and his other women as Marcello did in this classic moment from *8½*; Woody had spoofed this specific shot in his very first movie, Pussycat.

The lighting Woody employed for most scenes in the movie, including Gordon Willis's black-and-white images of a grotesque party in a surrealistic field Sandy and Daisy (Jessica Harper) stumble into . . .

yet they still don't mean anything to him." But those approaching the film without benefit of an audience with Allen saw something else. Bea Rothenbuecher, in *Christian Century*, noted that "Allen indulges in some disturbingly acid humor targeted against sycophants and ever-fawning hordes of autograph-seekers—all grotesquely caricatured but ultimately seeming to include the real life audience." In *The Nation*, Robert Hatch wrote that "Allen has hired a group of the ugliest people I can remember having seen on the screen. Grotesquerie of features is all that most of them have to offer; it is pitiful and, as a celebrity's view of his public, it is mean." Pauline Kael added that "Woody degrades the people who respond to his work and presents himself as their victim. . . . Woody Allen has

often been cruel to himself in physical terms—making himself look smaller, scrawnier, ugly. Now, he's doing it to his fans."

Most depressing of all, Woody depicts his persona as being a superior creature to those (mostly Jewish) people who adore him. As Kael noted, whenever they mention how much they enjoy his funny films, they are portrayed as being superficial and unable to grasp his more serious work; whenever someone mentions he enjoyed one of the serious films, he always turns out to have foolish reasons for doing so. "He anticipates almost anything you might say about *S.M.* and ridicules you for it," Kael continued. "Finally, you may feel you're being told you have no right to *any* reaction to Woody Allen's movies." In the same mood, Richard Corliss of *Time* called the film "an elaborate mechanism of self-abuse, a Rube Goldberg dildo, a film about a dead end that *is* a dead end for this prolific, personal filmmaker."

206

. . . recalls similar scenes like this one from Fellini's 8½, in which circus clowns invade real-life situations and turn the actual world into a place of fantasy.

In the movie's magnificent opening, Sandy finds himself on a train full of uglies, wishing he were making the symbolic trip through life on a neighboring train filled with beautiful people, travelling on parallel tracks.

At another of those "enormous restaurants," Sandy feels drawn to the straight, wholesome side of life when he enjoys a family-style afternoon with Isobel and her children (Vanina Holasek and Michel Touchard)...

...but he cannot resist the allure of a troubled, neurotic beauty like Daisy, especially if she begins their relationship by announcing: "I'm trouble!"

Part of the problem was that Woody couldn't see the forest for the trees. *S.M.* offers ample proof of how technically proficient he had become at everything from his work with actors to creating textural and atmospheric effects, making his previous films look downright primitive by comparison; but they worked despite their technical flaws, while *S.M.* is, for most viewers, an empty experience despite the technical virtuosity. As early as 1972, critic Stephen Mamber had noted: "As Allen matures as a filmmaker, it is likely that the uncertainties of style will become less pronounced, but there's always the risk that assured, controlled comedy is not suited to the nature of his humor....I hope Allen doesn't become too good." In *S.M.*, he became too good, which is another way of saying bad. Besides the anarchic spirit of the earlier films, something else was missing: Woody's unique humorous approach, grounded in self-deprecatory wit "Although many comedians depend on humor poked at members of their audiences," Morley Gillan wrote of stand-up comic Woody way back in 1967, "Allen makes himself the brunt of his own jokes."

Woody apparently saw it the same way: "I'm one of life's great self-haters," he said at the 1975 *Love and Death* press conference. "It figures you've got to hate yourself if you've got any integrity at all." Correspondingly, Woody's characters in the early films share that quality: they are self-critical and self-deprecatory, which is essential to their appeal. In *S.M.*, that quality no longer exists in the character or the tone of the movie that contains him—or, one might conclude, in the filmmaker himself. Critics and fans have been telling Woody Allen he is a genius for so long that he here appears to believe them. When in *Manhattan* Isaac Davis is accused of considering himself God and bluntly admits, "I've got to model myself after somebody," we laugh out loud; it's funny because Woody pokes fun at his own ego. When in *S.M.* a member of the audience calls out that he's a bit of a Narcissus, and he corrects him, insisting: Zeus!" we do not find it funny, because there is no apparent irony on the part of the filmmaker toward the attitude of the character.

The surface of the film certainly shimmers: anyone not familiar with *8½* would probably be impressed with the semi-surreal look, the way in which everyday life is given a circus atmosphere. But it all seems so much form without content *S.M.* is full of obvious, outlandish statements of a sententious nature, undoubtedly meant to make it clear that this is heavyweight stuff; but despite the light, airy attitude with which it elegantly won over audiences, *Manhattan* actually said much more about the human condition

209

Part of the reason Sandy cannot commit himself to married life is the nightmare vision of it he sees every time he visits his sister (Anne De Salvo) and her husband (Jaqui Safra).

Sandy complains to his cook that he does not eat rabbit, though like everyone else he is part of an enormous restaurant in which each creature is devouring something smaller and being devoured by something larger. Dorothy Leon plays the cook.

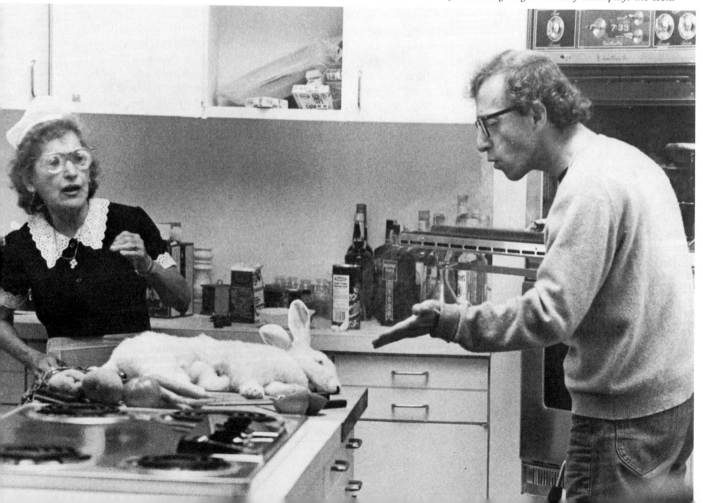

The Curse of Celebrity: Sandy tries to talk the police into not arresting his chauffeur.

while appearing, at first glance, to say very little. "A great pleasure in all Allen's work," Diane Jacobs has written, "is its deceptive simplicity." Though this is an accurate description of Woody's best films, the word "all" seems wrong considering *Interiors* and *S.M.* One of the key reasons *S.M.* fails to please is that its surface seems so complex while its essence is rather simplistic and self-aggrandizing. Grotesque-looking characters are constantly saying things like, "What's the matter with him. Doesn't he realize he has the greatest gift of all—the ability to make people laugh?"—that is, saying the very things people (the public and critics alike) had said of *Interiors*. And they are presented as buffoons.

No wonder John Simon accused him of a "virulent misanthropy that masquerades as amusement at the human show," while Judith Crist, who had allowed one of her famed film weekends (and herself as well) to be portrayed in the film, felt badly used: "What we have here falls into the category of kvetch." All great comic films laugh at the absurdity of the world, but laugh most of all at the comic's persona: Chaplin, Keaton, Lloyd, and early Woody Allen all have this in common. But in *S.M.*, there is

nothing funny about Sandy Bates, though he does occasionally come out with lines that are supposed to be funny but which are only sardonic and glib in a way his best lines are not. Woody portrays Sandy as deep and sensitive (he's always worrying about the starving people in India) and everyone else as corrupt and greedy (they can only think of making money, even at the expense of Sandy's art). Unlike Isaac Davis, who is sympathetic because he is a sometimes weak and uncertain man struggling to live a decent life, Sandy has nowhere to go; already enshrined as a hero before the drama proper begins, he cannot waver but can only cluck his teeth in disgust at all those inferior people around him. There is no comparable moment here to the one at the end of *Manhattan*, when we sit on the edge of our seats wondering if Isaac will make the right moral move and go back to Tracy. Sandy Bates can only parade about, making judgments on everyone else—which might not be so bad if Allen only gave us some sign that he does not necessarily accept or condone what Sandy is doing.

The best moments in the movie are the first and last sequences; viewed out of context, they constitute classic Allen bits. The opening is one of the most perfect expressions of Woody's vision of life, communicated wordlessly through the language of

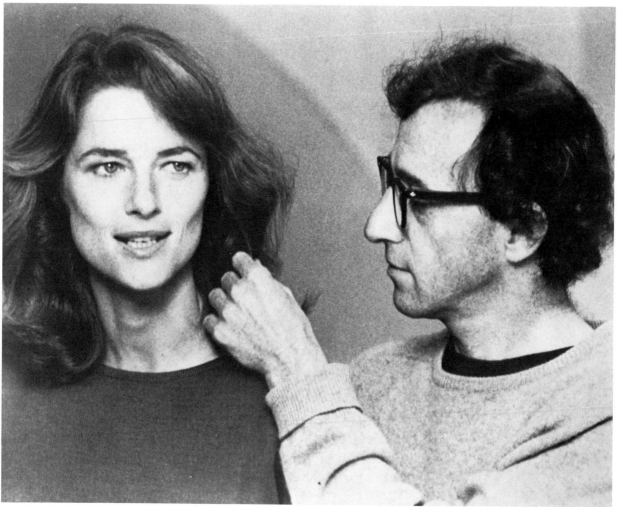

A fatal attraction: Sandy and Dorrie.

the cinema. Sandy/Woody sits on a train, waiting to pull out of the station. He looks around and notices unpleasant-looking people with him. Then, across the way, he spies another train on a parallel track, which presumably he could also be on; this one is full of beautiful people, having a great time. He jumps up to change trains, but it is too late: he must make his journey on this glum one, which wouldn't be nearly so bad if he hadn't had that glimpse of the possible alternative. The trains, of course, symbolize the ride of life, and this is the root of Allen's anhedonia: there is always that briefly glimpsed vision of a delightful life journey other people had the good sense to get in on, and which he has somehow just managed to miss.

Just as striking is the ending, with the romantic idealism it implies: Sandy recalls one wonderful moment when, on a quiet Sunday in New York, he read the *Times* while Dorrie sat across from him, looking incredibly elegant. The calm and peacefulness of that moment was an epiphany, a revelation of what all of life ought to be like. But it was only one wonderful moment, gone before it could even be completely comprehended. One remembers that similar moment in *The Great Gatsby* when Gatsby momentarily thought Daisy was forever his: "At his lips' touch she blossomed for him like a flower and the incarnation was complete," as the ideal becomes, for a brief second, real. But reach out to grasp it, and you find it gone. No wonder that in this film, Allen gives us a heroine with the same name as Fitzgerald's most famous woman: Daisy.

Allen's various themes are present here: the marriage theme, evident in his desire to marry Isobel and his inability to commit himself to her; the celebrity theme, further developed here than it has been before, in which fans constantly badger him, though when he finally gives in and tries to use his celebrity status to avoid a citation from a cop, he ends up in jail. In an apparent fantasy sequence, the "celebrity" is shot dead by a fan who walks up and says, "Sandy, you know you're my hero." Indeed, death haunts the film in the guise of an old friend who passed on just before the story starts, reminding Sandy of his own mortality. But when he again uses the line from *Annie Hall* about being depressed because the universe is breaking down and eventually there won't be anything left, it seems tiresome, at least within this film's tone of cruelty and cynicism.

Food, of course, is a key metaphor. The first time we see Sandy and Dorrie start to kiss, she mutters, between embraces: "Why don't I just run down and get some food? We'll stay in and *cook!*" Her reading of that word suggests she actually has other things in mind, and the sophistication of her sexual prowess is stated in the European gourmet delights she suggests preparing, even as they continue to kiss: "I could do my mother's recipe...fillet of beef...sweet-potato casserole..." Later, he returns the favor, cooking for her. "Your spaghetti could have used another 20 minutes," she tell him. Solidifying the link between food and sex, he looks at her askance and asks, "You don't want a limp noodle, do you?" At the resort hotel, Sandy finds a girl in his bed, as the intellectual groupie tries to score with him; first, though, she hands him a plate of brownies. And, of course, there is the obligatory scene in which the characters go to a movie; in this case, Sandy and Daisy take in *The Bicycle Thief*.

One of the most interesting scenes in the film (and most reminiscent of the old Allen) comes when we get a look at one of Sandy's movies, and it's an Allenesque comedy about a man who has a homely but sweet girlfriend as well as a mean but gorgeous one; to create the perfect woman, he transfers the brain of the beast into the body of the beauty. There is in that notion an element of the romantic sensibility that has gradually risen to the surface of his movies, with its comical approach toward the Allenesque hero who wants the ideal and cannot understand why it's so impossible to attain. A shame he did not make that film instead of *S.M.*, and a double shame since the idea was stolen, becoming the basis for a sloppy Steve Martin comedy.

Judith Crist kept count of the films Woody had directed and, noting that his work on *Tiger Lily* constituted half a picture, caustically suggested that *S M* could be called Woody's *9½*. At one point, Sandy picks up a theme already sufficiently explored in *Annie Hall* when he mutters: "You can't control life—it doesn't work out perfect. Only art...art and masturbation...two areas at which I'm an expert." In *Manhattan*, Allen proved he was indeed an expert at art. And in *Stardust Memories*, he likewise proved himself an expert at masturbation.

At Two with Nature:

A MIDSUMMER NIGHT'S SEX COMEDY

An Orion Pictures Release (1982)

CAST:

Woody Allen *(Andrew)*; Mia Farrow *(Ariel)*; Jose Ferrer *(Leopold)*; Julie Hagerty *(Dulcy)*; Tony Roberts *(Maxwell)*; Mary Steenburgen *(Adrian)*; Adam Redfield *(Student Foxx)*; Moishe Rosenfeld *(Mr. Hayes)*; Timothy Jenkins *(Mr. Thomson)*; Michael Higgins *(Reynolds)*; Sol Frieder *(Carstairs)*; Boriss Zoubok *(Purvis)*; Thomas Barbour *(Blint)*; Kate McGregor-Stewart *(Mrs. Baker)*.

CREDITS:

Producer, Robert Greenhut; executive producer, Charles H. Joffe; production designer, Mel Bourne; director, Woody Allen; associate producer, Michael Peyser; writer, Woody Allen; music, Felix Mendelssohn; art director, Speed Hopkins; set decorator, Carol Joffe; director of photography, Gordon Willis; editor, Susan E. Morse; casting, Juliet Taylor; costume designer, Santo Loquasto; animation effects, Kurtz and Friends; Flying Machines and Inventions by Eoin Sprott Studio, Ltd.; 94 minutes; Rating: PG.

"I'd rather die than live in the country," Woody told *Time* magazine in 1979; "I've always been a two with nature" goes one of his oldest gags. Understandably, then, *A Midsummer Night's Sex Comedy* is his most willfully perverse film, for it belongs to a genre that runs from Shakespeare's *A Midsummer Night's Dream* to Ingmar Bergman's *Smiles of a Summer Night*: the light-hearted bucolic love story in which city people enter the enchanted world of an Arden forest and find themselves falling under the spells of romance that the spirit-folk cast, causing these self-assured sophisticates to act in the silliest of ways. The "perversity" of Woody Allen working in such a genre derives from his being "at two" with the very premise, which would certainly seem to require an abiding love for nature and the natural world.

In fact, *AMSNSC* is in many ways the inverse of his masterpiece *Manhattan*. The country film is shot in

The ensemble includes Woody Allen as Andrew Hobbs (top left) and, clockwise, Mia Farrow as Ariel Weymouth, Jose Ferrer as Leopold Stugis, Mary Steenburgen as Adrian Hobbs, Tony Roberts as Maxwell Jordan, and Julie Hagerty as Dulcy Ford.

glorious color, whereas that city film was done in muted black and white; the country film is set against the ecstatic sounds of Mendelssohn's classic compositions, while the city film was accompanied by the jazz-drenched compositions of Gershwin. Moreover, the city film, generally accepted by critics and audiences alike as Woody's valentine to the Big Apple, was

nonetheless described by him as a depiction of New York City as "a metaphor for everything wrong with our culture." In comparison *AMSNSC* is an attempt to do the opposite, to take a subject he has consistently criticized (the country) and show its good points, its enchantments, its magic.

There is another tie connecting the two films: they are the ones that most clearly reveal a Renoir influence. This aspect of Allen's work has never been properly discussed, since critics have been too busy comparing him (favorably or unfavorably) to Chaplin or Bergman. *AMSNSC* has less in common with the Shakespeare play and the Bergman film, instead re-

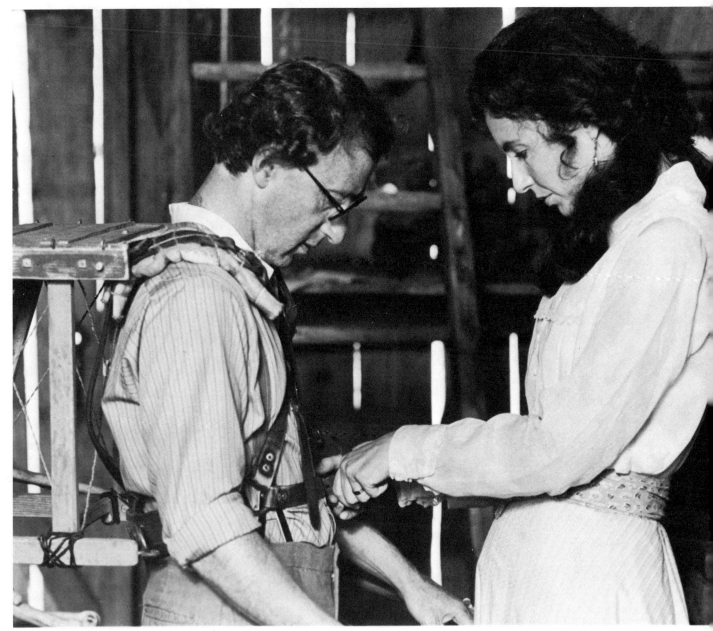

Adrian helps her husband Andrew prepare for the maiden voyage of his latest flying machine; his immense creative juices grow in part from his frustrated sex life with his wife.

sembling (in intent, if not effect) Renoir's *A Day in the Country*, that filmmaker's bittersweet study of city manners running up against country mores. The difference is, Renoir portrayed city and country with equal enthusiasm. Woody seems a stranger in a strange land, a lost, lonely filmmaker attempting a studied but dispirited and even sterile exercise in a genre which, by its insistence on a glorification of the natural, appears all wrong for him.

Indeed, though Woody wanted his film to have the look of the country, he found a location only a half-hour north of Manhattan so that he could drive back to his beloved New York every night. Though the movie is, in his own words, "about the country, summer, and sun," he doesn't care for any of those things and his predilictions are clear in the movie's unenthusiastic attitude.

The film concerns six people who spend a fateful weekend together in upstate New York, circa 1906. Leopold (Jose Ferrer) is a pompous, narrow intellectual who is about to marry young Ariel (Mia Farrow), a spirited beauty who years earlier almost (but

Andrew and Adrian lead their house guests on a trek into the woods for a summer day's picnic; unfortunately, they will find themselves at two with nature.

not quite) had an affair with Andrew (Allen). He is a stockbroker and amateur inventor who lives in isolation in the woods with his wife Adrian (Mary Steenburgen), who can no longer sexually relate to her husband for reasons she has not dared to tell him about: She had an affair with Andrew's best friend Maxwell (Tony Roberts) some time ago, and guilt over that indiscretion has caused her to become unresponsive when her husband tries to touch her. Now, Maxwell—a compulsive womanizer who has been unable to commit himself to a lasting relationship with any one woman—is coming to visit, bringing a free-living, easy loving nurse, Dulcy (Julie Hagerty), along with him. Seemingly the least serious member of the crowd that assembles, Dulcy

soon turns out to have an instinctual intelligence which her more educated companions lack; she is without neuroses, and calmly but wholeheartedly approaches sex as an enjoyable means of gratification.

But no one else in the sextet is able to achieve such peace of mind. Anhedonically, each manages to make him/herself miserable, wanting the one person he or she can't have. Maxwell quickly loses interest in the always agreeable Dulcy (her sexual attitude is just too healthy to make her very intriguing) and instead pursues Ariel, who would like to reignite her old relationship with Andrew. Adrian tries to grasp if she is still hung-up on Maxwell, while Leopold sets out to seduce the ever-willing Dulcy. Everyone has, at the outset, an attractive, appealing partner; everyone is miserable because he or she is thoroughly convinced someone else's partner would be the perfect one to be with; everyone wastes the time that could be spent in happy appre-

216

The Romantic Moment: Andrew and Ariel attempt to rekindle the lost romance of their youth, to recapture the moment that they let slip through their fingers; they will be sorely disappointed.

ciation of the one he or she is supposed to be with by recklessly pursuing someone else. Everyone who actually manages to pull off a tryst soon falls prey to romantic depression because the actual affair falls so far short of the anticipated experience.

To work, what the film needed was a joyous if ironic attitude toward these characters and what they do. The film needs to communicate a sense of fun, while never taking the characters at their face value, insisting on a wise as well as witty approach to their affairs of the heart. But it only seems leaden where it ought to be light and likable. This is a pretty film and an occasionally pleasant one, but it's also precious: slight in substance, too self-conscious in style. He misses the impressive essence of Renoir's *A Day in the Country* by trying painstakingly to reproduce the surfaces. Renoir's film was airy; Allen's is constantly striving to be airy.

In spite of all the romantic couplings and sexual frustrations, the major conflict is a philosophic rather than comic/dramatic one: between Leopold as the strict realist, believing only in the here and now ("Nothing is real but experience—that which by science can be proved," he announced in the opening scene) and Andrew, who believes there is more in heaven and earth, Leopold, than dreamt of in your philosophy ("You will admit there's more to life than we perceive with our senses," he says). In her book...*but we need the eggs*, Diane Jacobs insists that Woody's films, short stories, and plays all contain a single theme: the discrepancy between "reality—or life as it is—and magic—or life as one's (usually Woody's) mind and imagination can transform it." In the earlier movies, that theme is implied rather than stated outright. Yet *AMSNSC* seems so completely schematized along the lines of this theme (indeed, for many, over schematized!) that Jacobs' theory appears prophetic; it's too bad her book was published before *AMSNSC* was released, because this film is literally the culmination of that theme. Then again, there is always the possibility that Woody read her book, was influenced by her theory, and became self-conscious about it when he made *AMSNSC*. One of the reasons the film ultimately fails, though, is that it makes obvious what was better left implicit. If that theme did indeed give the earlier films a subtle meaning, it here hits the viewer point blank. The film never quite clicks as an engaging entertainment, but only sweetly creeps along, apparently leading to some sort of comic confrontation that never takes place. The paradox principle is in clear evidence, since Woody, who in film after film played the character who apparently believed in a nihilistic notion that all is blackness and, ultimately, a void, here insists on representing the attitude that we are not lost in the stars, that there is something out there. God may be an underachiever, but there seems no doubt about his existence.

Most of the scenes with Tony Roberts are recyclings from their confrontations over women and values in earlier films, which Woody wants to make fresh again by placing in a new context. The trouble is, it's not enough of a variation to make this seem something other than an old ploy dragged in once again, presented without the inspiration of the earlier efforts. A major miscalculation is the attempt to create humor by having the characters sometimes speak and act like contemporary types, at other times trying to perform in the "period" during which the film is set. This same technique was quite uproarious in, say, *Love and Death*, where Boris and Sonia would at one moment speak in a Hollywood costume picture conception of Russians during the Napoleonic wars, only to crack us up with anachronistic dialogue a moment later.

In *AMSNSC*, though, such an approach is only half hearted. Since the period is not all that remote—since fashions resembling those from 1906 are occasionally worn by hip people today—the effect is not so much comically delightful as totally confusing. Allen only implies, rather than insists, that the year is 1906, so many viewers spend the early portion of the film trying to understand if the film is set in the past (and, if so, what year) or if these are 1980's people engaging in a weekend's charade during which they drive around in old cars, sporting yesteryear's clothing. Also disconcerting is that Mia Farrow, who has always projected a distinct image all her own, here is directed to act as though she is Diane Keaton (as, to a lesser degree, are both Mary Steenburgen and Julie Hagerty) and the effect is bizarre. It is as if Allen, having accepted the break in his personal relationship with Keaton, did not so much fall in love with another woman as he tried to turn that other woman into his earlier love. This is the ultimate romantic urge on the part of a male, the desire to make the ideal real by capturing the lost moment. If Allen the artist was perhaps guilty of that in his direction of Farrow here (though not necessarily in

their later films), Allen the writer likewise created a story which is even more philosophically "romantic" than *Manhattan*.

For what haunts the lives of Andrew and Ariel is the notion of what could have been, the missed opportunity Andrew calls "the saddest thing in life." Ever since that moment when he did not act—did not make love to her—he has regretted his hesitation, and is aware that had he simply reached out as he wanted to, "both our lives might have been different." Adding insult to injury is the fact that Andrew had restrained himself from seizing the moment only because he believed Ariel to be pure and virginal, though in secret she had actually been a sexual profligate. Like Gatsby, Andrew wants to go back and do it over again, finally experiencing that wonderful moment he let slip through his fingers; like Gatsby, he will be sorely disappointed.

"The moment was so perfect," he keeps saying, though we know he is overinflating it. Ariel has become in his mind a kind of goddess, but like Daisy Buchannan—who, remarkably enough, was played in the film version of *Gatsby* by the very same actress—she is only a vulnerable, uncertain, ultimately self-interested girl. Thoroughly convinced that his entire life has been something of a mistake because of his failure, at the most crucial moment, to *act*, Andrew now acts; and, ironically, finds that action can be as big as mistake as inaction. When, toward the film's end, he and Ariel slip off into the woods—to that very spot, as only an arch-romantic would have it, where they *almost* made love years ago—they are unable to achieve orgasm. "It wasn't what I thought it would be," Ariel sighs. "Heard melodies are sweet," Keats wrote, "but those unheard sweeter…" Fitzgerald said of Gatsby: "He wanted to recover something, some idea of himself perhaps, that had gone into loving Daisy."

But like Scott Fitzgerald, Allen is at once a romantic and an anti-romantic, emotionally prone to romantic yearnings and intellectually sophisticated enough to take himself to task for his excesses of the heart. The great tragedy, he says here, is not that Andrew failed to act at the crucial moment (though in Andrew's naïve mind, that is the tragedy), but that Andrew has wasted his life mourning over the loss of what never could have worked anyway. He is sad because he didn't make the right move that would have let him spend the rest of his life with the woman who was precisely right for him, only we see (and, toward the very end, perhaps he does too) that she wasn't really right for him, after all. The wife he has been neglecting is in fact the right person for him, and when in the end they attempt to rekindle their relationship, the film sug-

Max finds himself attracted to Ariel, who is engaged to marry Leopold, who has begun to lust after Dulcy; anhedonia among American aristrocrats.

gests both a sense of hope for the future (now that they have knocked the romantic illusions out of their head) and a growth toward maturity on the part of Andrew.

"You still have that little boy look," Ariel tells Andrew, continuing the child-man theme hinted at in earlier films and carefully developed in *Manhattan*. There, we believed Isaac's purity, as opposed to every-

one else's corruption, because he did look almost as young as the woman-child Tracy he was dating; here, Allen is once more playing Salinger's Holden Caulfield, a catcher in the woods who does not want any emotionally and intellectually (if not necessarily sexually!) pure children to fall over the ridge and into the abyss of contemporary pseudo-intellectualism.

His characters are still subject to anhedonia. "Why does a beautiful day like today give me a sad feeling?" Adrian asks. His heavies can still, like Yale and Mary with *Manhattan*'s Academy of the Overrated, debunk the greats in order to conversely make

219

Leopold and Dulcy make plans for a secret tryst, not knowing that each of their partners is doing precisely the same thing with someone else.

themselves feel important: "Balzac—vastly overrated!" Leopold huffs. Marriage is still a key issue: Maxwell calls it "the death of hope," but considering the source (Maxwell is charming but superficial), we should perhaps withhold ascribing that statement to the artist himself, since at the end Allen leaves us with a very hopeful vision of marriage, as Andrew and Adrian— no longer prisoners of the past—work to reclaim their romance within the context of marriage. Marriage, the more mature Allen seems to be saying, only destroys romance if we let it.

Sex and creativity are still closely related. Early in the film, when Adrian will not sleep with Andrew, he pours all his energy into his flying machines. "Because of my trouble in bed, I can now fly," he whines, giving us an inverse of the scene in *Annie Hall* where, after making love to a beautiful woman, he sighed: "As Balzac said, 'Well, there goes another novel.'" When he has the sex, he feels guilty that it will sap away creative juices and not let him produce art; when he has the creative outlet, he feels frustrated that there is no sex. And Woody's sex and death theme

Andrew explains to his guests that the natural world is alive with spirits and magic, though the realist Leopold does not agree.

reaches its apex when Leopold literally dies during lovemaking, something the Allen films have been leading up to all along: "At the highest moment of ecstasy," Dulcy tells us, "he keeled over with that smile on his face." Before that, Maxwell shot himself when he realized he was desperately in love: "Wouldn't you die for Ariel?" he asks Andrew.

Food is the key metaphor for sex. When his wife jealously cross-examines Andrew about his previous relationship with Ariel, Andrew nervously tells her, "I went out with her *once*...had a couple of lob-sters...that's *it!*" But the audience knows from watching *Annie Hall* that lobsters are Allen's symbol of an irresistible attraction: The sexual attraction between Alvy and Annie was cemented when they had to boil the lobsters before they could eat them and, in the process of killing and eating, the two realized their love was the real thing. Love affairs are symbolized by lobsters, but marriage means more mundane meals. Midway through *AMSNSC*, Adrian decides to "take" Andrew on their kitchen table: "We can *not* have intercourse where we eat *oatmeal*," he shrieks.

Fascinating details abound in the film. The Tony Roberts character's name is Max, whereas in *Annie Hall*, Tony Roberts decided (for no apparent reason) that Max would be a good nickname for Alvy Singer.

221

Sadly, though, *AMSNSC* reads better than it plays. For a movie in which Woody loudly announces his belief in magic, there is a discernible lack of magic in the moviemaking; instead, the effect is mild, like one of those overcultivated art-comedies the earlier, more energetic Allen used to poke fun at.

The movie is reserved where it ought to be at least slightly ribald; the camera work is fancy, but there is too little fun in the film. In many scenes, Woody will train his camera on a room and allow the characters to come and go, rather than follow them; in *Manhattan*, it was with just such an effect that Allen made clear his key theme, that the place was as important a subject of the film as the people who inhabited it. Here, the same effect comes off awkwardly: the viewer wonders if Allen has lost interest in his characters.

With its continuation and even resolution of key Allen themes, the movie is of course of great interest to anyone interested in Allen as an *auteur*; it's a cornucopia for the student, the critic who has accepted *a priori* Allen's importance and is concerned with interpreting rather than evaluating the films. But for the critic unconcerned with Allen's entire artistic vision and only interested in the degree to which a film "works," *AMSNSC* falls flat. Following the irritating *Stardust Memories*, *AMSNSC* seemed something of a relief—an easy to take, easier to forget comedy that at least tried to be agreeable and never insulted the audience. Still, despite the rather obvious presentation of serious themes on the film's surface, it's an unimportant film, a comedy without many laughs, a film so softspoken that it lacks punch. There is none of the infectious charm, the absolute theatre magic, that suffuses the Shakespeare, Renoir, and Bergman origins and makes them—despite their seemingly frivolous surfaces—significant works of art.

Critic Peter Rainer complained: "Wan and featherlight....It's as if Allen had decided he could no longer be the handwrenching Bergman of movies like *Persona*, so now he's trying for the lyrical Bergman of *Smiles of a Summer Night*." In *Time*, Richard Corliss complained: "No Woody Allen comedy should mosey for arid stretches without a well-turned gag....Woody Allen has chosen to jettison those aspects of his comedy that made him a national endearment." David Ansen in *Newsweek* called the film a "classy but tepid pastiche." Colin L. Westerbeck, Jr., wrote in *Commonweal* that "the plot is about as clever as a porn flick with the explicit sex left out," while Pauline Kael scoffed in *The New Yorker* that "I began to look for a little of the messiness of his early pictures; who can be funny in tableaux that suggest the Nelson Rockefeller collection of imitation works of art?" In *National Review*, John Simon referred to it as "an utterly misbegotten item in which there is little sex and less comedy...the coup-

lings or near-couplings are drably mirthless.... Moreover, Allen's gags are sparse, old, repetitious, or crude...." In *The Nation*, Robert Hatch wrote that "the atmosphere is wrong. Allen, it would seem, has brought his cares with him, and they are incompatible with the bucolic revels....The strain appears in the direction, which seems not unlike that of a hostess who fears the soufflé will not rise. The players gambol, but as though on instructions to do so." Stanley Kauffmann, conversely, praised Allen's direction in *The New Republic*, calling this "easily his best-directed film," noting Allen's clear (and long sought-after) confidence with the camera. For Kauffmann, the problem was in the writing: "Allen uses some of the most trite pastoral symbols, and not paradoxically: a rabbit, a leaping deer, an owl on a branch swiveling its head as humans below argue. All that's missing is a huge close-up of a dewdrop falling from one leaf to another."

Allen now had two failures in a row. For a comeback, he would need a film that would bowl over critics the way *Manhattan* had. Allen would shortly provide just such a powerhouse with *Zelig*.

The Great Gatsby as Schlemiel:
ZELIG

An Orion Pictures Release (1983)

CAST:

Woody Allen *(Leonard Zelig)*; Mia Farrow *(Dr. Eudora Fletcher)*; Ellen Garrison *(Older Dr. Fletcher)*; Mary Louise Wilson *(Sister Ruth)*; Stephanie Farrow *(Sister Meryl)*; John Doumanian *(Greek Waiter)*; Erma Campbell *(Zelig's Wife)*; Jean Trowbridge *(Dr. Fletcher's Mother)*; Deborah Rush *(Lita Fox)*; Contemporary Interviews: Susan Sontag, Irving Howe, Saul Bellow, Bricktop, Dr. Bruno Bettelheim, Prof. John Morton Blum *(Themselves)*; Announcers: Ed Herlihy, Dwight Weist, Gordon Gould, Windy Craig, Jurgen Kuehn *(Themselves)*; Narration: Patrick Horgan.

CREDITS:

Producer, Robert Greenhut; executive producer, Charles H. Joffe; production design, Mel Bourne; associate producer, Michael Peyeser; writer, Woody Allen; photography, Gordon Willis; art director, Speed Hopkins; editor, Susan E. Morse; director, Woody Allen; optical effects, Joel Hyneck and Stuart Robertson; stills animation, Steven Plastrik and

Woody Allen as Leonard Zelig, the Human Chameleon. (PHOTO BY KERRY HAYES)

Zelig and his great love, analyst Eudora Fletcher, return to America as international heroes. (PHOTO BY KERRY HAYES)

Computer Opticals, Inc.; casting, Juliet Taylor; costume design, Santo Loquasto; music, Dick Hyman; running time, 79 minutes; Rating: PG.

At the end of *Stardust Memories*, a fan steps out of a crowd of well-wishers, smiles at the celebrity-hero Sandy Bates, whispers "I've always been you're biggest fan!" and blows him away with a handgun. At about the same time the film was released, a fan walked up to John Lennon outside his New York apartment and similarly shot him dead. What Woody Allen had conceived as the ultimate nightmare image of a popular celebrity's relationship with his audience turned out to be less paranoid than prophetic.

Woody Allen's films have always contained in them the theme of celebrity, dealing with the power and (paradoxically) vulnerability inherent in such a status. In *Stardust Memories* he had attempted to take this strain in his work and make it the central thrust of a project. But despite moments of perception and fascinating insights, the film failed. In *Zelig*, he revived the celebrity theme while expressing it through a

Leonard Zelig in one of his more relaxed moments. (PHOTO BY BRIAN HAMILL)

character who would not immediately be identified with himself: Leonard Zelig, a celebrity of the 1920's and thirties who is not (like Allen or Sandy Bates) a comic turned filmmaker but a very different sort of celebrity—a human chameleon who could take on the qualities of anyone he happened to be talking to at the time. In the presence of Republican businessmen, Zelig would suddenly be seen wearing a three-piece suit and sporting short, neatly trimmed hair. But if he entered a jazz club, he would quickly turn black and appear to be wearing funky clothes. Zelig's lack of a personality caused him to exhibit this bizarre quality; this, coupled with his desperate desire to fit in with any group he happened to find himself momentarily a member of, forced him to make fast metamorphoses.

On the eve of the film's release, Woody told journalist Michiko Kakutani that Leonard Zelig's existence as a human chameleon represented ''a minor malady almost everyone suffers from—carried to an extreme.'' In other words, this was a movie about conformity. ''It's that need to be liked,'' Woody continued, ''just to keep people around you

225

An incredibly intricate photo-mixing process was employed to allow Woody, as Zelig, to appear to be visiting with such real-life personalities of the era as Eugene O'Neill.

pacified. I thought that desire not to make waves, carried to an extreme, could have traumatic consequences. It could lead ultimately to fascism." Indeed, in the movie, it leads directly to that; near the end of the film, the Jewish Leonard Zelig is glimpsed at a brown shirt rally for Hitler. By making Leonard Zelig literally turn into a fascist before the film's end, Allen makes his figurative point in the language of the movie medium.

Much of the film's brilliance comes in the way Allen ties the two seemingly polar themes—conformity and celebrity—together in a paradoxical relationship. In Allen's negative view of celebrity status, he portrays mass worship growing not out of an appreciation for talent or wisdom or even beauty, but for a terrible kind of freakishness. Allen once said that "my one regret in life is that I was not born someone else," and in *Zelig* he was able to make that attitude the subject of a film. Like Allen, Zelig wants to be like those people around him; unlike Allen, who always remains uniquely himself, Leonard Zelig is

Mia Farrow as psychiatrist Eudora Fletcher. (PHOTO BY BRIAN HAMILL)

actually able to lose himself in the crowd.

But if the premise of the film is fanciful, that cannot be said for the style of filmmaking. *Zelig* marks a clear return to the approach of Allen's first directorial effort: the mock documentary. But whereas *Take the Money* was clearly a crude, likable early experiment, *Zelig* is the sophisticated filmmaker's return to this technique. We see his growth, both as a thinker and a craftsman, in the way he approaches relatively similar stuff. Peter Biskind likened the film to two others of roughly the same time when he called it a "cross between *The Elephant Man* and *Dead Men Don't Wear Plaid*," the former another sympathetic portrait of a celebrity freak, the latter an interesting experiment in which Steve Martin appeared to enter the world of old gangster movies through clever editing and trick effects.

But if Allen's work was effectively part of a popular movement toward heightened realism in the popular arts (docudramas often monopolizing the movie and made-for-TV-movie forms), Allen's approach was uniquely his own. His fascination with the styles of the past (the Gershwin music in *Manhattan*, the black-and-white style of shooting he loves to employ) lent themselves beautifully to this story of the first half of our century, and of a man who came to represent what was best and worst about it. Allen's growth in skill as a technician is even more in evidence here than it was in *Manhattan*, as he painstakingly supervised the compilation of still photographs and film archive material onto which his fictional character would be superimposed.

In *Take the Money*, the documentary effect was occasionally dropped for comic interchanges between the characters. But in *Zelig*, Woody confined himself completely to the mock documentary: There is no interchange between any of the characters—mainly Zelig and his psychiatrist, Dr. Eudora Fletcher (Mia Farrow), with whom he falls in love—that could not have been logically recorded. This caused some long-time Woody Allen fans to be disappointed, since there are few dialogue sequences in the film. It is an absolutely seamless imitation of a TV documentary, including interviews with people who knew the character and comments from experts about what the subject meant to the public. Everything is as it would be in a documentary film except the subject, who never existed.

More than just exhibiting mastery of craft, though, this becomes the key to the meaning of the film. "The skill," Stanley Kauffmann wrote in a rare word of praise for Woody, "is so clever as to approach brilliance. I ignore dozens of gifted artists and technicians when I single out Santo Loquasto for costume designs that combine accuracy with slyness. Allen, as a director, shows a keen eye for the way people looked, and thought they looked, in the period: the way they glanced at cameras, posed themselves for photographs, or invented 'business' for newsreels. Behind all this is not only a careful study of period materials, which many directors have done, but a sensitivity to cultural change. Allen, looking back from the present, perceives that this moment is a point of transition from the film camera as an ornament of civilization to a central component of consciousness."

A few critics tried to turn the film's technical brilliance back on itself, suggesting that Woody had created an effective but ultimately innocuous experiment. "The most daring idea for a film Woody Allen has had so far," John Simon applauded. But his mood quickly soured: "The film is supposed to be a fable about fame in the U.S.A., about the fickleness of the public...the technique is fascinating and a triumph for Gordon Willis, the excellent cinematographer, who here has surpassed himself....Altogether, *Zelig* is a curious example of a film with too much cleverness for its own good....The art of assemblage, instead of enhancing the semblance of reality, proves an inadequate way of dissembling: the cunningly joined snippets challenge us to peer behind them and discover the central hollowness." However, the "central hollowness" of Zelig is the *subject* of the film, not a failing of Allen's artistry. The point of the picture is that inside every celebrity there is a hollow man who feels the status he has achieved goes far beyond anything he deserves.

So Simon's criticism seems less correct than Jack Kroll's praise when, in *Newsweek*, he glowingly reported that this was "a brilliant cinematic collage that is pure magic, and allows Woody to satirize all sorts of things, from nostalgia, psychoanalysis and The American Dream to critics, himself and much more....His Zelig is a romantic who desperately wants the supreme cocktail of realism mixed with glory—the Great Gatsby as schlemiel." Kroll's last phrase is more than just a clever quip. Throughout his career, Woody has attempted a romantic statement, and his characters have often bordered on a Gatsby-ish vision of life: longing for the ideal, feeling vaguely disappointed with the possible.

Woody insists on the Gatsby connection here by beginning and ending the film with quotes from Scott Fitzgerald. The most romantic of twentieth century American writers is, according to the narrator, the first person of note to comment on Leonard Zelig, first seen hobnobbing with the high society of the late twenties, then conversing with the kitchen help. At the film's end, it is Fitzgerald who is again our source of information and opinion:

228

Zelig meets heavyweight champion Jack Dempsey and immediately adjusts by turning into an athlete himself.

"Wanting to be liked, he distorted himself beyond measure." Thus, the framing device for the film is Fitzgerald's voice, and Woody understandably allows Zelig a romantic adventure Fitzgerald would have understood. After all, Zelig conforms in order to be accepted, but comes out of his defense mechanism when encouraged to by the woman he loves. She is played by Mia Farrow, Allen's current inamorata and the actress who portrayed Daisy in the contemporary film version of Fitzgerald's *The Great Gatsby*. Gatsby, of course, is a character who like Zelig repressed his own personality in order to be accepted by the society of that time.

All the same, Zelig can express Allen, just as his earlier persona in a documentary-style film—*Take the Money*—did. For instance, early in the film, Zelig turns into a gangster, a jazz musician, and a psychiatrist. Woody expressed interest in becoming the first as a child, has constantly worked as the second, and maintains an abiding interest in the third. Zelig tells us that, as a child, he wanted to be a ballplayer, which doesn't sound very different from his creator. When his doctor takes him off to the woods to try and cure his strange malady, Zelig tells her under hypnosis, "I hate the country...the grass and the mosquitoes...," sounding very much like the comedian/filmmaker who is "at two with nature." His food fetish is also in evidence: "Your pancakes," Zelig tells Eudora while under hypnosis, "I drop them on the ground when you're not looking...your cooking is terrible...I love you... you're the worst cook...I love you." Fortunately, bad food does not here preclude good sex: Zelig and Eudora are well suited to each other.

As Gatsby was for Fitzgerald, Zelig is a created character through whom Allen can dramatize some of his most pressing personal concerns. One of those is the tendency of critics to overinterpret his work. An ironic contrast appears between an author who has written a book called *Interpreting Zelig* and, a moment later, Susan Sontag (playing herself), author of *Against Interpretation*. Just as each doctor who tries to determine the reason for Zelig's strange condition insists it has to do with his own specialty, so too does each "expert" insists that Zelig can be be explained from his own specific field. Noted analyst Bruno Bettelheim asks the question, "Was Zelig a psychotic or extreme neurotic?" "All the great themes of our culture were there," Irving Howe insists, interpreting Zelig as he interprets everything else. The French critics, we are told, had a heyday, for in Zelig they saw a symbol for everything.

Amazingly, Allen was able to persuade many prestigious figures to appear in what amounted to satires on themselves. Interesting also is the fact that Allen's use of "experts" to talk about the past and

very often contradict one another on key points spoofs the technique employed by Warren Beatty for *Reds*, his monumental film starring himself and Diane Keaton, formerly Woody's leading lady on camera and off.

"Certainly," Michiko Kakutani wrote, "Zelig's gradual discovery of his identity mirrors Allen's own discovery, as a writer and director, of a distinctive cinematic voice." Woody did indeed become a celebrity-director by parodying the filmmaking styles of others, symbolized in the film when Zelig achieves fame by becoming more like those around him. In *Annie Hall* and *Manhattan*, Woody found his own voice, just as Zelig manages to break himself of the habit of imitating others. But in *Interiors* and *Stardust Memories*, Woody reverted to imitations of Bergman and Fellini, just as Zelig experiences a relapse. A totally different but extremely ripe possibility is that Zelig symbolizes the Jewish American experience, seduced by the appeal of assimilation into the mainstream. Most fascinating is that the film comfortably supports all these various interpretations, in part because it is prismatic: various ideas, themes, and meanings may be logically deduced from it, though the film itself is not limited to any one of these ideas.

Vanity Fair viewed *Zelig* as the natural end product of two of Woody's longest running concerns: "After years of working thinly disguised autobiography and a documentary style into a vision of filmmaking as therapy, Woody Allen has come up with a movie in which he says as much about himself as he does about art." It is, incidentally, the most focused image he has yet provided of the therapeutic experience, one in which he sees it as being parallel to a love affair; although the analysis does not completely cure Zelig, it does indeed help him understand himself better.

When Zelig is in the presence of his analyst, he of course thinks of himself as an analyst, and what he says is noteworthy. "I'll try to help, but we can't promise anything," he warns the doctor who is posing as a patient in order to break through. His temporary role-playing as an analyst allows Woody one of his few characteristic gag lines: "I broke with Freud on the concept of penis envy," he wryly tells us. "He felt it should be restricted to women." Like the mainstream masterpiece *Manhattan*, this arthouse experiment is a stunning success mainly because Allen includes a few such gems while limiting the number of them, achieving that perfect balance he had so long sought between his comic talent and his serious intentions.

Most critics lauded the picture: "It's a summation and a perfection of methods and ideas that have been turning up in all his films," Vincent Canby wrote in *The New York Times*. Certainly, the idea that

Zelig, the elder statesman, meeting with former President Calvin Coolidge (left) and President Herbert Hoover.

Zelig is a man who would rather be anyone other than himself can be seen as the ultimate extension of characters like Allan Felix in *Play It Again, Sam*. In *Time*, Richard Schickel noted that Allen's concern with language is also an issue here: "Acutely satirizing mediaspeak, the film hilariously exposes the vulgarizations and misleading distortions of that language."

Whether it's the people who proudly mouth the most obvious ideas when interviewed on the streets or the ponderous sound of the narrator's voice as he tries to imply connections between Zelig and his times that may be forced or fanciful, this—the most visual and cinematic of all Allen's movies— is also, paradoxically, his most perceptive statement about how the beauty of the English language is degraded by its popular misuse. "Everything in the jazz age moves too quickly," the narrator insists, "like Red Grange," as the camera cuts to a newsreel shot of the great football player in action.

231

But everything in the jazz age did not move too fast (certainly, political and social reform did not), and those things that did move fast had nothing whatsoever to do with Red Grange, who was an isolated phenomenon. It was an easy metaphor, quick and obvious and seemingly an unassailable truth that in actuality is totally false.

Allen's long-time love of a different branch of the media is also clear. At two different points in *Zelig*, we see scenes from the Warner Brothers motion picture version of his life, *The Changing Man*. What's remarkable is that Allen not only captured perfectly the look and the sound of that particular studio's style, but by contrasting these two key scenes from the movie version with the "actual" incidents, reminds us of how much the biographical films played with reality. Zelig and Eudora are portrayed by far more attractive people in the film; everything is simplified and sentimentalized in the movie version, as the syrupy music and arch dialogue reduces Zelig's unique story to grist for The Dream Factory's mill. Allen captures the charm of such hokey old films while also parodying their excesses. This type of bit is what keeps Zelig from running out of steam. There was the possibility (and some critics argued this was the case) that the film would state a fascinating premise, hold the audience for a while, and then have nowhere to go except endlessly to repeat its basic gag. What keeps that from becoming a problem is the way Allen makes this a series of variations on a single theme: each divergence on the basic *Zelig* premise allows him to express yet another of his earlier themes in a new way, and in many cases round them out.

Leonard Zelig is lauded, marketed and exploited; hated, forgotten, rediscovered; he is the perfect symbol for all celebrities, but especially those who achieve their status by allowing an audience to glimpse, in that image onscreen, something of themselves. "He was amusing," one of the experts says, "but he also touched a nerve in people." The same could be said of Woody Allen.

Thematically complex and technically astute, *Zelig* may have failed to delight the mass audience (which still hoped, apparently, for another *Play It Again, Sam*) but certainly dazzled the audience Allen always aspired to: the intellectuals. Though they compared it to *Citizen Kane*, the even happier truth is that *Zelig* is in many respects the purest expression of Allen's own unique sensibility, a one-of-a-kind film, an absolute original that mixes just enough of Allen's peculiar sense of humor to qualify it as a comedy with his particular concerns about everything from the value of relationships to the effect of media on the audience that experiences it.

The Gospel According to Woody:

BROADWAY DANNY ROSE

An Orion Pictures Release (1984)

CAST:

Woody Allen *(Danny Rose)*; Mia Farrow *(Tina Vitale)*; Nick Apollo Forte *(Lou Canova)*; The Carnegie Deli Comics: Corbett Monica, Howard Storm, Morty Gunty, Sandy Baron, Will Jordan, Jackie Gayle, Jack Rollins *(Themselves)*; Milton Berle *(Himself)*; Howard Cosell *(Himself)*; Joe Franklin *(Himself)*; Craig Vanderburgh *(Ray Webb)*; Hugh Reynolds *(Barney Dunn)*; Paul Greco *(Vito Rispoli)*; Frank Renzulli *(Joe Rispoli)*; Edwin Bordo *(Johnny Rispoli)*; Gina De Angelis *(Johnny's Mother)*; Gloria Parker *(Water Glass Virtuoso)*; Bob and Etta Rollins *(Balloon Act)*; John Doumanian *(Waldorf Manager)*; Leo Steiner *(Deli Owner)*.

CREDITS:

Producer, Robert Greenhut; executive producer, Charles H. Joffe; production designer, Mel Bourne; associate producer, Michael Peyser; casting, Juliet Taylor; director, Woody Allen; writer, Woody Allen; photography, Gordon Willis; editor, Susan E. Morse; costume designer, Jeffrey Kurland; Rating: PG; running time, 85 minutes.

In many respects, the character Allen plays in *Broadway Danny Rose* is an extension of Jerry Wexler, a supporting figure in Allen's play *The Floating Light Bulb*, an extrovert who comes on like a hot-shot agent but is only an ever hopeful huckster, his biggest client being a talking dog. In a generally dismal review of that show, Frank Rich of *The New York Times* wrote that this character, played by Jack Weston, was the most convincing: "Allen clearly knows such small-time show biz hustlers to their bones. Weston is full of big talk—he has met Jimmy Durante and Cesar Romero—but his own clients turn out to be fleabag acts that play 'the mountains.' Still, he's more than a tired flim-flam artist: he's also a sad, overgrown momma's boy who lacks the courage to seize the moment...." Most critics concurred this particular character provided the high point of a play that was otherwise Allen's ineffective attempt to imitate Tennessee Williams' *The Glass Menagerie*. Allen obviously agreed: three years later, he

Woody Allen as Broadway Danny Rose.

built an entire film script around just such a man, this time giving him the necessary courage to "seize the moment."

The anecdotal quality of the film combines the complex narrative techniques of Joseph Conrad (it's a tale overheard, and the audience to whom the story is being told strongly affects the tone of the story itself) with the texture of Damon Runyon (assorted New York types, humorously presented as they scurry about the Big Apple in search of the big time). More a short story than a novel on film,

Broadway Danny Rose is low key in its approach and might be viewed as one of Allen's minor works, a mere trifle. But as a genre piece, this is completely satisfying and thoroughly charming, a bittersweet moral fable that has the audience laughing aloud early on, then emotionally moved toward the end. Into this Runyonesque world, Allen was able to project all his own concerns; while the "form" of the film may be a pre-existing genre, the "content" is uniquely Allenesque.

According to Michiko Kakutani in *The Sunday Times,* Allen was inspired to write the film when, several years earlier, he and Mia Farrow were having dinner in a New York restaurant. Also enjoying the Italian cuisine that night was a woman who perfectly

233

The Comics: (clockwise, from top left) Corbett Monica, Jackie Gayle, Sandy Baron, Will Jordan, Howie Storm, Jack Rollins, Morty Gunty.

incarnated a type, the kind of bleached blonde in dark sunglasses who chainsmokes as she sits on the edge of a seedy show biz shadowland. "Mia mentioned it would be fun to play that kind of woman—just to try, and I took her seriously," Woody told Kakutani. "I think she somehow, down deep, felt—maybe without knowing it herself—that she could do that kind of thing. I'd always wanted to do something about that whole milieu, and when she mentioned that, one thing led to another in my mind over a period of time and it sort of fell into place." Certainly, Mia Farrow's performance in the film is the most fascinating screen work she has ever done. Her delicate, ethereal beauty is almost unrecognizable as the cheap blonde who inhabits a twilight zone existence somewhere between the top levels of a Mafia lifestyle and the lower periphery of the entertainment world.

But the film is something more than a vehicle for Mia Farrow to demonstrate a previously untapped talent. Vincent Canby would call it "a love letter not only to American comedy stars and to all of those pushy hopefuls who never quite make it to the top in show biz, but also to the kind of comedy that nourished the particular genius of Woody Allen." In specific, Canby refers to the small clubs and side rooms where struggling singers and hopeful comics once plied their trade.

The movie begins in the Carnegie Deli, where

234

seven middlingly successful comic veterans congregate, seemingly by accident, and begin to swap wistful, whimsical stories of the good old days, and those people who struggled to make the big time, came within reach of the golden apple, and somehow never quite managed to seize it. Their conversation, and the yarns they spin (especially about one pathetic but sympathetic agent, Danny Rose) all have an edge of nostalgia to them, belonging to a Runyonesque period from the clouded, charming terrain of the imperfectly remembered past; yet the clothing and the cars all suggest the story is taking place now. The effect is not so much disconcerting as it is delightful: *Broadway Danny Rose* allows us to feel nostalgic about the present.

One of the comics (Sandy Baron) tells the greatest Danny Rose story of all: how Danny, who always represented clients no one else wanted (a husband and wife team who twisted balloons into dachsund shapes, a woman who played songs on glasses), tried to stage a comeback for a washed-up Italian balladeer named Lou Canova (Nick Apollo Forte), who back in the fifties briefly had a single hit record and has since degenerated into an overweight, egotistic alcoholic. Owing to the nostalgia craze, Milton Berle has agreed to catch Lou's act and consider using him on a TV show. But after hustling this opportunity for Lou, Danny learns that his nervous performer will not be able to go on stage at all unless his girl friend, Tina Vitale (Mia Farrow), is there. Since Lou's wife will be present, it's Danny's job to act as The Beard and bring Tina. Danny's attempts to get the tempermental Tina to the show are underscored by an irony: Danny's problem has always been that whenever an act he pushes actually makes it, the first thing that happens is the dropping of Danny Rose in favor of a big-name agent. Tina has already introduced Lou to just such an agent, and if Lou scores well during his performance, Danny will be out.

Talking about the early Allen personas, Diane Jacobs wrote "they have perfect comic faith in the efficacy of their most ludicrous illusions, which take them out of the realm of despair and into crime, revolution and, a bit more successfully, romantic love." Replace revolution with show business, but keep everything else she mentions, and you have an apt description of *B.D.R.*, which reveals a great deal not only about the central character but also the conception for this project. Though Woody remains, on a technical level, at his most sophisticated, the story is in many respects a throwback to his earlier work, the kind of funny films the aliens in *Stardust Memories* told Sandy Bates they wished he were still making. In a sense, then, *B.D.R.* is a perfect compromise—a film that satisfied Allen the artist by allowing him to create those highly sophisticated black-and-white visual schemes he so loves, and which satisfied his fans by giving them the blend of humor and sentiment they most enjoy. As Jonathan Baumbach argued in *Commonweal*, the film "disguises its ambitions in apparent modesty. Next to the innovative *Zelig*, *B.D.R.* seems a skillful entertainment, an interlude between serious projects. [But] the film's seeming offhandedness is its disguise. Almost all of Allen's obsessions, emotional and artistic, make appearance."

There is no more obvious Allen obsession than food, and no Allen film that is more filled with images of food than *B.D.R.* The movie begins and ends with an image of the Carnegie Deli, and all the storytelling takes place over plates of kosher meat. When, early in the anecdote, Danny visits Lou at a third-rate club where he's performing his "Great Crooners of the Past Who Are Deceased" medley, he offers to forego his agent's fee until Lou can get back on his feet. "You gotta live, too," Lou insists as he downs a plate of food, "*you* gotta eat!" Eating will, before the picture's end, become the key metaphor for human contact: for friendship and for love. As Sandy Baron's narrator quickly tells us, "Danny did everything for Lou…picked his clothes with him…even *ate* with him." But in the enormous restaurant of contemporary life, Danny is one of those small fish and, as Hecky Brown once warned Howard Prince in *The Front*, the sharks are everywhere. Out of loyalty to Lou, Danny compromises himself by lying to Lou's wife and insisting, over dinner, that the blonde he will bring to Lou's performance is his own girl friend. "Fantastic fettucine," he tells her while almost choking on it, and his own lies.

He is not the only small creature in the film in danger of being eaten by something larger; indeed, one of his clients, a trainer of exotic birds, complains that his act cannot go on because "Pee Wee's been eaten by a feline." More than just a good but unrelated gag, it serves as the central metaphor for what Danny (and, for that matter, all the other Allen personas) live in constant danger of. More than anything else, it is the crazed Mafiosi (mistakenly believing Danny has taken Tina away from their brother who loves her) who threaten to devour him; significantly, they are first glimpsed, at the lavish Italian party to which Danny follows Tina, as they (and everyone else) heartily down piles of food. Even as Tina is seen speaking on the phone in the foreground of a shot, we can clearly see a crowd of people in the background stuffing themselves.

Escaping them, Danny and Tina move tentatively toward the love that will eventually blossom, as they sit in the most appropriate of places, a diner. All the

235

Lou Canova (Nick Apollo Forte), overweight, alcoholic, and egotistical, tells his agent Danny that he must act as a "beard."

Danny attempts to guide Lou through the performance that could spell a comeback for him.

Lou, briefly a singing sensation back in the fifties, may ride the wave of nostalgia to a comeback on Milton Berle's TV special.

while, people around them devour plates of food, though Danny and Tina apparently eat nothing, even though they work up a hunger for each other that neither is yet clearly aware of. But when the threatening brothers suddenly appear outside, Tina is quick to use food as a metaphor for death as well as life: "Do what I tell you," she warns Danny, "or you'll end up on a meathook." In flashback, we also learn that her hunger for Lou's success leads her to a restaurant meeting with the agent who may replace Danny. From this shot, the camera cuts to the two threatening brothers, stopping their pursuit momentarily to stuff themselves with pizza. Every character in the film has a hunger—for love, for success, for revenge—and each hunger momentarily is represented onscreen by the universal hunger for food.

"All my life, I never got in any trouble," Danny squeelingly tells Tina. "I ate the right *foods*." But that does not protect him from the dangers of the moral spiderweb he stepped into when he agreed to act as Lou's Beard. At the end, when Lou has succeeded and immediately dumps Danny, we see the nearly destitute agent still caring for his pathetic clients, and the means of expressing his love is again food: The lovable losers sit around his apartment, unwrapping frozen turkey dinners for their Thanksgiving meal. Remarkably, the scene is handled with such finesse that it doesn't become cloying; it is touchingly humorous and at the same time quite sad.

Tina, at last realizing she's in love with Danny, shows up and is at first rebuked. Quickly, though, Danny realizes his mistake—however fallable and flawed a person she may be, she is still worthwhile, and her growth in moral understanding is clear from the very act of showing up—so he pursues her onto the street.

They meet, quite perfectly, in front of the Carnegie Deli, the very place where the comics will eventually tell the story of Danny Rose. Danny and Tina break through to one another in front of the restaurant that, while not enormous, still has a huge appeal for Woody, symbolizing as it does a beloved link with New York's wonderful history of show business's second string. And as a reward for his saint-like "acceptance, forgiveness, and love" (as his

237

Danny must take Lou's mistress, Tina Vitale (Mia Farrow) to the show if Danny is to go on.

Tina is furious because she has heard a rumor Lou was seen at the race track with a cheap blonde; she has no idea that she herself is the cheap blonde.

During their brief adventure, Danny and Tina argue constantly, not realizing they are falling in love.

uncle once commanded him to treat other human beings), Danny Rose gets the perfect enshrinement for a film that's been dominated by food imagery: "They named a sandwich after him," one of the comics pronounces in the film's final line. Danny Rose has lived out the unconscious aim of every earlier Woody Allen hero: He has become food.

In the Catholic church, the ritual of eating the communion wafer is meant to symbolize the eating of Christ's flesh; in this Jewish agnostic's profoundly moral (and, in his own way, religious) vision, the eating of that sandwich by the multitudes who congregate in the church called The Carnegie Deli will likewise be partaking of the saint-like Danny. As Jack Kroll noted in *Newsweek*: "In Danny, Woody's classic schlemiel becomes a kind of saint, watching over his stable of lame acts like Francis over the animals. Like all saints, Danny must be rejected.... When Lou, goaded by his hard-as-nails mistress...dumps Danny for another agent, it's Judas time

in the gospel according to Woody." Paradoxically, the Jewish intellectual among modern moviemakers is also one of the few interested in making movies that are Christian allegories. Of course, the notion of any artist writing for himself a role so clearly Christlike could be viewed as an act of extreme egotism, but the criticism falters when one closely examines Danny and the way he operates. He is no saviour, pure and simple; he has his dark side, as he lies to Lou's wife and agrees to a deceitful action he feels in his heart is wrong (he seems aware, throughout, that it is his own guilt that causes all his problems with the mob and even legitimizes the eventual betrayal by Lou). When the mob boys string him up, he gets them to go away by throwing out the name of a totally innocent man, Barney Dunn, insisting he's the guy they really want. This is almost forgotten by him and by the audience watching the film until Danny is abruptly confronted with the fact that as a result of Danny's desperate attempt to save himself and Lou, Barney was brutally beaten. To keep from being devoured by a larger fish, Danny devoured a smaller one; survival has its price. *B.D.R.* is about learning to live with the consequences

239

of one's actions; it's also about that long-held Allen concept of courage. He has admitted, in interviews, his fear that he would not bear up well under torture by enemy agents, and Danny is the figure who most completely represents that fear onscreen.

But if he is neither pure nor simple, he is indeed a saviour: like so many of the Chaplin characters, who have their dark sides but are far purer than the morally ignorant crowds around them who feel neither guilt nor remorse for their failures of nerve, Danny is, at least in comparison to everyone else in his world, a kind of radical innocent. That gives him, like the Chaplin hero, a therapeutic quality: by mere exposure to him, the female character can come to a new kind of consciousness. *B.D.R.* could be subtitlted "The Education of Tina," since it is about her growing consciousness: the way she becomes worthy of Danny. In this sense, the film is the most romantic Allen movie yet. Previous Allen heroes held ideal images of the women in their heads, then gradually had to come to grips with the distinction between their romantic notions and the realities of those women. Danny Rose apparently thinks of Tina as little more than a cheap blonde, but his "realistic" image of her turns out to be false when she at the end proves to be more of a "romantic" figure than he ever hoped for by giving up everything to be with him.

At the Carnegie Delicatessen, the comics swap stories about the legendary Danny Rose.

"You've got to have a little faith in people," Tracy told Isaac at the end of *Manhattan*. Whether Isaac was able to learn that lesson or not, we'll never know, but certainly that is the lesson Danny has learned. Most of the people he has faith in do not deserve the emotions he lavishes on them, yet he continues to do so anyway. Danny may, at a crucial moment, have a failing of courage, but never of faith. That quality is what lends Danny the stature that this pipsqueek of a loser has amassed by the movie's end. Jonathan Baumbach of *Commonweal* tags the film "a comedy about mythmaking," and that it is. The stories Danny inspires may be funny, but they are also reverential; and in our secular society, what befits a legend more than having a sandwich named after him in the shrine of the Carnegie Deli? It may be the greatest immortality any Allen character has yet achieved.

Immortality carries with it the notion of death. "He's a dead man," one of the toughs says early on of Danny, and we believe throughout that the threat is a real one. At his worst moments, Danny survives by becoming like Leonard Zelig: At the big Italian party, he attempts to say what everyone wants to hear. And, speaking of Zelig, there is at least a touch of that documentary quality that has always haunted Allen's films: The presence of Milton Berle, Joe Franklin, and Howard Cosell, all playing themselves, lends the film authenticity, a touch of the real-life backdrops into which Zelig's fictional story was set.

*Mia Farrow's delicate, ethereal beauty is unrecognizable as she
plays the vulgar, gum-snapping, hip-swinging Tina Vitale.*

241

Allen here deals with concepts that were present in earlier pictures. The notion of a friend cheating on his wife is a variation on a theme introduced with Yale in *Manhattan*; the notion of the Allen hero becoming interested in the girl who "belongs" to his buddy relates to both that film and the earlier *Play It Again, Sam*. The entire concept of The Beard can hardly help but remind us of the basic dramatic device in *The Front*. The vulgar Tina turns out to be a would-be interior decorator, creating a link to the mother's profession in *Interiors*. All of the violent problems are caused by Tina's tendency to flirt, without ever considering the consequences; though the context here is comic, that was also what led to the violent confrontation between Flynn and Frederick in the dramatic *Interiors*. Tina's marriage is in many ways the ultimate image of all those earlier Allenesque visions of a union so terrifying one must flee from it. And there is Allen's tendency to draw on movie mythology: In *Stardust Memories*, *The Bicycle Thief* is not only cited but heatedly discussed; in *B.D.R.*, a scene from that film is virtually replayed, as Tina goes to an elderly Italian lady who serves as a medium and fortune teller.

There is a resemblance between Danny and some of the early, insecure Allen heroes: "I'm never going to be Cary Grant," he admits to Tina, though she (like previous incarnations of the Allen heroine) quickly tells him she's never cared much for handsome men, and is turned on by intellect. Still, Richard Blake of *America* saw him not so much as a recycling of the early Allen heroes, but an intriguing step in a new direction: "Danny is a fast talker and as slick as an eel in chicken fat, but he is loving and loyal....In *B.D.R.* he is no longer the perpetual underdog; he is the guardian angel of underdogs." Like Gatsby, Danny is pursued for a sin he didn't commit rather than for the one he did; and while Tina Vitale may be the inverse of Daisy Buchanan—rough and vulgar instead of soft and sophisticated—Mia Farrow brings to this character, as she earlier did to Daisy, the notion of a woman who sees herself quite differently than anyone around her does. She may not, like several earlier Allen heroines, announce immediately "I'm trouble," but she certainly is just that, which adds to her fascination.

Guilt, that key aspect of earlier Allen films, haunts this one: "It's important to feel guilty," Danny says, "otherwise you're capable of terrible things." Then brilliantly deflating what could be an overly ponderous statement, Allen undercuts it with comedy: "I'm guilty all the time, and I never did anything." When Danny and Tina get lost, it is in nature, which both appear "at two with"; the ugly flatlands ("My husband's friends used to drop bodies here," Tina calmly explains) looks like a cross between T. S. Eliot's The Wasteland and The Valley of Ashes from *Gatsby*. When Danny says, "We all want what we can't have in life," he is truly speaking of the gospel according to Woody. When he and Tina have their major moral argument, we see the dichotomies of this moral fable. "*My* philosophy—you've got to suffer," Danny says. "*My* philosophy—do it to the other guy before he does it to you," Tina replies. Before the picture is over, she will have been won over to his view. Courage is everything, the test; in the last scene, she will at last get passing grades. When Danny pursues her from his apartment to the street, the travelling shot of him running takes on extra resonance by reminding us of an earlier, similar run. This is a replay of Isaac's frantic race to Tracy's apartment in *Manhattan*, played out here with lowlife rather than high society characters.

"For Woody Allen fans," Linda-Marie Delloff wrote in *The Christian Century*, "this film is a joy. It heralds a return to his earlier style of verbal comedy joined with some action-slapstick humor, while at the same time retaining the serious thread that has run through his more recent films." A few critics were rough: Stanley Kauffmann wrote in *The New Republic* that "we have the paradox of a nervous realist writing about a sentimental domain that no longer exists and dealing with it harshly," while Pauline Kael of *The New Yorker* complained of a "curdled Diane Arbus bleakness," insisting this "is the only time a Woody Allen picture has made me feel he was writing down—trying for a crowd pleaser." But the paradox Kauffmann complains of is better taken as an apt description of Allen's complex and highly unique vision; and while Kael is correct about the Diane Arbus quality (Arbus and Allen have a legitimate resemblance as artists), she is wrong in saying Woody is "trying" for a crowd pleaser. He is, in fact, effectively producing one.

In her review of the previous Woody Allen film, *Zelig*, Kael had written: "If it's a masterpiece, it's a masterpiece only of its kind...like a teeny carnival that you may have missed—it was in the yard behind the Methodist church last week." But the essential unfairness of such a condescending attitude toward a filmmaker who successfully creates self-consciously small works is offset by Richard Corliss's appreciation of that very style in *Time*: "To the honor roll of artists who worked in miniature—Vermeer, Webern, Faberge, the medieval philosophers who squeezed a chorus line of angels onto the head of a pin—add Woody Allen's name." In other words, "little" does not necessarily imply "small."

I Lost It at the Movies:

THE PURPLE ROSE OF CAIRO

An Orion Pictures Release of a Rollins-Joffe Production (1985)

CAST:

Mia Farrow *(Cecilia);* Jeff Daniels *(Tom Baxter, Gil Shepherd);* Danny Aiello *(Monk);* Irving Metzman *(Theatre Manager);* Stephanie Farrow *(Cecilia's Sister);* David Kieserman *(Diner Boss);* Ed Herrmann *(Henry);* John Wood *(Jason);* Deborah Rush *(Rita);* Van Johnson *(Larry);* Zoe Caldwell *(The Countess);* Eugene Anthony *(Arturo);* Ebb Miller *(Bandleader);* Karen Akers *(Kitty Haynes);* Annie Joe Edwards *(Delilah);* Milo O'Shea *(Father Donnelly);* Dianne Wiest *(Emma);* Helen Hanft *(Movie Viewer).*

CREDITS:

Producer, Robert Greenhut; executive producer, Charles H. Joffe; production designer, Stuart Wurtzel; associate producers, Michael Peyser and Gail Sicilia; casting, Juliet Taylor; director, Woody Allen; writer, Woody Allen; photography, Gordon Willis; set decorator, Carol Joffe; editor, Susan E. Morse; costume designer, Jeffrey Kurland; original music, Dick Hyman; Rating: PG; running time, 81 minutes.

In Woody's award-winning short story "The Kugelmass Episode," the sexually starved humanities professor of the title enters Flaubert's novel *Madame Bovary,* becoming romantically involved with literature's most ravishing heroine. However, people then reading the book cannot understand why a contemporary Jewish guy has inexplicably leaped into the classic storyline. Likewise, when Emma Bovary leaves her book to join Sidney Kugelmass in New York, she has as much trouble adjusting to "the real world" as Sidney had trying to exist in her aesthetically re-created Paris. The premise was precisely right for a short story: "Kugelmass" was conceived of and constructed as a piece of prose because this medium perfectly fit the message. Still, many critics cited "The Kugelmass Episode" in their reviews of Woody's thirteenth film as a writer-director, *The Purple Rose of Cairo,* for it was clearly the motion picture equivalent of

"Kugelmass"—the film that says about film what that work of literature said about literature.

The title refers both to Allen's movie and to a movie-within-a-movie, one of those slick, sleek black-and-white *divertissements* that briefly brightened a few hours of people's mundane lives during the difficult days of the Great Depression. In particular, *"The Purple Rose"* is peopled by a group of cardboard cutout high-life Manhattanites (the men always wear tuxedos, the women are invariably glimpsed in evening gowns) who take up with a gentle explorer, Tom Baxter (Jeff Daniels), trekking in Egypt in search of a rare flower. *The Purple Rose* focuses on Cecilia (Mia Farrow), a battered wife and beleaguered waitress who spends one-third of her waking hours at the movies, one-third of them talking about the movies, one-third silently daydreaming about the movies. Essentially, Cecilia symbolizes the American public of the 1930s, people whose lives were so drab that they gladly grew hooked on the glamorous, glittery alternate world (life idealized, though the impossible perfection was made to seem achievable) in a way no other generation quite has; it's not for nothing the best-loved, most warmly remembered American movies were made during the troubled Thirties. That was the era when, as a people, we needed movies most and appreciated them best.

Writer-director Allen employs Cecilia to symbolize this syndrome by exaggerating it to the point of absurdity, allowing us to better understand the implications. The movies are so vivid and vital to Cecilia that one day, as she watches *"Puple Rose"* for the umpteenth time, Tom Baxter actually turns to the audience and addresses her directly, scampering down from the screen and slipping into her life. (There is no explanation for this miracle other than, as one character whimsically puts it, "In Jersey, *anything* can happen.") As Tom and Cecilia run away together, the others onscreen at the Jewel Theatre find themselves unable to continue the story without this key character, while the audience seated in the shabby little theatre grows angry that the story has stopped. Even as Allen examines the chaos brought to a work of art when an essential element is eliminated, he also slyly investigates the fascinating implications of a fictional character's treating real life as he would a series of movie situations. When Tom kisses Cecilia, he expects a conventionally discreet 1930s fadeout that doesn't occur; when he attempts to pay for a meal in a restaurant, he's shocked to learn play money won't do. Conversely, when the tables are turned and Cecilia joins him onscreen, she discovers her night on the town in Manhattan goes by in a matter of seconds, as a dissolve-montage effect that, in the classic Hollywood style, swiftly suggests the passage of considerable time.

The Purple Rose received some of the most ecstatic

243

reviews of Allen's career. In *Newsweek,* Jack Kroll called it a "gem, one of the shrewdest, funniest, most plaintive explorations of movies as dream machine and escape mechanism," while in *Time,* Richard Schickel similarly hailed it as "one of the best movies about movies ever made." In *The New York Times,* Vincent Canby insisted it offered "pure enchantment...a sweet, lyrically funny, multi-layered work that again demonstrates Woody is our premier film maker." A few critics were less thrilled, though even they were not harsh: Molly Haskell writing in *Vogue* dismissed it as "slight but charming"; David Denby in *New York* claimed it "wears thin pretty fast"; Bruce Williamson in *Playboy* argued that "movie fanatics and incurable

Woody Allen buffs are far likelier than anyone else to derive maximum enjoyment." But near-constant Allen critic Pauline Kael of *The New Yorker* called it "the most purely charming" of all Allen's films, "the fullest expression yet of his style of humor," insisting *P.R.* was both "gentle" and "complex," rating as "the first Woody Allen movie in which a whole batch of actors really interact and spark each other." Indeed, that's basic to this film's success: for the first time since the disastrous *Interiors,* Woody attempted an ensemble film in which he himself did not appear. This time, he pulled it off.

Canby continued: "I'd go so far as to rank it with two acknowledged classics, Luis Bunuel's *Discreet Charm of the Bourgeoisie* and Buster Keaton's *Sherlock, Jr.,* both of which it recalls though in no way imitates." Certainly, in his least successful films (*Interiors, Stardust Memories*) Allen attempted to impose his personal

During the Great Depression, ordinary Americans forget about their problems by going off to see glamorous movies like "The Purple Rose of Cairo." (Photo by Brian Hamill)

Cecilia (Mia Farrow) and her sister (Stephanie Farrow) work as waitresses but spend their time daydreaming. (Photo by Brian Hamill)

In ''the film within a film,'' glamorous explorers (Edward Herrman, John Wood, Deborah Rush) slip into an Egyptian Tomb. (Photo by Brian Hamill)

vision on an ersatz transcription of a great work by some artist he admires (Bergman, Fellini); at his most successful (*Manhattan, Zelig, Broadway Danny Rose*) he (as Canby aptly phrases it) recalls past masters (Renoir, Welles, Damon Runyon) without appearing to imitate them. In addition to Bunuel and Keaton, there are other influences here: in dealing with characters who self-consciously discuss their roles in the film they are trapped in, Allen may be influenced by Pirandello's *Six Characters in Search of an Author.* No wonder that in *The New Republic,* Stanley Kauffmann contended that *P.R.* "begins, as usual, with an arresting idea, new for [Woody] though not new in the history of film."

To a degree, that's a fair description of how Allen works. In another sense, though, the device employed in *P.R.* is not new even to Woody, for the film

Jeff Daniels as Tom Baxter and Gil Shepherd, a character in a glossy Hollywood movie and the actor who plays him. (Photo by Brian Hamill)

marks a conscious return to (and adjustment of) his approach in *Sam.* There, the unhappy Allan Felix was guided through his unexciting life by an irresistibly romantic figure from the movies, Bogey; in *P.R.,* Cecilia (Mia Farrow, made up to resemble the young Woody Allen) has much the same experience. Here, other people besides Cecilia actually see Tom Baxter step down off the screen; in *Sam,* Bogey's presence existed merely in Allan's imagination. "My whole life," Cecilia says after entering the magical world of movies, "I wondered what it would be like to be on *this* side of the screen"; "My whole life," Allan Felix admits after saying to a woman what Bogart tells Bergman at the end of *Casablanca,* "I've been waiting to say that to somebody." The films develop parallel plotlines and explore what Kauffmann calls Woody's major theme, "the sovereignty of fantasy even in the humblest." Where the films differ significantly is in their endings, and the opposite implications of what they "say."

For *Sam* concluded on a relatively optimistic note. In the play, Allan is last glimpsed entering into a serious relationship with an attractive young woman, having finally gone beyond his need to rely on Bogart and the movie mythology Bogey represents. *P.R.* offers a considerably darker view: we last glimpse Cecilia, having been courted by both Tom Baxter the movie character and by Gil Shepherd, the actor who plays Tom. Having lost them both (and, presumably, once more living with her lazy lout of a husband) she is back at the local Bijou, watching yet another fantasy on film. It's as if the older Allen felt the need to go back and correct, in maturity, the implications of his earlier statement. In his youth, Woody may have believed he (and we) could go beyond our need to rely on the vicariously experienced ideals of Hollywood films; in his later, bleaker adjustment of that vision, he tells us we will never make that great escape. Though Cecilia has come to understand the essential hollowness of Hollywood hokum, she remains hooked on its shimmering surfaces. She may have learned firsthand that this is only an empty if elegant illusion, but the dawning of this realization does not free her from a dependency on the opiate offered by the silver screen. Understanding that it's a drug does not end one's habit; knowledge, this appealing but demanding film tells us, does not bring freedom.

Interiors failed because Allen thought it necessary to temporarily suspend his comic gifts to ensure the proper degree of darkness for his statement; *P.R.* succeeds in large part because he came to see the two are not necessarily at odds. *P.R.* is filled with funny lines, but that doesn't take away from what's ultimately a tragic vision. The final image of Cecilia, robbed of her innocent dreams but not freed from her need for them, can bring an audience to the brink of tears.

In true Woody Allen fashion, her plight is schematized through her relationship to food. It's not for nothing Allen makes her a waitress rather than assigning her some other equally drab job (sales clerk, secretary). Early on, we see her mumbling mindlessly about her movie-fed fantasies even as she none too effectively serves food to a very real, and very hungry, clientele. At the greasy spoon diner, Cecilia daydreams about those people glimpsed eating at the Copacabana. Understandably, then, her relationship with her husband is defined by images not of affection or even marital responsibility but of food: "Any more meat loaf left?" is all Monk (Danny Aiello) wants to know. The highest compliment he can extend refers to a successful meal: "That stuff you made yesterday was delicious." When Cecilia considers leaving him, he's less worried about losing her sexually (he's already sleeping

Where do movies leave off and where does real life begin? Two characters (Zoe Caldwell, Van Johnson) in the "film within the film" stare back at the audience watching them. (Photo by Brian Hamill)

In comparison to the preferred world of Hollywood illusion, Cecilia must inhabit the real world where a vulgar husband (Danny Aiello) mistreats her. (Photo by Brian Hamill)

with someone else) or even her financial support (she works, he doesn't) than his stomach: "I want my supper" is all he can say to a wife desperately walking out the door.

Monk exists in contrast to Tom. Yet when Tom enters the real world, he too grows hungry: "I left the movie before the Copacabana scene," he explains to Cecilia. Naturally, she gets him appropriate food for someone associated with the movies: popcorn. Back at home, her husband expresses growing discontent through his negative reactions to the food she puts in front of him; stuffing himself with spaghetti, he complains, "There's too much pepper in the sauce." When Tom's double, actor Gil Shepherd, first meets Cecilia, she is in the process of buying food for Tom; when Gil gets interested in Cecilia, the conversation immediately shifts to food: "Can I buy you lunch?" he eagerly asks and, after *Manhattan,* we know all too well the sexual implications of *that* particular meal. Like all Woody Allen movies, *P.R.* is about hunger: the emotional starvation

The thin line between illusion and reality shatters when Tom Baxter (Jeff Daniels) walks off the screen and into Cecilia's (Mia Farrow) life. (Photo by Brian Hamill)

of Cecilia is ironically underscored by her necessity to serve literal, physical foodstuffs to every other key character. Importantly, she is the only one in the movie who never gets to eat anything.

Mostly, Cecilia is starved because of her abysmal marriage, a variation on a traditional Allen theme; marriage has served as a point of focus since the beginning of Woody's career. Cecilia's own marriage may be a brutal shambles—a sketched-in nightmare image of a blue collar marriage that might have been borrowed from James T . Farrell—but when Cecilia talks about Hollywood with her sister, she focuses on her fantasy image of star *marriages;* squealing with delight at Lew Ayres' possible coupling with Ginger Rogers, explaining why his previous union couldn't work. Later, we learn that no matter how unconventional Cecilia's imagination may be, her morality is most conventional: "I'm married," she insists to Tom when he tries to romance her. Indeed, marriage creates problems even for the characters still waiting to continue with the movie-within-the-movie: "I'm tired of

249

Cecilia (Mia Farrow) finds her humdrum everyday existence invaded by a character from the movies. (Photo by Brian Hamill)

250

Cecilia's idol from films (Jeff Daniels) and her husband (Danny Aiello) fight over her. (Photo by Brian Hamill)

marrying you every night," Van Johnson says to Zoe Caldwell. "We never even get to the bedroom." As in earlier Allen vehicles, the institution designed to (among other things) insure and enshrine sexual release in fact only gets in the way of it; Allen's attitude does not appear to have softened any over the years.

Woody's thematic maturity is countered by a parallel growth in technical accomplishment. Working with Gordon Willis, he created two unique and separate visual "worlds" here: the b & w of the movie-within-the-movie (*"The Purple Rose"* exists

midway between mimicry and nostalgia, a loving satire on thirties styles) and a carefully controlled color scheme for the movie itself. Pauline Kael could complain that "The Depression thirties was the era of Deco dishware and cheap and cheerful primary colors....The deep *Godfather* browns here are too serious." But she misses the point: this is, after all, not Woody's attempt at a docudrama re-creating the "real" 1930s (an era he did not, in fact, experience as an adult firsthand, and so could not accurately portray from personal experience), but rather Woody's visual statement about the thirties: what it means to him and to the rest of us who look back on it from today's

The ''stars'' of the movie within the movie: Jeff Daniels, Edward Herrmann, John Wood and Deborah Rush. (Photo by Brian Hamill)

The characters in "the film within the film" feel trapped behind the screen; from left to right, Milo O'Shea, Deborah Rush, John Wood and Edward Herrmann. (Photo by Brian Hamill)

perspective. Simply, we know that period primarily through movies like *The Godfather*, so in *P.R.* the thirties are perceived through the prism of recent movie images of that era. Actually, Woody created a witty contrast: the b & w of "*The Purple Rose*" is so varied, so richly textured in shades of gray (as so many movies of that period were) that the film almost appears to be in color; on the other hand, *The Purple*

Rose is so glum and unglamorous in its washed out hues that its color photography appears less colorful than the film within the film.

This visual distinction between the romantic and the realistic conveys, in the wordless language of the cinema, the movie's (and Allen's) basic theme. As Shickel wrote, "Movies like [the one] delicately parodied here proposed not just the possibility of perfect love at first sight but of permanent romantic transcendence." And that transcendence is the consistent subject of Allen's work. His sensibility is akin to that of F. Scott Fitzgerald when, in *The Great Gatsby*, he gave us that archetypal American romantic,

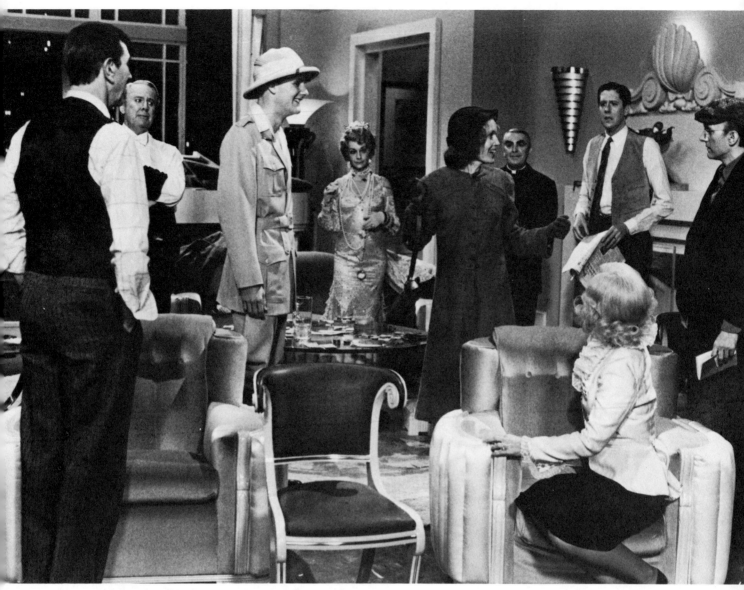

In the movie within the movie, the cast of characters (joined by Cecilia) prepare to go to the Copacabana. (Photo by Brian Hamill)

Jay Gatsby, but also created Nick Carraway, the realist who forms a necessary balance. At first, it seems Cecilia will be this film's romantic figure: "You're going to like ('The Purple Rose')," she tells her sister, "better than last week's —it's more romantic!" But when Tom makes the ultimate romantic gesture—leaving his fictional universe to join the woman he's fallen in love with in her real world—Cecilia feels the need to temper his romantic ardor with realism. "We'll live on love," he exclaims; "That's just movie talk," she sweetly reminds him. Indeed, Tom's rampant romanticism actually brings out the realist in Cecilia. "People get old," she

tells him about her world, adding: "and never find perfect love."

Importantly, then, Tom and Cecilia do not physically consummate their passion: their perfect idyll in the woods remains a platonic, pastoral moment, unsullied by experience. They remain like the figures on Keats's Grecian Urn— "Heard melodies are sweet, but those unheard are sweeter," so their sexual song remains unheard. Tom is clearly a total innocent, experiencing wonderment at the smell of a rose as though he were a figure from a poem by Shelley; he's the ultimate child-man, Wordsworth's child as swain, born into the world with a man's physique and intellect and a child's honest instincts. Cecilia's internal conflict is not between Tom and

her lout of a husband, but between Tom and Gil. They may look the same, and Gil may even affect a kind of nonchalant innocence that makes him seem to be one and the same with Tom. But Gil can only act innocent, while Tom *is* innocence. Cecilia's tragedy is that she sends Tom back to the screen, telling him they had a beautiful moment—a moment of romantic transcendence—which the romantic in her loved but which the realist in her knows cannot be made to last. With Gil, there is at least the hope of a permanent, ongoing relationship. But as soon as Gil has accomplished his task—getting Tom back on the screen where he belongs—he deserts Cecilia in a way Tom never would. Confusing an actor with the roles he plays, Woody reminds us, is dangerous.

Alone in the theatre at the end, Cecilia has learned the hard way that perfection exists only in art; but needing perfection, she resumes her addictive moviegoing. She is a person of romantic sensibility tempered by a realist's awareness: She is Woody Allen. We can at last understand, then, the source of Allen's famed anhedonia. It stems from romantic melancholia; he is forever wistfully nostalgic about a dream of perfection which he's intelligent and sophisticated enough to know is a sham. That knowledge, though, does not free him of the dream; he continues to instinctively yearn for its incarnation into reality, while forever consciously aware the ideal he longs for is unattainable. Thus, he experiences the worst of both possible worlds: a romantic's innocence and idealism, a realist's cynicism and pessimism. Which explains why describing him as our most significant comic filmmaker seems such an understatement.

A Resilient Organ:

HANNAH AND HER SISTERS

An Orion Pictures Release (1986)

CAST:

Woody Allen (*Mickey*); Michael Caine (*Elliot*); Mia Farrow (*Hannah*); Carrie Fisher (*April*); Barbara Hersey (*Lee*); Lloyd Nolan (*Hannah's Father*); Maureen O'Sullivan (*Hannah's Mother*); Daniel Stern (*Dusty*); Max Von Sydow (*Frederick*); Dianne Wiest (*Holly*); Sam Waterston (*The Architect*); Tony Roberts (*Mickey's Friend*); Helen Miller, Leo Postrel (*Mickey's Parents*); Bobby Short (*Himself*); John Doumanian (*Thanksgiving Guest*).

CREDITS:

Producer, Robert Greenhut; executive producers, Jack Rollins and Charles H. Joffe; associate producer, Gail Sicilia; director, Woody Allen; screenplay, Woody Allen; director of photography, Carlo Di Palma; film editor, Susan E. Morse; production designer, Stuart Wurtzel; costume designer, Jeffrey Kurland; color by Technicolor; running time, 115 minutes; Rating, PG-13.

Even before the public release of *Hannah* in February, 1986, advance word from Hollywood screenings boasted that the film would be perceived as 'accessible' to a mainstream audience in a way Woody's previous half dozen movies (even those which enjoyed a favorable critical reception) had not. This wave of positive pre-release publicity was articulated in *Newsweek*, which announced that *Hannah* "seems destined to have the greatest popular appeal of any Allen movie since *Annie Hall*." In the same story, Woody himself responded with charmingly characteristic negativism: "If you make a popular movie, you start to think, where have I failed? I must be doing something that's unchallenging, or reinforcing prejudices of the middle class or being simplistic or sentimental."

In fact, he was again being harder on himself than necessary; for once, a film lived up to its advance hype. *Hannah* immediately registered as a solid box-office success while the critics fawned. "Flat-out wonderful," claimed *Newsweek's* David Ansen. "A

beguiling new comedy," Richard Corliss called it in *Time*; "a great film, rich and complex," David Denby echoed in *New York*; "Allen's most ambitious work," Brian D. Johnson wrote in *MacLean's*. Even Pauline Kael paid it something of a backhanded compliment, hailing *Hannah* as "an agreeably skillful movie" in *The New Yorker*.

Longtime Allen detractor Stanley Kauffmann cast one of the few minority opinions in *The New Republic*: "The script gives the impression that Allen, who wrote it, keeps notes ... Allen, much like Neil Simon in method if not tone, deals in recognitions. We spot the hang-ups as we spot the locales." But such highbrow condescension misses the appeal of Allen at his best (or, for that matter, Simon at his best), and *Hannah* is most definitely Allen at his very best.

Essentially, the appeal of *Hannah* is twofold. On the one hand, it's a traditional Woody Allen film, full of those elements an audience associates with him: an obsession with death, a quest for love, a skeptical study of marriage, a glowing affection for both Manhattan and The Movies of a grander age, the importance of art and the creative process, and a fascination with food as a metaphoric bridge between the possible extremes of sex and death. Here, the most significant scene between the title characters takes place in "an enormous restaurant," where over lunch they at last reveal the long-repressed emotional anger these blood-bound women have been experiencing. Like Mia Farrow in *Purple Rose*, Woody's character Mickey resolves his problems while at a movie (it's the Marx Brothers in *Duck Soup*), while music associated with a grander age (from Bach to Basie) magically rises from the Manhattan streets.

Even Tony Roberts makes an unbilled appearance as Mickey's oldest friend, an agreeable reminder of their relationship in earlier films. On the other hand, *Hannah* marks a departure from Allen's previous pictures. At 115 minutes in length, *Hannah* is his longest film, something of a surprise from an artist who appeared content working to be in miniature. The cast was likewise the largest he had yet assembled, also suggesting an expansive canvas. For the first time, Woody played a supporting role in a broad ensemble rather than either creating an ensemble in which he did not appear or fashioning a film in which he was the central character. Important too is that the film was not photographed by Gordon Willis (who was unavailable), but by Carlo Di Palma, whose more muted photographic style gave Woody's recurring concerns a visual freshness.

This balance between a continuation of the old

Like Chekhov and Bergman before him, Allen concentrates on three sisters: Hannah (Mia Farrow), the perfect wife and actress; Lee (Barbara Hershey), the misunderstood beauty; and Holly (Dianne Wiest), the neurotic would-be artist.

Essentially a study of artists, commercial and ''pure,'' the film allows us to study the different approaches to life of April (Carrie Fisher), a song 'n' dance performer, and Frederick (Max Von Sydow), a serious and solipsistic reclusive painter.

and a move toward something new can be seen in the film's relationship to *Interiors*. That glum, unmemorable film told the story of three sisters, attempting to communicate Allen's key themes through the relationships of the women and their parents. The sisters here have strikingly close parallels to the sisters in the earlier film: Hannah (Mia Farrow) is a successful artist and therefore self-assured in her relations with men; Holly (Dianne Weist) has all the angst of an author but, she fears, none of the talent; Lee (Barbara Hershey) is the beauty, which causes her to be perceived – however unfairly – by everyone around her as superficial. As in *Interiors*, the husband of the serious artist in time grows distraught over a neurotic fear that he is not good enough for his talented wife, and attempts a seduction of his wife's beautiful sibling. Though not incest in any technical, scientific sense of the term, the seduction of a wife's sister becomes a key moral concern for Allen, implying as it does a man's divided loyalties between a sense of family and a healthy heterosexual fascination with female attractiveness.

But whereas the earlier film was depressing and downbeat, solemn in effect instead of serious in impact, the new one effectively made its points with telling humor. As Ansen wrote, "Anyone bemoaning the disappearance of adult matter from the movies need look no farther. Here Allen single-

As in so many earlier Allen films, a character cannot understand why attaining all he wants fails to make him happy: Eliot (Michael Caine) is not satisfied in life, despite winning the woman of his dreams, Hannah (Mia Farrow).

handedly restores glamour and substance ... He juggles these overlapping stories with novelistic finesse, counterpointing hilarity and pathos with almost faultless tact." It's as if Allen, alone among contemporary filmmakers, can learn from his own mistakes, which is why even a muddled mess like *Interiors* has its value: without it, we may never have experienced the pleasures offered by *Hannah*, for which the earlier film seems an awkward, uncertain dry run. If it took Allen an extremely long time to find his own metier, his special style, the wait was clearly worth it. The false starts and dead ends were necessary experiments; the masterpiece that is *Hannah and Her Sisters* was the prize waiting down the road.

Like *Interiors*, *Hannah*'s concentration on three sisters reveals Allen's continuing indebtedness to such past masters as Chekhov and Bergman. Now, though, he seems less an imitator of his idols than a mature artist who works in their league. "Finally absorbing the lesson of Chekhov all the way," David Denby wrote, "Allen sees comedy and drama not in his old fashion, as separate moods, but as

Mickey (Woody Allen), previously married to Hannah, is a death-obsessed neurotic, something the healthy Hannah cannot comprehend.

The Thanksgiving celebration, which has become as significant a symbol in Allen's films as Christmas was in the work of Frank Capra, is lorded over by Hannah's father (Lloyd Nolan) and mother (Maureen O'Sullivan).

While enjoying the catering that the "potato-salad Picassos" have created, a practical artist (Sam Waterston as an architect) flirts with April (Carrie Fisher).

inextricably mixed, with laughter growing out of the painful incongruities and humiliations of life, and pain falling helplessly and brutally from pleasure. The two theatrical masks have joined into one, with an immense gain in power."

Likewise, Pauline Kael noted that "Like Ingmar Bergman's *Funny and Alexander*, which was also about a theatrical family, the film is full of cultured people, and it has a comfortable positive tone.... Like Bergman, Allen shows his intellectuality by dramatizing his quest for meaning and then shows his profundity by exposing the aridity of that quest." In *Hannah*, Woody neatly schematizes his vision by having the film open on a Thanksgiving dinner, then concludes (and frames) the story two years later when a similar dinner is held by the same

family in the same apartment. The use of Thanksgiving itself is significant: this holiday is (much like Christmas in the special lexicon of Frank Capra comedies) repeated until it takes on a personal meaning within the body of the artist's work. Woody employed Thanksgiving when, at the end of *Broadway Danny Rose*, the poor talent agent and his sad little band of friends enjoyed their humble TV dinners together, while the appearance of Danny's lost ladylove suggested that he, like his friends, had much to be thankful for.

The characters in *Hannah* are, of course, quite

different: upscale New Yorkers, enjoying two turkeys in Hannah's Central Park West apartment. But for this gathered congregation, as for the uglier and less successful one in *B.D.R.*, the message is the same: there is, despite the overwhelming negative evidence to the contrary, much to be thankful for. This is neatly reflected in the way his character here, Mickey Sachs, serves as a recapitulation of all the earlier Allen heroes, but goes further in his journey toward self-knowledge than any of them. Like Isaac in *Manhattan*, Mickey is a successful TV producer who gets out of the rat race; like Alvy Singer, he is a hypochondriac obsessed with death. But Mickey moves beyond self-absorption and a failed marriage (to Hannah), eventually marrying her sister Holly. When he at the end shows up for the lavish Thanksgiving dinner, he may seem a far cry from poor Danny Rose, but this is rather the same scene, played out on a different level of society; like Danny, he has accepted life, with all its faults, turning his back on such possibilities as suicide, Hare Krishna, and the Roman Catholic Church as avenues of escape. What he is attempting to do at the end is live life fully; the large family and the plentiful food suggest Mickey's (and Woody's) understanding of the need to rejoin the human community.

Just as there are three sisters, so are there three men, and it would be a mistake to see Mickey (since he is played by Allen) as the Woody Allen character in the film. Essentially, each of the three male characters represents one portion of Allen's personality; only when taken together do they add up to Allen himself, for he once again relies on the device of splitting himself into aspects of his own personality which can be more efficiently dramatized. Mickey is the mass media celebrity who questions the lasting value of what he does and attempts to opt for a more simple life. Eliot is the successful businessman obsessed with any beautiful woman he has not yet possessed. Finally, Frederick is the glum solipsist, an island unto himself, superior and sad, pure and impotent. Frederick is a cross-reference to an identically named character in *Interiors*, while the casting of Max Von Sydow is a confident nod to the Bergman influence, now so firmly under control that Allen can employ Bergman's favorite actor without appearing either to emulate or to imitate that director but rather, as his equal, to share the talents of that star.

In addition to one of the facets of Allen's own personality, Frederick also represents an aspect of the idea of the artist, and there are many in this film: Hannah's parents (Lloyd Nolan, in his last role, and Maureen O'Sullivan, real-life mother of Mia), who are musical-comedy entertainers, now retired;

Caught in a pensive mood, Mia Farrow plays Hannah, the Earth Mother and perfect woman . . . whose suffocating perfection drives the men she loves away from her.

Hannah herself, a serious actress willing to allow her career to suffer so she can be with her children, suggesting life may take precedence over art; Holly, who tries both acting and writing but seems most successful as a caterer, where in the tradition of *Don't Drink the Water* she can be a potato salad Picasso ("The Stanislavksi Catering Co.," she coyly calls her "method" for serving meats), uniting life and art by making an edible masterpiece; Dusty, the rock star who wants to buy paintings to legitimize his success; Mickey, whose *Saturday Night Live*-style TV show is an artistic success within a commercial medium; and the architect (an unbilled Sam Waterston) whom both Holly and her actress friend April (Carrie Fisher) date. But the two poles of the picture are formed by Frederick, who insists on such purity in art that he can no longer function within the human community, and Mickey, whose art is essentially public and commercial, and must please the masses every week. The other characters each fall somewhere between the extreme possibilities for the creative sensibility.

The contrast between serious art and the passingly pleasing is driven home when the hermit-like Frederick (Max Von Sydow) refuses to sell his paintings to the rock star Dusty (Daniel Stern). Barbara Hershey (left) and Michael Caine (right), Lee and Eliot, witness the abortive transition.

Intriguingly, Allen's own character Mickey appears to belong to another film from the rest of the characters, who are tightly knitted together. Other than the fact that he was once married to Hannah, he seems to be functioning in an alternative universe, so peripherally is he related to them, until at the end he shows up for the Thanksgiving dinner, this time matched with Holly. He is amazed to realize that when, a few years before, he attended a similar dinner, he could not conceive of loving anyone but Hannah; now, here he is with her sister. Lee, as we saw in the film's main plot, did not think she could live without Frederick, but left him for Eliot, whom she did not believe she could live without, discovering in time that she preferred her college professor, as so many previous Allen women (including Annie Hall) have realized before. "Love fades," the little old lady told Alvy Singer on a New York street nearly ten years earlier.

The plight of a person who has the sensibility and anguish of an artist, but quite possibly none of the talent, is powerfully dramatized by Dianne Wiest as Holly.

261

Eliot (Michael Caine) strikes up an affair with Lee (Barbara Hershey), his wife's sister; the contrast between a normal attraction and loyalty to a friend or family member has been basic to Allen's plots since his earliest work.

Barbara Hershey as the beautiful, but not necessarily superficial, Lee.

But in *Annie Hall*, that simple truism seemed impossible for Allen — or his persona — to accept; he was embarked on a romantic quest for perfect love in a world where other people's emotions were superficially fickle. The most remarkable thing about *Hannah* — the true breakthrough — is that this is no longer the case. Indeed, almost the opposite is true: before the film even began, Mickey possessed perfection in the form of Hannah, who is a great artist but also a great mother, sister, friend, and wife; Hannah is a second cousin to one of those Madonna-like women in the early Bergman films who are the source of all truth and beauty in the world. Farrow deftly plays the character not as a stereotype, but with such a cutting edge of irony that we completely understand why Mickey left her, and why Eliot needs to cheat ... earlier Allen films complained that perfection did not exist in this world, whereas Hannah understands that it does, and that it is suffocating.

In describing the film's photography, Brian D. Johnson wrote that "unlike his film *Manhattan*, which worshipped New York's streets in rapturous black and white, *Hannah* reveals the soft colors of the place and weaves them subtly into the narrative"; David Ansen similarly commented that as compared to Gordon Willis' usual romantic approach, Di Palma's "warmer palette and somewhat less studied lighting help give *Hannah* its deceptively casual grace." Visually, as well as thematically, this film is Woody's breakthrough picture, in that for the first time he rejects the very Romanticism he has emotionally and aesthetically steeped himself in. Pauline Kael could snidely, smugly suggest Woody should take "a long break from his sentimentalization of New York," but in fact every image of the film suggests otherwise. Here, his love for New York is filtered through a less flamboyantly glamorous eye than in *Manhattan*.

Kael's comment makes about as much sense as suggesting that Renoir ought not to have made *Rules of the Game*, or Ernst Lubitsch *Trouble in Paradise*, but that rather they should have moved on to some theme other than glorifying the glamorous twilight hours of European aristocracy. If either had taken such advice, we would of course have been denied two of the greatest 'high comedies' of all time. And it is just such a twilight that Woody is simultaneously celebrating and criticizing in *Hannah and Her Sisters*; as David Denby wrote, "the West Side apartments" provide "furnishings that offer the memory of a slower, more gracious and ample style of New York life now largely vanished but still available to a few." This is Woody's terrain, his demi-monde; he conveys it with the same percept-

iveness with which Renoir and Lubitsch chronicled the fading hours of its European counterpart.

Certainly, the city is still far and away his favorite place, the antithesis of L.A.; but no longer does his appreciation of it seem the product of an intelligent adolescent mind. He knows what's right and what's wrong about the people who live there; he loves them, but can see their failings, and his own. So the key line of dialogue — the three words that unlock the real meaning of this movie, and Allen's sensibility at the time when he made it — come at the very end, when Mickey realizes, with the combination of humor and acceptance which lead to true wisdom, that though love fades, new loves are constantly being born. He, like the others, is susceptible to that. After all, the only alternative is becoming like Frederick, which means hiding in a hovel from reality.

"The heart," Mickey concludes with a happy twinkle in his eye, "is a resilient organ." With the acknowledgement and acceptance of that, Woody

As Eliot, Michael Caine looks and acts, for the first time in his career, like a British Woody Allen, which makes sense since he is portraying one side of Allen's personality; in Allen's first film, What's New, Pussycat?, *Peter O'Toole played a similar role.*

Allen at last passes from romanticism to realism. With that philosophic and aesthetic metamorphosis, he has transformed from an artist of great potential into a mature filmmaker. Having experimented with entertaining comedy in his early work, then stumbled awkwardly but steadily toward a more serious vision, he is at last an auteur who has completed the first film of the third and most important phase of his career. He is, at last, sitting at the Grown-ups' Table. Better still, the success of *Hannah* puts him at the head of the table. Considering the autobiographical element of his work, it wouldn't be a bad idea if, at the next Thanksgiving dinner he chooses to film, he showed himself carving.

Allen Amarcord:

RADIO DAYS

An Orion Pictures Release (1987)

CAST:

Julie Kavner (*Mother*); Wallace Shawn (*Masked Avenger*); Seth Green (*Joe*); Michael Tucker (*Father*); Josh Mostel (*Abe*); Joy Newman (*Ruthie*); Hy Anzell (*Mr. Waldbaum*); Dianne Wiest (*Bea*); Kenneth Mars (*Rabbi Baumel*); Mia Farrow (*Sally); Tito Puente (Latin Bandleader*); Danny Aiello (*Rocco*); Jeff Daniels (*Biff Baxter*); Kitty Carlisle Hart (*Radio Singer*); Tony Roberts (*Emcee*); Diane Keaton (*Singer*).

CREDITS:

Producer, Robert Greenhut; executive producers, Jack Rollins and Charles H. Joffe; director, Woody Allen; screenplay, Woody Allen; director of photography, Carlo Di Palma; film editor, Susan E. Morse; production designer, Santo Loquasto; costume designer, Jeffrey Kurland; Color by DuArt Film Lab; running time, 91 minutes; Rating: PG.

Following the stunning critical (though at best lukewarm commercial) success of *Hannah and Her Sisters*, Woody Allen again found himself in the bind he'd been in several times before: having produced an acknowledged masterpiece, he was expected (however unfairly) to top himself the next time out. The filmmaker who wanted to be able "to fail occasionally in front of the public" clearly had less lofty ambitions for his project than for *Hannah*, and the relatively mild reception *Radio Days* received may in fact have less to do with any failings in the film itself than in its inability to measure up to expectations engendered by the previous ensemble epic on modern Manhattan lifestyles.

If *Hannah* provided Woody's scathingly satiric yet sweet spirited study of how we live today, *Radio Days* can be seen as a kind of complement: in comparison to *Hannah's* sharpedged realism, this film offers a dreamlike reminiscence of the way we were—or, more correctly, of how Woody (and those who share his vision, the people whose collective sensibility Woody articulates) chooses to recall us as being. Though Allen does not appear onscreen during the course of the film, he does speak a voice-over narration, as we watch a child called Joe (Seth Green), clearly a stand-in for the young Allen, growing up in Long Island's

Rockaway district during World War II. Like Neil Simon's play *Brighton Beach Memoirs*, Woody's movie focuses on the family and immediate friends of the youthful hero: most importantly, his iron-willed mother (Julie Kavner), whose strength of character and personal convictions just barely hold the family together; the pleasant but passionless father (Michael Tucker), forever dreaming of get-rich-quick schemes but barely able to bring in enough money to keep the household going; and Aunt Bea (Diane Wiest), the extremely attractive maiden aunt who invariably proves unlucky in love.

Unlike Simon, though, Woody has (as his title indicates) something else up his sleeve, to be expected from the one-time budding magician. His trick here is introducing another entire ensemble of characters, who contrast drastically with the humble working class Jews. These are the celebrities of the radio during its golden days, when—before the advent of TV—it stood at the center of the nation's consciousness, informing our attitudes as a people while reflecting an idealized vision of ourselves. Not only music and news broadcasts entered every waking hour of these people's lives, but also soap operas, serious talk shows and lightweight chit-chat, high drama and low comedy, adventure serials for the kids...radio was, simply, at the heart of popular culture, able (because a radio could be carried anywhere, experienced on a picnic or drive as well as in the living room) to pervade a person's life even more significantly than television does today. Radio personalities ("stars" seems a less correct word to describe what they meant to, and how they were perceived by, the public) were, simply, more an everyday part of the lives of people at that time, in that place, than the loftier silver screen stars, who seemed remote and untouchable.

In previous pictures, ranging from *Play It Again, Sam* to *The Purple Rose of Cairo*, Woody comedically explored the relationship of normal, everyday people to larger-than-life idealized images of human behavior. But Allen was as much a product of the golden age of radio as the golden age of Hollywood, so *Radio Days* seems something of a long overdo cinematic statement about the effect of this significant mass medium on him—and, by process of abstraction, on us.

So he cuts back and forth between Joe's family and parallel anecdotes involving the radio people they constantly listen to. These include cameo characterizations by such Allen stock company regulars as Wally Shawn, Tony Roberts, and Diane Keaton. Chief among the performers is Sally White (Mia Farrow), a dumb blonde from Canarsie who wants to crack into show business and begins by selling

A family from the forties: (front, left to right) William Magerman, Seth Green, Leah Carrey; (rear, left to right) Michael Tucker, Julie Kavner, Diane Wiest, Joy Newman, Renee Lippin, and Josh Mostel. (Photo by Brian Hamill)

Writer-director Allen scouts locations for a shot in Radio Days. *(Photo by Brian Hamill)*

cigarettes (and getting used and abused by the men who promise to "help" her) but eventually becomes the leading radio star of the day. While the visions of Joe's home life are presented as nostalgic recollections of situations he experienced firsthand, the episodes involving Sally and her ilk are reported more in the style of show business myths. The voice-over makes clear here that what we see is not necessarily what actually happened but rather oft-told tales, greatly embellished by the very nature of an oral tradition of storytelling.

Allen's developing sophistication as a film direc-

In the final New Year's Eve sequence, when the family members are in their humble home listening to the radio, the celebrities are high atop a modern Manhattan skyscraper where a female vocalist (Diane Keaton) entertains them—and the entire nation. (Photo by Brian Hamill)

tor can be seen in his effective use of two distinct approaches. The sequences involving Joe's family are all shot "on-location," in what appears to be the actual Rockaway district, little changed in over forty years, with just the right dreamy atmosphere added to make visually clear that this is not absolute realism but bittersweet nostalgia. On the other hand, those sequences featuring the radio performers are all done with a far more stylized look, so we sense—just from viewing them—they are not meant to be taken as literal truth.

Most critics noted Allen's mastery of technique, but some found it oppressive: concerned that in developing a subtle directorial style, Woody had backed off from something more primitive but, perhaps, more significant, a gutsy, iconoclastic substance. In *The Nation*, Terrence Rafferty noted, "The film, charming at first, becomes puzzling after half an

Aunt Bea (Dianne Wiest) finally meets a nice man (Robert Joy), though he turns out to be a homosexual. (Photo by Brian Hamill)

hour or so of 'I remember this, I remember that' vignettes, finally infuriating as we realize there isn't going to be a point—that Allen's ramblings are as random and unmotivated as Joe Franklin's. ...The great mystery of *Radio Days* is why Allen insists on telling us yet again everything we already know about him." Of course, artists have traditionally offered, in successive works, a series of variations on recurring themes, but Rafferty missed the rough-edged quality of Woody's earlier variations, which he felt had here degenerated into slickness, causing him to recall "an energetic intelligence that expressed itself in edgy, startling jokes rather than in elegant camera moves and editing transitions." Pauline Kael, of *The New Yorker*, arrived at a similar conclusion, insisting that "the protagonist of [the earlier Allen] comedies was fuelled by hostility and neuroses," but now Allen only makes his childhood innocuous...reduces everyone to harmlessness. It's pure nostalgia—the past sweetened and trivialized.... Commenting on the old neighborhood, he's like the curator of Woody's childhood...while you're watching it you feel he wants too

much for you to like it.... Woody has found in himself the heartfelt coyness of Louis B. Mayer—without the redeeming vulgar joyfulness. Allen goes for the lump in the collective throat, carefully, tastefully."

But that sort of criticism may be unfair, taking Woody to task for being at another stage in his progression as a person—and as an artist—than when he produced works which perfectly expressed an earlier era in his public/private development. Understandably, then, not everyone agreed. Near-constant Allen fan Richard Shickel of *Time* had only words of praise, seeing large thematic ambitions beneath the film's unpretentious surface of simple comic storytelling. Admitting the clear autobiographical link between Allen and his diminutive redheaded hero, Schickel nonetheless insisted: "Rather than a personal history or an exercise in nostalgia, it is a meditation on the evanescence of seemingly permanent institutions [like radio's powerful but temporary role in the national consciousness or anyone's own family unit]....In the most delicate way imaginable, the snippets drawn from the seemingly great world of broadcasting and those from the little world of listening shed the most affecting and provocative light on each other. Somehow, one thinks of Chekhov, and is once again astonished by the complexity and clarity of Woody Allen's vision."

267

The two worlds briefly come together in an Allen "incarnation" when the family's Aunt Bea wins a radio contest and receives a prize from the announcer (Tony Roberts). (Photo by Brian Hamill)

But while Schickel may have been reminded of Chekhov, the majority of movie lovers were in fact reminded of someone else: Federico Fellini, the world-class Italian film director Allen has always emulated and occasionally imitated. Just as *Stardust Memories* struck all but the most charitable critics as Allen's attempt to offer his own *8 ½*, so did *Radio Days* seem to them to bear a similar relationship to *Fellini Amarcord*, that director's own nostalgia-tinged reminiscence about his boyhood in rural Italy. With its slight narrative line and large canvas of warmly recalled characters, vividly recreated incidents, and richly detailed settings, *Amarcord* certainly appeared to be the model for Allen's latest. Just as *Amarcord* plays as a mellower, milder, more easily accessible diversion compared to Fellini's more obscure and demanding works, so does *Radio Days* seem slight stuff after something as lofty in ambition and execution as *Hannah*. Then again, an artist has the right to his lighter moments. Fellini and Allen both deserve the opportunity to indulge in more modest work, just so long as the quality of craftsmanship remains high.

And the Allen themes are clearly here: the maudlin marriage seen in contrast to the horror of living alone; the populist-Romantic impulse of ordinary people to penetrate the sacrosanct world of their "gods," the media celebrities; the disparagement of life in the present in contrast to a dimly remembered and admittedly idealized image of the past. Understandably, then, *Playboy's* Bruce Williamson praised *Radio Days*, claiming: "Almost plotless but not pointless, this tuneful tribute to golden oldies on the airwaves during America's age of of innocence ranks in the collected works of Woody Allen as a trivial pursuit—which makes it approximately twice as funny and meaningful as a magnum opus by anyone else."

What remains problematic is whether Woody is an authentic artist, able to come up with his own conceptions, or merely a copycat assuming the forms a primary innovator like Fellini develops. *Stardust Memories* still strikes me as a sad disappointment not because of the overall similarity to Fellini's film, but because Allen also reproduced Fellini's individual flourishes: the tinny Nino Rota rococo musical style, the harsh and angular black and white photography. The effect was like watching a virtual remake of *8 ½* with Allen standing in for Marcello Mastroianni. But that's not the case with the *Radio Days/Amarcord* relationship. While Woody has as-

Sally (Mia Farrow) works as a cigarette girl in a posh club, where the various men (including Daid Warrilow, left) promise her much, give her little, and take a lot. (Photo by Brian Hamill)

Father (Michael Tucker) and Mother (Julie Kavner) in one of their glum moments, providing yet another variation on Woody's recurring theme of the woes of marriage. (Photo by Brian Hamill)

sumed (consciously or otherwise) Fellini's essential format, he makes this movie his own. The difference between the Fellini influence on *Stardust Memories* and *Radio Days* is as significantly distinct as the influence of Bergman's *Cries and Whispers* on Allen's *Interiors* and *Hannah*: both films were clearly inspired by the Bergman classic, though *Interiors* was a glum, artificial attempt to reproduce the Bergman film whereas *Hannah* played as Woody's unique and acceptable equivalent to it. If *Stardust Memories* is in the same lackluster league as *Interiors*, *Radio Days* works because it belongs to the same mature period as *Hannah*. Clearly, Woody can now be influenced by one of his idols without turning out a patent carbon copy of the original.

Still, the similarity to Fellini's film did not sit well with all critics, as some found Woody's film considerably less effective. In *Maclean's*, Lawrence O'Toole wrote: "What is missing in *Radio Days* is the exuberant spirit..Fellini brought to his 1973 childhood-memory film ..., which *Radio Days* uncomfortably resembles.... Allen's point of view lacks the dreamy perspective of man a looking back: his hindsight is essentially prosaic. And the constant use of old broadcasts and music becomes grating, like living in a house where the radio is always on." Few agreed, though, that there was anything wrong with the "spirit" of Allen's vision of the past, or that he failed to offer a proper dream-like vision; indeed, many other critics noted those very qualities in passing, even as they then proceeded to pick at other problems in the film.

New York's David Denby, frequently an Allen fan, called this "a mild and very minor reminiscence," insisting that "we get a series of brief vignettes held together only by some vague connection to broadcasting...there are dozens of tiny anecdotes, and since they don't build or comment on one another, they can be enjoyed only in a limited, blackout-sketch way....*Radio Days* is exquisitely crafted, but the picture is suffused with mediocrity." In fact, though, the anecdotes do build, though the effect is cumulative rather than neat and schematized. What Denby complains about—the "vague" connection of anecdotes—is basic to the film's appeal, for the title itself suggests Woody's belief that the high, low, and in-between points of people's lives were suffused by the radio listening experience. It makes sense, then, that one of Aunt Bea's dates would be ruined when, as she necks in a parked car with a possible candidate for marriage, he is panicked by Orson Welles's *War of the Worlds* broadcast, which he takes as literal truth, as numerous real-life people did. Or that during the height of a family fight, they—like the rest of the country—are brought into what McLuhan would have called a global (or at least continental) community by endless broadcasts of information about a little girl who is trapped in a deep well. Or, perhaps most characteristic of Allen, the family's teenage daughter (Joy Newman) dressing up like Carmen Miranda and, dancing about their humble abode, performing marvelous lip-synch impersonations of the fiery Latin star. At those moments, the bridge between Joe's family and the faraway voices are linked; the incarnation—when, for a fleeting second, everyday reality and the ideal become inseperable—is briefly theirs, as the real woman and the romanticized one merge, however temporarily. As the men in Joe's family slip into the mood by lip-synching the male chorus's song-lines, they too briefly turn their lives into "art." The desire to do that—to become one, if only for a second, with either popular or classic art—has been at the root of Allen's characters since his very first film.

Likewise, with mixed emotions but a far more charitable tone, *Newsweek's* David Ansen wrote: "Though in some ways it's only an elaborate doodle—a minor work in the Allen canon—it's nice to report Woody remains oblivious to the pressure to repeat his former successes. *Radio Days* turns its back to genre and to any claims to Importance." Ansen noted, then, that the episodic quality made this more uneven than any Allen film since *Everything About Sex*: the quality of the individual anecdote, and the degree to which it had been thought through as a film (rather than a written) vignette, determined the success or failure at any particular moment. The gag about the baseball pitcher who continues to lose appendages is funnier in conception than in execution and might have been better as a piece of short fiction; the opening bit about burglars winning a radio contest while robbing an apartment is pure cinema as well as pure Allen. "Like a box of sampler candies," Ansen concluded, "*Radio Days* offers a wide assortment of bite-size goodies. They can't all be to your taste, but the sweetness lingers from the best."

There was the occasional totally negative review, as when Tom O'Brien of *Commonwealth* complained: "The story stinks and the so-so acting can't hide it....There is not enough plot to sustain a single genuine role." But that judgment seems naïve, based on the incorrect notion that *Radio Days* is meant as a conventional narrative (it isn't) with traditional forms of acting. Though the film (and Allen) is certainly not above or beyond criticism, it must (to be fair) be criticized for failing at what it is supposed to be, not measured against some arbitrary yardstick that has nothing to do with the film (or filmmaker's) intentions. Certainly, Woody proved with *Hannah* (just as Fellini had with *La Dolce Vita*) that he could deftly create a varied ensemble of believable and full-bodied characters; in *Amarcord* and *Radio Days*, such a spectrum of three-dimensional people was not needed (and, to a degree, would have been all wrong), since what we see is not "what happened" but rather a visualization of the narrator's mental dream-construct of the past. To succeed at what they are up to (and I believe they both do), Allen and Fellini necessarily make us "see" their sketchy recollections of those people. Only one character from each world—Dianne Weist's aunt and Mia Farrow's radio celeb—is developed fully, which is precisely what Allen requires to successfully realize this specific project. After all, each is the one Woody/Joe found most intriguing in their place, and so the one who emerges as fully realized in any onscreen depiction of his mental reconstruction of that era.

O'Brien comes closer to the truth of this film's limitations when he insists that "*Radio Days* is painfully superficial." When one truly understands Woody's specific, limited ambition for this project, we cannot complain about the superficiality with which certain characters are drawn (they are perfectly realized in terms of their context), but we can about the comment on radio, which seems awfully obvious. Though Woody offers a great deal of pleasant reminiscence much in the manner of a Jean Shepherd memoir, the fact is that Allen is widely considered a major American artist, not merely an agreeable entertainer like Shephard. With that in mind, one wishes his film had a bit more substance, a sharper cutting edge, a fresher statement about what radio meant than we find here. One can come away from the film delighted by what Woody offers and still a little disappointed by the fact that our supposedly central artistic consciousness did not offer insights more original than what many others have already said, if less charmingly so. Only a mean-spirited cynic could deny that *Radio Days* is fun, yet only a shallow observer could fail to notice it's a bit more frivolous than it absolutely needs to be.

Cinematographer Carlo Di Palma (second from right) confers with Woody as they attempt to get a shot just right. (Photo by Brian Hamill)